Niche

MOMUS

a memoir in

pastiche

Niche

FARRAR, STRAUS AND GIROUX: NEW YORK

Farrar, Straus and Giroux
120 Broadway, New York 10271

Printed in the United States of America
First edition, 2020

Library of Congress Cataloging-in-Publication Data
Names: Momus, 1960– author.
Title: Niche : a memoir in pastiche / Momus.
Description: First edition. | New York : Farrar, Straus, Giroux, 2020.
Identifiers: LCCN 2020012290 | ISBN 9780374144081 (hardcover)
Subjects: LCSH: Momus, 1960– | Musicians—Biography. | LCGFT:
    Autobiographies.
Classification: LCC ML420.M5568 A3 2020 | DDC 780.92 [B]—dc23
LC record available at https://lccn.loc.gov/2020012290

Designed by Richard Oriolo

Our books may be purchased in bulk for promotional, educational,
or business use. Please contact your local bookseller or the Macmillan
Corporate and Premium Sales Department at 1-800-221-7945, extension
5442, or by e-mail at MacmillanSpecialMarkets@macmillan.com.

www.fsgbooks.com
www.twitter.com/fsgbooks • www.facebook.com/fsgbooks

10 9 8 7 6 5 4 3 2 1

Preface

Dead writers are unemployed. It's a shame, because they could be put to better use than rotting and being forgotten. Think of all the talents a dead writer might have: a way with words, a flair for drama, an interest in other people's lives, a disarming honesty, a shocking originality, the power to connect us with ancient worlds or imaginary places, good metaphors and maxims, a distinctive voice, a gift for publicity! Why waste all that?

Dead writers are dead, of course. But dead in what sense? Culture is humanity's greatest invention: a machine that overcomes distance, difference, and death, by connecting us to people who are far away, or unlike us, or no longer alive, and making them seem alive and close by and like us. Thanks to culture we can feel as if we've lived for thousands of years, and that's because, even as they enliven us with their work, we're giving these corpses a little spasm of new life by letting their thoughts seep into us.

That sounds a bit spooky, but I like spooky things.

I'm Nick Currie. A Scot born in 1960. I've spent most of my life as Momus, a music artist, a singing writer. I never really planned to set down a memoir. I know it's the sort of thing successful musicians do in later life, but I've never really had the sort of mainstream fame that would justify a standard rock memoir. So that's not what this is. It's more of a phantom choir with some memories suspended in a cloud of dry ice.

In the summer of 2018 I came back to Europe after eight years in Japan. In Osaka I'd spent most of my time cycling, making music, uploading videos to YouTube, and collecting old foreign-language paperbacks from shabby secondhand bookshops. When I arrived back in Europe my life was all up in the air: I had no idea what to do next. I made for Berlin because it's a city I feel comfortable in. A friend there had an apartment I could sublet.

One day I got an email from Jeremy M. Davies, the editor responsible for signing my first novel, *The Book of Jokes*, to Dalkey Archive Press. He was coming to Berlin and suggested lunch. Although we'd been working together for a decade this was our first meeting. I took him to Smart Deli, my favourite Japanese café in Mitte. Jeremy told me about his new job at Farrar, Straus and Giroux and said the New York publishers would be interested in reading anything I showed them. I took that as a kind of politesse, a rote invitation; I was focused on the pop record I wanted to make and didn't really have any literary plans. After lunch we went to see Brecht's grave in the Dorotheenstadt Cemetery. Brecht and his wife Helene Weigel lie under two rough-hewn stones, their names picked out in white sans serif. The windows of their Chausseestraße apartment overlook the site on one side. On the other is a student canteen where I sometimes grab a cheap lunch.

Jeremy returned to New York but kept sending emails urging me to pitch an idea. Maybe an account of all the scenes I'd been peripherally involved in? Postcard Records, Creation, Shibuya-kei, Berlin, the New York art world. There was even money in it! He named the biggest advance I'd ever been offered and my mind suddenly focused. But what to propose?

The first pitch was an ironic memoir about my struggle with drugs. The joke being that I've never done any. Amazingly enough this got accepted and the first tranche of money arrived from New York. But when I sat down to write, the idea quickly fizzled. The joke was undermined by its own punch line, and the whole thing seemed disrespectful to the musicians—obviously legion—who really have struggled with drugs.

Then I had a brilliant idea. The musty smell of old paper sends my pulse racing. Paperbacks are really my drug of choice; there's always one concealed somewhere about my baggy clothes. The thing I get high on is text from dead writers. So why not get them to recount my life story? Pastiche, after all, has always been a part of what I do as the musician Momus. I mock, I copy, I channel.

It turned out to be great fun to make the book this way. I would sit down to write each day thinking: "Now, what year have I got up to, what happened to me then, and who should cover it?" As David Bowie once put it: "Who can I be now?" And in a sense the book wrote itself, because I learned to listen to what these authors seemed to want to talk about. "What would x do?" is a question artists at an impasse often ask, x being some artistic hero. Would x get honest here, or direct or visionary or poetic?

Often the writers I chose were people with higher and nobler concerns than mine. They changed the way I wrote about my life, tugged me towards elegance or grandeur or lyricism or directness. Many had been part of the landscape all along. These were figures who really did intrude into my life as I grew up. Sometimes they were people I was aspiring to be like, since writers were always my role models, along with musicians and visual artists. (I know: dysfunctional, solitary, impoverished, vain, neglected, and self-harming, artists are the worst role models ever.) Sometimes they were just the paperback in my pocket.

Of course this superpower I'd given myself, this license to raise the dead, produced absurd juxtapositions. Hubris and bathos. Imagine Proust coming back to life—becoming a somebody again—just to talk about me, a nobody! How would he feel, to be invoked at some weird séance and forced to lend his voice, reputation, and talents to this hackwork, this propaganda? I can tell you that Norman Mailer was furious to be woken from his eternal sleep by a schmuck. Now that I think about it, it's a very similar scenario to the one in *Popppappp*, my last novel, which describes two graphic designers forced to work for a fundamentalist sect. They spruce up the beheadings on television, add a bit of clarity to the fonts. Maybe humiliated and compromised artists are a good metaphor for humanity? We're all working way below our potential.

Raising the dead is dangerous sorcery. One probably shouldn't reveal the secret. It's never quite clear how the speakers in *Niche* get reanimated. More than one of the writers speculates that it's a punishment: that having to talk about some indie singer is one of hell's lesser tortures. Each ghost gets just one chance to speak before being consigned back into oblivion.

Sometimes the point is to mimic the writers' voices, sometimes their names just appear because their books were to hand when something happened in my life and their themes overlapped with mine. Please don't worry if my impersonations get threadbare from time to time and you can hear my own voice coming through: pastiche and parody will often crisscross with sincerity and story in these yarns. These strands are my warp and my weft. If it were nothing but pastiche there'd be no storyline. If the writers weren't present it would just be a press release.

So here they are, my heroes, brought back to life. They're discussing me. What narcissistic arrogance! Did this idea occur because David Bowie, in 2013, actually spent three words in an email (at a time when he seemed to be in a liminal zone between life and death himself) praising my cover of his song "Where Are We Now"? "That's so cool!" It was one of the highlights of my life, because cool is exactly what he'd been in my eyes.

It's not *totally* arrogant of me to have my heroes narrate my story. Maybe my life isn't inherently terribly interesting, and maybe I'm not culturally important enough for a book like this. In that case you can read the authors talking about themselves, expanding on their own themes and concerns. There's something more than me, me, me.

At its worst this book might be like scanning someone's recommendations on Goodreads, if they did them in funny voices. Or a much-expanded list of a musician's favourite books. One good thing about never getting too famous is that I've had a lot of time on my hands. A lot of rainy days to fit musty books into.

Niche is, as it says on the cover, a memoir in pastiche. The big form I'm pastiching is obviously the oral history. I enjoy oral histories like *Please Kill Me* or Dylan Jones's book about Bowie. They're informal, punchy—a cat's cradle of anecdotes. You hear the voices in your mind's ear as you read. As far as I know no one's ever made an oral history narrated by ghosts. At one point I thought of using the title *Ghostwritten*. I googled and found it had been taken. Hmm, how about *Momus in the Bardo*?

Niche works because it sounds like my name, Nicholas. And because it perfectly describes my position in culture and in commerce. A niche is a recess into which you fit a statue—the representation of a human body—but it could also be a grave; the ashes of human remains are stored in a cremation niche. Death lurks in the wings as you scribble away at a memoir. I'll be sixty when this book comes out. I will obviously at some point in the not-so-distant future join my great dead.

A memoir is a way to back up data before a great crash. To say thank you to old living friends and possibly hello to future dead ones. And I like the idea of portraying myself as a footnote to the pantheon. Like Momus, who was a minor god in ancient Greece, employed on Olympus to mock the others. (Aphrodite made too much noise with her feet, apparently.)

I worry that literary culture is becoming a redundant form, like the DAT tape or slide transparencies. I'm not sure whether people have the time or the attention to read books now, or if they have

the same respect for "the best which has been thought and said."
(I should squeeze Matthew Arnold into *Niche*, I used to quote him
in interviews!) For a while I considered giving the book a title that
would pastiche the one Nabokov chose for his memoir: not *Speak,
Memory!* but *Speak, Library!*

There are no solid targets in *Niche*. Everything is recounted by
ghosts, and these sprites are unreliable narrators. This is something
I've done in my songs too. It prevents my tales from becoming confessions. Confession seems a bit too much like self-betrayal, self-
incrimination. Sure, the narrators in my songs—some of them rogues
and scoundrels—were probably more reliable than I wanted to admit. As masks, they were sometimes brittle. But I do enjoy that mar-
gin of doubt. "Chaucer is singing this, not me! Isn't that obvious?"

Aesop tells us that Momus suggested Prometheus should put a window in man's chest so that the gods could keep an eye on what
humans were thinking. The fictional narrators here serve a higher
purpose: a small lie can tell a bigger truth. The ventriloquism and
the impressions provide cover for a higher degree of honesty. Allow
me this self-protective measure of art, of persona, please! I love
to play with voice and style and irony—it gives me some reflexive
distance from myself and the tyrannous idea that personality is destiny. But in the end I'm just installing a window, and trying to keep
it clean.

Not everybody shares the same moral standards. We don't all agree
on taste or definitions of the good life, and not everybody is indul-
gent and forgiving. Especially now, when we seem more judgmental, more riven and squabbly, than ever. But people who read and
write books do seem to be working on it. They've been doing this
for hundreds of years, talking to us about their lives and helping

us to find parallels in our own. *Humani nihil a me alienum puto,* as Terence put it: nothing human can be alien to me. Writers coax out empathy. Presumably that's why we let them haunt us. Speak, memory! Speak, library!

Momus, Paris, June 2019

1960–1970

I am deeply conscious of the presence of the

great company of the dead, and I am convinced

that could they make their voices heard they

would be with me in what I am about to say.

—Edward, Duke of Windsor, May 8, 1939

Dylan Thomas: First comes Paisley, and then Glasgow, and the mossmuffle of a basement in Crown Gardens, where N's first utterance is—so the story goes—"Lumumba," a name the Philips radio spins out that jackfrosted January of 1961 on silvered waves from Hilversum to Kalundborg. Patrice Lumumba, prime minister of the Congo, has been shot by firing squad. So N's first word is blood-spattered and red-breasted, full of the violence of this world, its vices and its voices. His second word is "car," and the black Alvis his father drives is also red-breasted with roadkill, and even its leathery insides reek of the cold blood of extinct salmon and trout and pheasant and hare and the damp hide of living dog. The Curries drive the taxi-like Alvis to Auchterarder, a Perthshire farm, and Old Bill Curriculum becomes a schoolteacher at Perth Academy, and for a while all is ferndamp in the pine forest where the wind whines and the wood pigeons gurn and grieve—*a POOR world, you fools! A POOR world, you fools!*—while burglars, cautious as night, creep over a pine needle floor to plunder the cottages of humble woodcutters. Baby N is a miniature grandee perambulated, and Old Bill a simulated country squire in tweed plus fours, flanked by Jo his gracious queen in flecked fifties wool and a Hermès headscarf. Custer is the dog, a piebald German setter, and Sukey is the cat, a brindled tabby. One day N pulls at the cord of a scalding iron and it tumbles from the board and cuts his face above the eye. Even things one does not remember can leave scars. When the weather is warm Jo pins her cloak with a brooch and they sit on the landing that juts out into the small loch; the calm is almost Swedish. But the rustling ditches of that placid county cannot long satisfy the three: the Grecian, Georgian city to the south is calling, still cheap and cobbled, still sooty but becoming festive. There Pericles walks still, cracking jokes with David Hume and Adam Smith, and Burns tickles the salon, and Jim Haynes shares a lewd tale with Ricky Demarco. And so the trio moves to Auld Reekie, tilted Athens of the North, agora of the wits and city of the great plain sandstone façade, where Bill has been summoned to stride robed along the trinian crenellations of George Heriot's School for Boys.

Fred J. Schonell: N learns to read on India Street. Mrs. Griffiths teaches him with my *Happy Venture Readers*. The text is big and simple. The books show Dick and Dora, Nip and Fluff. Nip is a dog and Fluff is a cat. Dick dresses in red. *Listen with Mother* plays on the radio. At home there are now five Curries: Bill, Jo, Nicholas, Mark, and Emma. They live at 6 Great Stuart Street. Their flat is on the first floor. The city is Edinburgh. Edinburgh is the capital of Scotland. Words help us to remember. Words make things happen in our heads. Heads enclose worlds. Books and pictures and music are like drugs. The people who make them are artists. It is good to be an artist, says Dick. When artists are dead they can still speak to us, says Dora. It is not good to be dead, barks Nip. But artists are ghosts, mews Fluff. G-g-ghosts are frightening, stammers Dora. But we like to be haunted, says Dick. *Whooooooooo*, whoos Nip, all jagged and electric. Everybody jumps.

Dr. Benjamin Spock: N was brought up according to the principles I outlined in *The Common Sense Book of Baby and Child*

Care. I told mothers to trust their own child-rearing instincts and not to overdiscipline; children given autonomy will tend to become adults of their own accord. For this reason I was glad to see that Jo allowed N to push the books in. That was his favorite thing to do: he would waddle dimple-kneed over to the big mahogany bookcase and just push the books toward the wall in fan-shaped arrays, delighting in the way that units could become waves, and rectangles curves. No attempt was made to stop him: as a librarian, Jo could certainly understand the pleasure of handling books, even when one doesn't actually read them. And as a matter of fact I believe one could say that N is still pushing books in today.

Robert Louis Stevenson: Great Stuart Street was just around the corner from where I'd lived a century before, in the same solid crescents of Georgian town houses facing private gardens. I based *Treasure Island* on a pond in Queen Street Gardens; N played there too, but was mostly confined to the gated dodecagon of Moray Place Gardens, running around the perimeter path as though, like me, he dreamed of voyages. Daisies poked through the clovered *pelouse*, which could—through squeezed eyes—become a sea. A tree stump contained a gazing face in fungal jelly, or so N swore to a half-listening parent. The New Town streets still boasted the lamps I'd described as Leerie lighting, although by the mid-1960s they were electric. I had been delicate in life, but in death was positively spectral; I craned to observe 1960s Edinburgh past my astragal glazing, and was pleased to note that the milk was still delivered by horse and cart, the newspapers still burst with potential plots for adventures, and coal men still crept from door to door with rough hessian sacks on their backs.

Elspeth Davie: I lived upstairs at 6 Great Stuart Street, and wrote short stories and novels which were published by Calder &

Boyars. We had come, my husband, George, and I, from Queens University in Belfast, where we knew Larkin. I was dry and self-effacing and resembled the French "new novelist" Nathalie Sarraute, who also published with Calder. My books were quite different from hers, though: not avant-garde, but careful, coherent, and concise. At Edinburgh College of Art I'd developed a flair for precise visual impressions and symbols of gentle alienation. A world of party hats and wallpaper shops. The Edinburgh we inhabited was ruled by old ladies. There may have been Jaguars and Rovers parked outside, but one still lived, essentially, in the nineteenth century. Above me was Miss Mackay, a teacher at Leith Academy. Next door, in the top flat, was Mrs. Dickson, who mostly sat by an orange gridded gas fire with her wire-haired terrier Binnie. She would prepare treacle pudding when N visited. Mrs. Dickson was always hoping that he would befriend her grandson Malcolm Martineau, who became an accomplished accompanist. But all that seemed to interest N was the marvellous maze of dividing walls, dim back gardens, and craglike tenements that he could glimpse on the vertiginous crawl through the bulge of the bay window that connected Mrs. Dickson's kitchen to her bathroom.

Colin Rowe: Many architects have seen interiors as an afterthought, an appendix to a façade, rather than the very womb and origin of a building. Le Corbusier, in *Towards a New Architecture*, talks about a building as a bubble blown from the inside, its perfection and harmony deriving from the steady and even distribution of the breath that creates it. While this evidently describes the genesis of domes and vaulted structures, it could stand in a wider sense as a principle for an ideal all-round approachability. The best buildings, it seems to me—as it did to Lewis Mumford—are as good from behind as before, if they even permit of such a distinction in the first place. I will illustrate this point with a slide of Ainslie Place, a handsome crescent in Georgian Edinburgh, which is all façade. Mumford provocatively called this "barracks architecture facing a catwalk" and chided its architects for their indifference to rear views—as though they were theatrical scene painters, or people making views to be reproduced on table mats. He imagined smallpox, shabbiness, and moral turpitude lingering in the rough-hewn stone backyards of these buildings, making them stand in microcosm for what Edinburgh itself was in the widest view: a city of unreconciled halves, one daubed in perfume and garlanded with fine frills and enlightened reason, the other suppurating in decay and infested with disease, a teeming warren of impulse and instinct. The distinction between New Town and Old, front and rear, became, for Mumford, the difference between "scene" and "obscene."

Sigmund Freud: Edinburgh at that time was quite similar to Vienna in 1900: behind the respectable scenography there were many examples of hysterical neurosis caused by sexual repression. It was in his apartment on the Größestuartgaße that I first witnessed a marked inclination towards exhibitionism in young N. He was cared for at that time by a succession of continental au pair girls. One evening his parents went out; N was in his bedroom, studying the poster on the wall. It depicted a scene from *Les Très Riches Heures du Duc de Berry*, the medieval book of hours painted by the Limbourg brothers. French peasants could be observed harvesting grapes in front of a pale and spindly castle. Some loaded barrels onto carts drawn by mules, others stood by eating stray grapes. Bored and skittish, N resolved suddenly upon a course of action: he carefully removed his clothes and walked naked, in a state of obvious sexual excitement, to the living room, where a particularly appealing au pair from Rotterdam was listening to the radio. "Jeanette," he asked, "when will Mummy come home?"

Margaret Tait: I am a round-faced lady, a bit of a character, an artist. If I were alive I would be 102 years old. For almost fifty years I worked on Edinburgh's Rose Street in a shabby studio with a sign on the door that read ANCONA FILMS. I made film-poems on a wind-up Bolex, thirty-two in all. I would record the sound separately, and splice my confections together as I pleased. In *A Portrait of Ga* (1952) there's a sequence of my mother on Orkney unwrapping a boiled sweet, reading a book, executing a playful little pirouette. What seems trivial right under your nose attains gravitas and beauty with time. A Bolex is a bee, turning the flowers into a sweetness you can store. I paid for everything myself; I filmed the captions and titles using children's tin letters, and ofttimes scratched images and shapes directly onto the film prints. I had connections with the islands of the north, but also with lands far to the south—the name of my production company came from the Via Ancona in Rome, where I lived when I studied at the Centro Sperimentale di Fotografia. My films give a marvellous sense of the sheer otherness of life in Scotland in the postwar period: the greens and the reds look deeper, the lorries are chunky and round-shanked, the books in the bookshop windows might be medieval, and yet you can recognise places and faces which still exist. There goes the poet Hugh MacDiarmid, walking up to the pub past tiny hatchet-faced men in caps, and here's George Street, right enough, a little sootier than you've seen it! This is the damp and smoky world into which N emerges. The scent of the brewery is pungent and all-pervasive. N's mother wears a head scarf and carries the oval wicker hen basket made popular by Brigitte Bardot. My islands are to the north, theirs are to the west: when the family catches a light aircraft from Glasgow to Tiree in 1963 it is N's first flight. On the pale sand of the beach—that singing sand which still sings when segmented in a jar—he draws the sleeper slats of a railway with a twig, giving himself license to become a small human locomotive.

Deprived of money, this is what we do: with just a couple of props we can give ourselves license.

Mickey Spillane: You're crumpled by the door of the john with blood slopping out of your nostrils like hot fudge, courtesy of some punk named Spivak. Then suddenly back it rushes: how your old man took you to St. Andrews to meet the Prof—Duncan was his name, Tom Duncan. You peered over the edge of the castle well together and saw green marbled ice far below, and the Prof said to your old man, see, hell really does freeze over. That green rock in the bottle dungeon had curves like a broad, if she were also the sky glittering above the Arctic at 5:00 a.m. They tortured men down there. They plugged a cardinal's body into a chest of salt. Scotland! Keep it, grunts Spivak. Your gut is getting gnawed by a thousand rats, but in your head there's a field of imperial emerald where your old man is handing you a tiny miracle, a four-leafed clover. You throw that damned thing away. Nobody told you it was rare. The Prof and the old man gasp and fall to their knees to search, but that's just how life is. We pluck it, we toss it. It comes once and goes, but don't you get to thinking it's anything special. Just ask Spivak.

Franz Kafka: N, when young, had two imaginary friends named Dougas and Dougar. It seems—although no one at the time would have suggested as much, and indeed to raise my name in any discussion of these creatures would have seemed strange—that they were quite similar to the assistants Arthur and Jeremiah, assigned to Land Surveyor K by the officials of the castle in my novel of that name. For they had apparently embarked on an endless succession of childish games, and seemed completely undifferentiated one from the other. N would pass a building, a basement in the Dean Village, for example, and casually tell his mother, "Here is where my friends Dougas and Dougar live." Every evening at dinner—

without fear of contradiction, and indeed in the expectation of a kind of benign indifference that is nevertheless an indulgence—N would indicate two empty chairs and inform the adults present that these places should remain undisturbed, for they were occupied by Dougas and Dougar, the assistants, who were perhaps at that moment—almost imperceptibly—engaged in some childish quarrel or pointless dispute.

William Burroughs: Shortly after my appearance at the Edinburgh International Writers' Conference of 1962—the moment at which my writing started to become more widely known—Bill Currie embarked on a Linguistics Ph.D. at the University of Edinburgh. His chosen topic was children's acquisition of language. Inspired by the theories of Chomsky and Bernstein, Bill decided to use his own children as guinea pigs in a linguistic experiment similar to the ones I was making myself at the time. One day he brought home a Uher Report 4000 reel-to-reel tape recorder and set it up in front of N. "Tell me a story," he demanded. "Make something up. Anything." N dictated into the microphone the following: "One day . . . there was a dog . . . and he ran onto somebody's roof . . . and then a bell came bouncing on the road and bounced on top of the dog's head . . . and then came a person and killed the bell . . . the bell rang ting-a-ling . . . like a fire engine . . . and the fire engine went past going n-n-n-n-n . . . n-n-n-n-n . . . they were in a hurry to get to the house on fire." The story appeared—as an example of something called "XH structure"—in *Discovering Language, Book V*, a textbook Bill published through Longmans. This was in 1964, the same year Grove Press put out my cut-up novel *Nova Express*.

Jean Genet: I became a thief out of necessity, but also because I was attracted to hard, brutal, dead-eyed men whose crimes appeared to me like minor miracles garlanded with flowers. Young N was not such a man, not by any stretch of the imagination. But he too was a thief. When he was first sent to the Edinburgh Academy's junior school at Denham Green there was a craze for pencil erasers shaped like trolls with vividly coloured hair. N stole one from a classmate and concealed it in his pocket. When the teacher learned of this and searched him, he tried to forestall her with lies: "Oh, you'll find a tissue in there!" There was no tissue, but instead a holy relic, the missing Norwegian troll, wedged deep in the warm pocket, poking up its pink hair. Later N stole a silver James Bond car—a Corgi model of the famous Aston Martin DB5—from his classmate Brian Muir. News of this crime rose to the highest levels of the Edinburgh Academy. The headmistress, Miss Taylor, telephoned N's parents. Perhaps a stretch in a tough Borstal—or a brutal prison in which men masturbate while looking at crude sexual diagrams inked on the flesh of their own arms—would have done him good. But instead N was merely instructed to borrow things rather than steal them. He wrote a pathetic letter—craven in its stolid bourgeois complacency—to the boy he had stolen from. "Dear Brian Muir," it began, "please can I borrow your James Bond car?" Presently an answer came, and it was, naturally, in the negative. N, disappointed, was in another sense relieved. The little Corgi with its ejector seat and retractable machine guns—the very image of respectability, and of murder in its service—would never be his.

Joseph Beuys: Creativity is humanity's true capital and everybody is an artist. In 1965 I performed my action *Explaining Pictures to a Dead Hare* at Galerie Alfred Schmela in Düsseldorf. Not many people were there, but it has since become famous thanks to photographs taken by Ute Klophaus. I sat cradling the body of the hare, with a mixture of honey and gold leaf spilled over my head.

(This was devised partly to disguise the fact that I was going quite bald.) After a while I stood up and, looking at the pictures on the gallery walls, explained each one to the hare in a quiet voice. It was a satisfying performance. That same year, N—at the time just five years old—is shown in a family photograph holding a dead hare very similar to mine. He is in the kitchen of the Edinburgh flat. His father has shot the animal and brought it home. The expression on N's face is one of mourning. The creature was running across the field, the shot rang out, the hare somersaulted several times and came to a halt, the dog retrieved it, the hare was brought to Edinburgh in the car and hung up in the kitchen. N was permitted to play with it briefly, and then it was skinned and cooked. Fifteen years later, when I came to Edinburgh at the invitation of my good friend Richard Demarco, N was sitting in the front row of a performative lecture I gave in solidarity with the hunger-striking artist Jimmy Boyle, who was serving a prison sentence for murder. Boyle was now the hare. I filled a blackboard with my spidery handwriting, and turned radical politics into a cosmology both spiritual and mysterious. We did not meet that day, but in the documentation of the event now stored in the Demarco Archives at Summerhall, N and I can be seen together in the same photograph.

George Davie: Soon after moving in, Jo Currie befriended Elspeth and me. She was a librarian, bright and well-read. She knew all about my book *The Democratic Intellect*, an account of Scottish education in the nineteenth century. Bill always seemed to be away—dressed in knickerbockers and country tweeds—fishing or shooting. Even when the children were being born, Bill somehow had important fly-fishing to do. On the modest salary they paid schoolmasters at Heriot's, Bill managed to afford a Bentley. It was a secondhand R-type saloon in dove grey, with a folding walnut drinks tray in the back. One afternoon I glanced out of the window and caught sight of N stepping into this grand car dressed as an Elizabethan. He must have been on his way to a fancy-dress party. He looked happy all got up in hose, with his incongruous sandals, ruff collar, and beret. Like his father he obviously enjoyed dressing above his station, beyond his means.

Jean de La Fontaine:
For human qualities animals provide the richest metaphor
In children's stories therefore beasts remain most popular
And so it was that, 'mongst these Curries here,
N was known as "tiger," Mark as "bear."
The tiger was above all for his frankness vaunted,
The bear for strength, but what much-flaunted
Qualities did "Little White Pet" suggest?
For such was Emma's nickname, 'til in jest
N—with tiger cruelty *infra dig*—
Amended it to "Little White Pig."

Eugène Ionesco: It was shortly after N began attending Scout meetings in the basement of St. John's Church on Princes Street that he noticed something was amiss. It wasn't just the pointless activities the boys were forced to waste their afternoons on—picking the poisonous beads off nettles one by one, or imitating the hoots of owls, in exchange for nothing more than tokens made of milk bottle tops and the chance to tick some item off a pink card—but the fact that they were clearly turning into armadillos. Yes, armadillos, I will not use rhinoceroses again! The armadillo is, if you insist, a tiny rhino, with the advantage that all its nutritional needs can be met by ants. Well, first it was little Nigel Barry who became an armadillo, still clad in his two-tone cravat and scout uniform. On miniature hooves he galloped through the assembly hall uttering shrieks and poking out a long pink tongue. Nobody said anything, although you could sense the boys watching Nigel out of the corners of their beady eyes, still at that point forward-facing. Nicholas Croan was the next to become a beast. *Tiddle-um-pum, tiddle-um-pum* came the sound as he trotted past on brittle hooves. And then—with a plop—Ian Gibson became a ginger-haired rhinoceros! I mean, forgive me, armadillo! A ginger-haired armadillo, galloping up and down the Scout hall, there at the west end of Princes Street, still wearing his scarf and woggle. It happened while the others were making the Scout pledge to Akela, the scout leader: "Akela, we'll do our best!" they chorused, like robots or rhinoceroses. Akela was explaining that the following weekend the Scouts would be doing "Bob-a-Job" at Palmerston Place, by the enormous cathedral. Bob-a-Job meant ringing people's bells and proposing to do some odd job around the house for a shilling. Those were innocent days in which such a situation led to very few sexual propositions, and the shillings were guaranteed to be handed over to Akela as soon as the boys returned to base. On returning from this trip—during which he had been made to polish up a whole set of doorstep brasses—N noticed that his left leg was beginning to shine, not like metal but like scaly skin. Imagine his relief on discovering that this was not because he was turning into an armadillo, but because he had lost control of his bladder. A yellow liquid was trickling down the inside of his bare thigh and into his thick green sock. Akela, we'll piss our leg! N raised his hand, pointed to the rank flow, and was permitted to visit the bathroom to clean up. After that disgrace he never went back to the Boy Scouts, but kept the pungent memory as a warning against conformity, totalitarianism, and other armadillisms.

R. D. Laing: Of course, in the sixties, LSD was everywhere, whether you were taking it or not. I certainly was; it was the ideal antidote to Scotland's dismal lack of color. In *The Divided Self* I had described the "schizogenic" nature of the nuclear family, and

N
I
C
H
E

in the process started—together with David Cooper—what came to be known as the anti-psychiatry movement. The idea was that society has a blind spot about itself, and prefers to punish individuals perceived as deviants (by lobotomising or medicating them) rather than confront its own collective madness. The way we drive people mad in families is with the "double bind": we exhort children both to do and not-do something; we forbid that which we also command. For instance, young N would have been aware that drugs were illegal, and yet everywhere he looked in the sixties he would have seen evidence that drugs were virtually de rigueur, a *rite de passage*. There they were in the songs of the Beatles and Pink Floyd, in the Asterix books, where the druid Getafix was busy strengthening the Gauls with his "magic potion," and in Lewis Carroll's Alice books, veritable pharmacopeias stuffed with shape-shifting, mind-altering mushrooms, pipes, bottles, and cakes. Psychiatric clinicians were of course replicating that message, and medicating what were essentially existential problems. If you knew where to look—and children do—it was clear that this society was not just maddening, not just intoxicating, but also toxic.

Karlheinz Stockhausen: N's uncle John spent most of his life working as a choral conductor. He also wrote the libretto for an opera version of James Hogg's *Private Memoirs and Confessions of a Justified Sinner*. His son Justin became a musician too, singing in a successful pop group called Del Amitri. My first impressions of John were alas darkened by a foolish misunderstanding. The Scottish musician invited me to give a lecture at the University of Glasgow and asked what I would require. I replied that I would just need a medium-sized lecture theatre, a reel-to-reel tape recorder, and two exits. After some difficulty John located a suitable room at the university; most had only one door. I'm not quite sure why he thought I needed two exits—perhaps I had enemies in

Glasgow and wanted to be ready to make a hasty escape, or perhaps I harboured a deep fear of getting trapped in a fire. Of course, my real meaning had been lost in translation. All I wanted was two outputs from the tape recorder, left and right. Isn't that just like a musician, though, to think that talking about our instruments is really talking about the world? It's as if I said "I want a big organ!" and you thought I was talking about sex. Perhaps you would not be altogether wrong.

Henri Michaux: In my book *Miserable Miracle* I invented a new term to cover the otherwise incommunicable world I saw while on mescaline: *anopodokotolotopadnodrome*. It's an interesting word to look at on the page, but in itself the word doesn't tell you what a mescaline trip is like, thereby illustrating Pessoa's formulation of every writer's dilemma: that things inside the reader's daily experience seem obvious, and things outside it meaningless. I am hoping N will take drugs at some point, as every adventurous artist—or curious layman, or spirit guide—ought to do. Not so that this memoir can take its place beside dull rock magazine interviews filled with chemical innuendo. Not even so that it can join interesting drug books like Huxley's *Doors of Perception*, *Junky* by Burroughs, *Opium* by Cocteau, or all that Hunter S. Thompson gonzo stuff. Rather, I want N to do drugs so that we can witness his response to the ultimate writing challenge: how to wrap words around those experiences—slippery as soap—which must inevitably remain beyond them.

Giles Telfer: My namo is Gilos Tolfor. I'm an Edinburgh occontric adoptod in tho sixtios by Diordro Bott, a friond of Jo's who livos on Alva Stroot. My choap typowritor prints ovory loworcaso *E* as an *o*. What's wrong with that, I hoar you ask? Indood, nothing. It's all to tho good! In fact, in 1968 tho Fronch writor Goorgos Poroc wroto a wholo novol without onco using tho lottor *E*. In Fronch it was callod *La Disparition*, in English *A Void*. It sooms to mo that my typowritor, by substituting tho lottor *o*, makos my toxt moro intorosting to road. Porhaps I havo boon using tho samo ribbon for too long. Povorty is at tho root of my trick, but tho rosult is a kind of richnoss. To amuso my frionds I'vo takon to spoaking that way too. If you'ro clovor you can loarn to spoak quito fluontly this way. And I am a clovor follow indood: I havo dogroos in goology and goography. I could oasily havo boon a toachor, ovon a locturor. Instoad I lurch around town liko a charactor from Samuol Bockott. I havo lady frionds liko Diordro. To koop thom choorful whon wo moot I talk to thom in my spocial lingo. Instoad of "Doan Bridgo"—that's tho bridgo that crossos tho Wator of Loith—I always say "Doan Bridgo." For somo roason, onco you hoar that you can novor again think of tho bridgo in tho samo way. It will always bo Doan, novor Doan. It's tho samo with Princos Stroot, and othor stroots of Auld Rookio. In your hoad you will bo saying, as you walk down Goorgo Stroot: "Now, what do I havo to buy today on Goorgo Stroot?" And you will laugh to yoursolf swootly, and romombor mo, Tolfor, now doad.

Enid Blyton: In 1966 N, Mark, and Emma, plus Poppy the dog, moved diagonally with their parents to 6 Ainslie Place, just across the gardens from Great Stuart Street. They lived in a big flat on three levels that stretched down from grand reception rooms on the ground floor to a warren-like basement featuring bedrooms, a kitchen, and a scullery. A stone staircase led from this basement to an even deeper level, a dank sub-basement which opened onto a steep garden. This soon became the children's subcultural lair, the base for all their most exciting adventures. The garden descended in turn to a wooded gorge bordering the Water of Leith. This was the private park known as Lord Moray's Pleasure Gardens. As a pretext for adventures in these gardens, N created an organisation called LEH: the Law Enforcement Helpers. I approved, of course, for it was very much in the spirit of my Famous Five and Secret Seven adventures, which mostly see groups of children becoming a sort of unofficial police force whose mission is to stop poor people bettering themselves through crime. I was busy with Noddy at the time, and unfortunately when I next cast a glance in N's direction his law and order organisation (for which he had even drawn up a beautifully lettered manifesto) had completely changed its nature, and was now dedicated to building traps for the packs of pugs led daily through the park by the old ladies who ran the Dog Aid Society at number 2. N organised this mischief by dragging the lids off drainage shafts and concealing the holes with twigs and grass. No pugs died, but I wish N had stuck to his first plan. Whilst I understand that there are few, if any, working-class criminals marauding through a locked garden in an upscale Edinburgh neighbourhood, pug-trapping is an irresponsible and potentially dangerous alternative to the apprehension of ne'er-do-wells. Dogs cannot be criminals.

Paul Klee: As a child there are several minor misfortunes that can befall you. You can get a splinter, or you can get an electric shock. Splinters live in wood, and electric shocks hide behind the wall. These are both animals with quick, sharp bites, and you will probably cry and run to Mummy, who will either take tweezers and pull out the splinter, or get angry with Daddy for not yet screwing the plate over the bare wires around the light switch—he promised to do it last week! And look, the children are now being electrocuted! Other things can go wrong. You can get something in your eye, in which case you will need the licked corner of a handkerchief dabbed on the white surface of your eye, which hurts more than the original speck. You can skin your knee, and it will take about a week for the skin to grow back under a flesh-coloured Elastoplast. Or you can catch some kind of highly infectious pox, which will cover your face with polka dots. The pox has a good side, for now you can stay off school for at least a week, and get everything you need brought to you in bed. Perhaps, between meals, you will sit up against a plumped pillow, grip a pencil in your small fingers, and start drawing what I call "spirit animals." Nearby—it serves as inspiration, no doubt—hangs a cheap print of my 1928 painting *Sinbad the Sailor*, which depicts a fisherman standing upright in a boat, jabbing a double-pronged spear into the bleeding mouth of a rampant motley fish whose two companions, hovering pink-scaled on a sea of blue cubes, look on in astonished dismay.

John Knox: N, as I observe from my station here in heaven, is a child without the title of Godliness, who nevertheless doth shew certain signs of Illumination. He hath in his eighth year a pungent and austere Tract prepar'd, and its name is *The Dive of Wealth*. This he illustrateth himself, and doth pass from hand to hand through his own family for the elucidation and improvement of all who do read it. Without mention of the Almighty, He from whom all Justice doth flow, N hath yet cursed those material Iniquities licensed by Greed and Worldliness. For though there be no Fire without Heat, nor Lamp without Light, yet may there be Righteousness without Bibles. Amen!

Fanny Cradock: As a staple, mince and potatoes may have its charm, *avec* or *sans* carrots and onions. But to serve it every night— no matter how elegantly Scandinavian the cutlery and crockery—is just too British for words. And my dears, when I say "British" I do not mean it as a compliment, certainly not where cooking is concerned. True, Jo alternates the dish with an Indian curry speckled with sultanas, and will sometimes add an approximately East

European dessert called Peasant Girl with a Veil (cream on fruit trifle). And granted, there is a lettuce or cabbage salad with "French dressing" which consists of simple oil and vinegar. N's job is to mix up the dressing in a measuring jug—everyone knows he will add too much wine vinegar, but no one seems to mind. There's also a delicious fish kedgeree—simple, yellow in colour, thick with butter—served frustratingly seldom. Of course, at this time Edinburgh has almost no restaurants. There are perhaps two: one is in a hotel, the other is Chinese, but does not dare to open on Sunday. Invitations to dine with friends seldom arrive, though there are cocktail parties galore. The shops stock industrial products like cornflakes, instant coffee, quick custard, and Creamola Foam—a lumpy, sulphurous concentrate with all the allure of rat poison. Of course Jo is run off her feet, with lodgers to feed as well as the family: there's Anders the Finn, Birmingham dolly Ginny Payne with her Triumph Spitfire, Olly Qwan, and John Muirhead the librarian, bearded and charming. Enough characters to make a sitcom. And of course no food complaints are forthcoming, for nobody expects Escoffier, my dears. Family and lodgers alike are happy to bolt the vittles then scurry back up to the sitting room to watch me, *The Magic Roundabout*, or *Rowan and Martin's Laugh-In*. At school N fares no better: the menu is a soggy Culloden of blood pudding and haggis. N asks Jo to provide him with a note saying he "cannot have the pink pudding"—a ghastly tinted semolina with a red dollop of industrial jam at the centre. Somehow he associates this pudding with his lewd classmate Jake, who takes every opportunity to pop his pink little cock out under the canteen table. The parental note is a plea for protection from both pinks, the pudding and the penis. Well, the producer is indicating that I have said enough. We'll be back next week with three ways to perfect a cauliflower gratin, won't we, Johnnie?

Francis Cadell: I am Francis Campbell Boileau Cadell, the painter. I should say "I was," but artists have a habit of lingering on after their physical death, haunting culture. We can even haunt houses. Fifty years before the Curries moved in, I was living and working in their house. My 1914 painting *The Orange Blind* shows the two main rooms of the ground floor at 6 Ainslie Place as I had them just before the Great War. In the foreground is a silver tea set placed before an elegant woman in a floppy hat. To the left you can see a Japanese lacquer screen. Through the double doors a man is seated at a grand piano. A chandelier is visible—exactly the same chandelier which was hanging there fifty-two years later, when the Curries took over. In my painting the rear windows—with their views over the Firth of Forth to Fife— are covered with orange blinds that fill the space with a womblike light, making it look like Matisse's *The Red Studio*, painted at Issy-les-Moulineaux three years previously. I love Matisse! I discovered his work when I went to study in Paris. Frankly, I think I decorated those connected rooms better than the Curries did. But how could they know, or compare? I died in poverty in 1937, and failed to haunt the 1960s very effectively. N didn't find out about me until much later, when he suddenly recognised his old home in a painting he found online. It's interesting that I would make such a Japanese environment in the house where N would—quite inexplicably—become such a Japanophile himself. Perhaps it was my ghostly influence, as I flitted around like a Fauvist phantom. N and I went to the same school, you know, the Edinburgh Academy. One of my best friends was the Scottish Colourist Samuel Peploe, and N was at school with his grandson, Guy Peploe. They vied to top the English class; Guy later became a character in Alexander McCall Smith's *44 Scotland Street* novels. He's represented as an art dealer specialising in the Scottish

Colourists, which is what he is in real life. And now I suppose I'm a character in this book N is writing, getting all ekphrastic about my own paintings.

Gertrude Stein: Now we are in the vicinity of the inside of the front door at 6 Ainslie Place, and 1960s life swirls around us like a magic roundabout, which is the name of the odd serial which precedes the six o'clock news, and features a white dog called Dougal and a hippie on a spring who drawls like a heavily drugged Bob Dylan, and whose name is also, incidentally, Dylan. And the whole thing is just an extrapolation by someone called Eric Thompson of what he thinks might be happening in a French series the BBC has bought, and they've thrown away the original soundtrack and got Eric to substitute droll improvisations, in a slightly sardonic actor-ish voice. And Bill is there in the drawing room, chopping at rolls of typeset with enormous brown scissors for his green and yellow fishing magazine *Rod & Line*, or dictating letters to Mrs. Fairweather, the secretary. Ginny Payne, the lodger, swinging daughter of a bacon magnate from Birmingham, with her green and blue Triumph Spitfire parked at the door, is in her room studying the outline of the blue and green hills of Fife, that room in which the children previously played Strip Jack Naked, which is a card game you play very fast, throwing the cards down and paying fines for the colored ones, four for an ace, three for a king, two for a queen, one for a jack, and some people call it Beggar My Neighbor. In this vicinity of the hall door, from which plunges a staircase to the floor below, past an inset window featuring a vase of pink-headed dried flowers, and arriving at a little piece of corridor that N somehow associates in his mind with the song "Massachusetts" by the Bee Gees, in this upper vicinity, as I say, a real act of beggar my neighbor occurs when N opens the door to a man his father has called a rat, and immediately says: "My daddy says you're a rat!" And at that the man turns and leaves immediately, returning, presumably, to his rat wife and rat children, to tell them, in a sad rat voice which possibly sounds as if it's being overdubbed by Eric Thompson, that he has been insulted by a six-year-old boy, who opened the door and called him a rat, when, as everyone knows, he is in fact a rat, and what is wrong with that?

Norman O. Brown: Freud told us that children are polymorphously perverse. It seems that N had been—his mother tells us—a shrinking baby who disliked to be touched. With the birth of his brother, Mark, however, a transformation occurs. The younger sibling becomes a playmate, a ready audience, a smaller doppelgänger, a bodily extension, an acolyte, a victim. There now appear for N new pleasures: of performance, of solidarity, but also of power—like the time N tries to make his sibling eat feces from his sister Emma's diaper. Mark refuses, teaching N a valuable lesson. Being bigger—or having the soft power represented by the ability to distract and entertain—is not enough, if exploitative manipulation is the aim. But here we are discussing power and dominance, issues better explained by my colleague Alfred Adler, or even the ethologist Konrad Lorenz.

Patrick Anson, Lord Lichfield: There's a photograph of the Currie family sitting on a bench in Moray Place Gardens. The year must be 1968. My diary informs me that I was actually at a society wedding in Kent that day, photographing Liz Taylor surreptitiously snapping the queen, a relative of mine. But if I'd been in Edinburgh with the Curries, I'd probably be using my Nikon F, the camera I prefer for location shooting. I would select the Nikkor Q 135mm f/2.8 lens, which creates beautiful background blur thanks to a relatively wide aperture for its focal length. I would approach the family as they sit ranged like safari wildlife on the bench. Emma is a baby, and Jo is cradling her lovingly. Bill looks charming, with a skinny tie, a handsome grin, and a strand of dark hair over one eye. Mark has a dimply smile and a generally supportive demeanour, with one knee resting against the green bench. N, waving a toy gun, wears sunglasses and a rictus grin—a mask he seems to pull whenever a photo is taken. Although it may hide shyness, there's something satirical in that face, with its exaggerated capitulation to the command to smile. "He was offered the choice of a new bicycle or a model Luger," Bill tells me, flicking a strand of hair from his eye. "And he plumped for the pistol."

Simon Dee: Although these days largely forgotten, I was a famous chat show host in Britain in the late 1960s. Sure, I later fell out with the broadcasting establishment, ran up huge debts, became a bus driver, even went to prison for a while. But in 1967 you could see me on your black-and-white TV set rolling up at the BBC Television Centre in an E-Type Jaguar filled with miniskirted, thigh-booted girls. Few men, in that era, seemed more visibly successful. Appreciative of my swinger image, N made a little votive installation in the wine cellar at 6 Ainslie Place, taping my photo next to an empty wine rack and lighting the installation with a road worker's candle lantern. He was looking for role models at this age, cool blond men, so I was in competition with Noel Harrison—scattering soft vowels across his spooky hit "The Windmills of Your Mind"—and Ilya Kuryakin from *The Man from U.N.C.L.E.*, played by David McCallum. Although assuming a Russian accent for the role, McCallum could pass as a cosmopolitan Scot, which in fact is what he was. *The Man from U.N.C.L.E.* featured urgent congas, globes, guns, flutes, plots of byzantine complexity, martini-dry zings, and exciting dissolves from one Cold War location to another. There were spin-off products to covet and collect: badges, toy cars, replica Lugers, posters. There was Robert Vaughn's silky voice, and a witty script. How could I, a mere chat show host, compete with that? I soon joined dorky Peter Tork of the Monkees in oblivion.

Vito Acconci: You're moving through a structure, a structure that is called Scotland. You're moving in a westerly direction, in a vehicle. You will visit grandparents in this scenario. Of the two sets, one is asymmetrical: your father's father, William, has already lost his wife, Elizabeth, to womb cancer. The old man lives alone in a dwelling near the sea, beneath eight layers of gray cloud. The town is called Prestwick, and the house is called Minicoy. It's a red sandstone bungalow divided from Mansfield Road by an impossibly tidy garden of seemingly tiny scale. It's probably raining, and the wind is probably rolling in from the Atlantic, across the Firth of Clyde. The iron railings bounding the little front garden were removed to be melted down for munitions during the last war, and never replaced. The grass looks like turf or moss. The gravel is pink. Everything is somehow Japanese in scale, manicured, pristine, and careful. A tall bald gentleman with fat lips answers the door. He is wearing National Health spectacles. He has been waiting patiently for your car, observing the street through net curtains. He seems to spend his whole life waiting. Like his son, your father, his name is William. He was born in the nineteenth century. He fought in the First World War. He did something with observation balloons, or weather balloons. He was in France, on the battlefield. He was traumatized by this experience and never spoke about it. When the Second World War broke out he had a sort of nervous crisis, and collapsed in the bathroom at Minicoy. Fortunately, he was by then too old to serve. Today he is dressed in a suit. His voice is calm, deep, and sibilant. He is kindly and often fulsome in his praise of your good qualities, whatever they may be. He is deeply Christian, a member of the Brethren. He used to be a lay preacher, and worked for the railways. Drink, for him, is the source of all evil. You have a tape recording of him somewhere talking about Moses. In Minicoy there is an ancient telephone made of black Bakelite on a stand in the hall. The bedroom is to the left, the parlor to the right. A parlor is a room for show and ceremony. There is a kitchen through the back, and a ladder to an attic loft room where brothers Billy and John used to live. Where was sister Molly lodged? Perhaps the parlor was another bedroom in those days. On a small bookshelf you can see *The Pilgrim's Progress* by John Bunyan in the Everyman's Library edition: "Everyman, I will go with thee and be thy guide, in thy most need to go by thy side." There's an outhouse just beyond the kitchen door where Billy used to dismantle prewar motorbikes. The back garden is as neat as the front, marked by green washing-line posts. Here there's a high wall protecting the property from the links beyond. The public space of the golf course is reached by a green gate. The terrain out there is flat and sandy, alive with warm, dampish air that wafts in with the Gulf Stream. William stands at his sink, washing the teacups, gazing out at the terra-cotta-topped wall protecting his back garden from the sea wind. Somehow you expect to see Rupert Bear pottering about out there, bending fox-glove stems to sniff at blooms. Later you will visit a tearoom in town and William, spotting a Negro on the street outside, will exclaim in his thick Ayrshire burr: "Look, a coal-black gentleman! It's rare to see a coal-black gentleman in these parts."

Timothy Leary: In 1968 Bill attends a summer school in Poznan, Poland. He comes back with a present for his eldest son: a small acoustic guitar. N has seen San Francisco hippies in a BBC documentary about flower power and feels sure he knows how to complete the look: he picks daisies in the garden and garlands his ears with them, hangs little bells around his neck on leather thongs, and stands in front of the mirror strumming the guitar. Something is missing, though: N heads up to Bill's desk—the place where his father pastes up his low-circulation fishing magazine, *Rod & Line*—and carefully letters the word "LOVE" in pen on a white mailing label. He peels off the paper backing and sticks it to his forehead. It looks ridiculous. I'm tired of being held responsible for everything that happened in the sixties.

Vance Packard: *The Hidden Persuaders* sounds like a TV thriller series, but it's actually my 1957 book on the advertising industry. The book does pack a thrill if you like to be horrified by the idea that American admen of the time were using "depth psychology," a "built-in sexual overtone," and "the psycho-seduction of children." As a conservative critic of the emerging consumer society I was keen to point out how advertising—drawing on the theories of psychoanalysis—was beginning not just to play on unconscious inse-curities, social anxieties, and emotional needs, but actually to create them, thereby increasing the sum of human unhappiness. The blue Pelican edition of *The Hidden Persuaders* warned its readers that what happens in America usually follows, sooner or later, in Britain, but the advertising dystopia I describe was necessarily muted—even glamorously rare—in a country with only one commercial TV channel. Nevertheless, Jo and Bill were worried enough about the "psycho-seduction" of their three children to ban all viewing of the commercial network. Snobbism may have played its part: ITV was vaudevillian glitz for the proles. Despite this blanket ban—and the fact that no advertising hoardings were to be seen anywhere near the Georgian crescents of Edinburgh's New Town—N developed a keen awareness of certain brands, logos, and slogans. He begged his mother, for example, to let him wear Tuff slip-on shoes, reluctantly tolerated by the Edinburgh Academy's uniform code. He tacked a Carlsberg logo to the wall of his basement bedroom (the open script on the letter "b" made him think for a long time it said "Carlsverg") without being quite sure what beer was. He also pinned up Union Jacks and RAF roundels, vaguely aware of the way the Mods were recontextualizing these red, white, and blue designs. But who exactly were the Mods? Did they have anything to do with the "I'm Backing Britain" campaign? Did they ride scooters, or fly with the Royal Air Force? Just because things are seductive, it doesn't follow that we understand them.

Richard Hamilton: The Americans like to think they invented Pop Art. In fact, the Scottish-Italian sculptor Eduardo Paolozzi and I were using mainstream commercial imagery in London several years before Warhol and Lichtenstein. As the sixties progressed and the Americans contented themselves with replicating the work we'd done in our 1956 show *This Is Tomorrow*, I got more interested in ironic prints and multiples. Like me, and like Eduardo, N was fascinated by any kind of printed matter published in series. And like the Independent Group—as we called ourselves—his interest in popular culture seemed to come in part from a peculiarly British distance from it. While other boys had action-packed comics, a dull educational magazine called *Look and Learn* was N's only weekly subscription. Rather than reading the red and yellow mag (filled with improving historical articles and a portentous sci-fi strip called *The Trigan Empire*), N ranged his copies neatly on a rug, deriving some kind of anal pleasure from the visual rhythms of repetition and variation. At this time I was blowing up small sections of postcards in my *People* series, and making my first images of *The Critic Laughs*—a Braun electric toothbrush attached to a pair of dentures. Critical laughter would become important to both of us.

Thomas Carlyle: What meaning lies in Colour! What glory it is—as the fictional professor Teufelsdröckh asserts in my diverting book *Sartor Resartus*—to "flow gracefully out in folded mantles, based on light sandals; tower-up in high headgear, from amid peaks, spangles, and bell-girdles; swell-out in starched ruffs, buckram stuffings, and monstrous tuberosities"! N in the 1960s is keenly aware of a resurgent Anglo-dandyism. For Christmas 1967 he requests, and is given, a pink shirt, which is considered daringly unmanly and possibly suggestive of proclivities still illegal in England up until July of that year (indeed homosexual acts would not become legal in Scotland until 1980). When his mother makes a trip to London, N asks her to bring back a pair of bell-bottomed trousers, and she chooses a child-sized pair of hippie loons in blue nylon piped with dark stripes. He craves a "cornerboy cap" from a boutique on Queensferry Street, but the jaunty headgear (which might have completed the freewheeling look, allowing him to pass for a junior member of the Incredible String Band or a child Donovan) is beyond the reach of his pocket money. Most of the time he's subject to the strictures of the Edinburgh Academy uniform code, a thin visual gruel scraped together at Aitken & Niven outfitters on George Street: a grey cotton shirt, blue and white tie diagonally striped, dark blue jacket and shorts held up by a pale blue elastic belt with a snake-shaped clip, thick woollen socks suspended by garters, and a braided blue cap featuring the school motif—a Parnassian laurel wreath picked out in glinting thread.

Norman Mailer: "N and his mother make a trip to London in 1968. They visit Carnaby Street, and N is excited to spot a member of the Tremeloes near Marble Arch." Why am I speaking this trivial garbage? Who put my name on this? Can somebody tell me? Where's my lawyer? Seriously, who the fuck is this schmuck we're having to describe and why, exactly, are we doing it? For money? This is a nobody, and we are somebodies. Sure, he's alive and we're dead, but what does that have to do with anything? Don't tell me we're in hell? Don't tell me this is our punishment? Forever? Hubris precedes nemesis, the peak the dip. I should have guessed it. Really. Oh no. I have to read this? This next one? "During a family holiday on the island of Colonsay N meets a London girl with long blond hair who sings the lines from 'Sloop John B' by the Beach Boys: *I want to go home, I feel so broke up, I want to go home . . .*" We all met fucking blondes with acoustic guitars in the sixties, so what? This is bullshit. This is everything that's wrong. Get me the fuck out of here.

Basil Bernstein: For some time young N confused the words "accent" and "accident": he amused his parents one day by saying that a West Coast friend had "a Glasgow accident." Listening to a tape recording of his own voice one day, N remarked with embarrassment how Scottish he sounded. "He says it in the tone of someone confessing to have dirt in his pants," his indignant father exclaimed to guests, as if to exonerate himself from the stigma of such snobbism. This was a topic Bill, as a linguist, knew a great deal about: his shelves heaved with books by Chomsky, Pit Corder (the expert on error who supervised his Ph.D.), and myself, Bernstein. My work on the class dimensions of linguistics broke down speech habits into Restricted and Extended Code. That corresponds roughly with working-class and middle-class usage. Speakers of Restricted Code use language like a series of redundant grunts and chuckles; Extended Code speakers, on the other hand, communicate new and personal insights with subtlety and fluidity. Bill probably found this distinction so compelling in his linguistics work because he was the first member of his family to become a student. Jo was a university librarian while Bill studied English at Glasgow University. The children were brought up with a slightly regional variant on the kind of standard English heard on the BBC Home Service. In the early days there were whimsical slang words: teeth were "toothy pegs," bed "the dowsy den," and the toilet "my potty." The children derived their own personal slang from Emma, the youngest sibling, and her productive mistakes with words. Money was "sixes," "because" was "acos," a monster was a "hoggy," and a killed frog "a deaded ribbit."

Keith Waterhouse: It's not that he lied, exactly. But N—and no doubt his distantly Irish blood was responsible—always knew that reality was as stretchy as knicker elastic. It was a betrayal of the truth to suggest that the truth need be dull. On the top deck of the 19 bus that ran from Charlotte Square to Granton—and that transition was already a kind of miracle—the old women recounted endlessly what "she says to me" and "I says to her" while the old men puffed cigarettes in stoical silence. Clutching his pink bus ticket, N liked to ask about the dream lives of his friends, those earnest Academy boys in their blue uniforms with their Captain Scarlet candy cigarettes. Then he would tell them about his own dream, the one in which badgers with machine guns barged into his basement playroom on the snow-quietened day when he built an entire city from a collection of Tree Top bottle tops, and laid out pencil-bounded streets traversed by flashing red vehicles made of hovering bicycle lights. It was always the future in his dreams, and in his games, but that's because things were always tilting towards the future in the sixties. The Concorde flew low over Scotland one afternoon on a test flight, and the Curries were there to watch it roar past. In Montpellier, in the summer of 1969, N witnessed Neil Armstrong walking on the moon from a student common room near the Jardin des Plantes. The family was in the South of France because Bill was teaching at a summer school. Amid the blazing orchids at the Jardin N noted a huge wasp and a film crew concocting a stop-motion movie, the kind that makes its actors seem to hover by asking them to hop each time a frame is shot. The Apollo mission seemed like an episode tacked onto Méliès's *A Trip to the Moon*. So anyway, the badgers wearing berets jump into the room—N is recounting this nightmare on the smoky top deck of the 19 bus, remember—with their Kalashnikovs poised, ready to spray the place with bullets and spatter everybody in N's model city to *passata di pomodoro*. But they just freeze and fade, for when you die in a dream you just wake up.

Melanie Klein: Towards the end of the second session of this child analysis, some interesting inhibitions and excitations began to emerge. N told me that he had been invited by his friend Bobo Pease to a holiday on a farm in Kirkby Lonsdale. It was the first time N had taken a holiday with a family that was not his own. On the first day, when evening fell, N hid under the bed, too shy to make an appearance downstairs in his pyjamas. When Mrs. Pease came up to ask what the matter was, N said: "This may sound silly, but I don't want anyone to see my bare feet." On another occasion, during a family holiday in France, N had sauntered up and down a beach for half an hour twirling his bathing trunks like a propeller in front of him, unwilling to strip naked in a public place. This inhibition turned to excitation in places where N felt secure, however. In Ainslie Place the front windows were covered with muslin curtains through which passersby could occasionally be seen walking past the clematis-entwined basement railings. Knowing that he could see these strangers without himself being seen, N voluptuously prolonged his morning dressing sessions, turning his semi-nudity into a kind of invisible striptease. But later, in London, visiting the home of the Hunters—metropolitan family friends who worked in the field of progressive journalism—N was disgusted to see Bernard, a boy his own age, parading about the house naked. Nudity, to stay exciting, had to stay shameful.

Dr. Heinrich Hoffmann:

See him strut, this little boy

This paradigm of Dr. Freud

Between a puritan sobriety

And the new "permissive society"!

The fun of sex (how well he knew,

As D. H. Lawrence cottoned too!)

Is all tied up with social order,

Legal boundaries and borders.

And so, delightfully guilt-ridden

N tingled at forbidden

Pleasures that, harmless enough

Were nevertheless not quite love.

And so began his lust for things

That Iggy Pop called "some weird sin"

The marginal, and not the central

The incidental, not the essential.

I have it here in a little note

That lovely Rosemarie Trockel quote:

"The fetishist, that human who

Wants just the shoe but must make do

With the whole woman."

Martin Esslin: The Theatre of the Absurd was only just beginning to be known in Britain at this time; Eugène Ionesco had been nominated in 1964 for the Nobel Prize in Literature, but lost out to Jean-Paul Sartre. There were, as usual, attacks: Ken Tynan said in his *Observer* column that Ionesco's anti-theatre was anti-realist "and by implication anti-reality as well. Here was a writer ready to declare that words were meaningless and that all communication between human beings was impossible." This idea—resisted or not, and perhaps indeed strengthened by the British sense that the new continental theatre was nihilistic and toxic—made its way, if only by accident, into a school play N was involved in during 1968. Mr. Britten, the headmaster of the Edinburgh Academy prep school, harboured artistic ambitions. He wrote a portentous drama called *Ultima Ora*, which is Latin for "the last shore." N was cast as Black Patch the Pirate. Onstage, kitted out with an eye patch, a tricorn hat, and a huge comb, N forgot all his lines and stood there, a pirate mime combing a mermaid's hair. The headmaster was furious, unable to appreciate that his old-fashioned symbolist drama had been much improved by the cosmopolitan—yet, to be perfectly honest, accidental—injection of Absurdism.

George Martin: There's an upright piano in N's sub-basement lair at Ainslie Place, a Bösendorfer. Before it stands, instead of a stool, an old trunk painted orange. Lying around are a leather airman's helmet, a pair of non-functioning headphones—they must be a relic of Bill's National Service training as a radar mechanic with the RAF—and a silver coronet with a dark blue velvet cover: the bardic crown awarded to Jo's grandfather Angus MacKechnie for a Gaelic poem about the Highland Clearances. On the piano are two hardback songbooks from France decorated with daisies and Art Nouveau typography: *Vieilles chansons et rondes pour les petits enfants* and *Chansons de France pour les petits Français*. There's a record player, but only one record: a copy of *Revolver*, which I produced with the boys at Abbey Road in 1966. It's been permanently "borrowed" from a family friend—a tall swinger in kinky boots. *Revolver*, as you know, is a psychedelic record. N ingests secondhand lysergic acid thanks to Strawberry Fields, Lucy in the sky, Emily at play. That feeling is everywhere. The first song N writes—at the age of seven, in 1967—is called "I Can See Japan." Bill records it on his Uher reel-to-reel, capturing N pounding on the Bösendorfer. At-

taching the mic to one of the piano's built-in candelabras, he leads
N through several takes, instructing him to try it "with less noise on
the piano and more singing":

> *I can see Japan*
> *I can see Japan*
> *I can see the mountaintops*
> *And I can see the villages*
> *And I can see your images*
> *And baby, best of all, I can see your love*

That's the whole lyric. The last line is spoken, Barry White style.
The vocal is nasal, the piano-playing plonky, clumpy. Lyrically, N is
copying the Who's "I Can See for Miles," which is actually a song
about surveillance and infidelity. But since this is 1967, Pete Town-
shend hints that he's keeping tabs on his girlfriend with the aid of
tabs of acid: "There's magic in my eyes." When the session is over, N
bounces on his bed to "Tomorrow Never Knows," imagining that its
Indian whoops, backward guitar parts, and sagelike paradoxes are
just what pop music sounds like, and the all-pervading ambience of
LSD perfectly normal. In 1967, perhaps, it is.

Georges Perec: In the eyes of the geometrician, a family with
five members must assume the ideal outline of a pentagonal form,
that is—if it is regular—a shape whose internal angles are 108 degrees and whose convex diagonals are in the relationship of the
golden ratio to its sides. When one fits this family into a car, one sees
a pentagon squeezed into an irregular rectangle, one in which the
parents—the reproducers—sit in two evenly spaced front seats and
the children—the reproduced—sit on a bench behind in a row of
three. If the car is an estate, there is possibly also a golden retriever
present in the area behind, bringing a hint of hexagonality and a

third tier in the hierarchy. The cars into which these creatures—collectively, the Curries—are squeezed are, in sequential order: an Alvis, a Bentley, an Austin, a Rover, a Volvo, another Rover, and then a succession of Volvos through a period in which the family splits into a range of separate cars: Volkswagens, MGBs, and so on. (N is the exception: he will never own a car.) During the period of classical pentagonal order the following sociological conditions pertain: Bill, in the front right-hand seat, drives. To him are therefore presented all the controls, and most of the authority. Jo, in the front left-hand seat, is free to survey the landscape, or the children behind, or her own face in the mirror that flips down on the passenger-side sun visor. The three children sit behind, a stunted proletariat hunched on a padded bench. Mark is often being sick, which gives him the bargaining power to oblige Bill to pull over to the left verge from time to time. N is often bored, turning the sound of the wind into a symphony, or imagining that his cupped fingers are architecture. But it's usually Emma who plucks up the plaintive courage to ask: "Are we nearly there yet?" To be powerless is to be waiting, somewhere beyond the lines of sight. Time seems to drag by more slowly for children than adults, due to their quicker metabolism and the fact that they have nothing to occupy themselves with during a car trip. In desperation the siblings tickle each other and assume silly voices. From time to time Jo has to twist around to control the hilarity, trying instead to interest the subversives in a stately home that is veering by at fifty miles per hour. The children don't even feign interest: it looks like a country version of the kind of town house they already inhabit, without the benefit of a surrounding city. And so the squeezed pentagon—this imperfect power structure, this species of mobile space—continues to whiz through the Scottish countryside, towards some dreary hotel or windswept reservoir.

Herbert Read: Although the influence of modernism on Britain was belated and relatively muted, the 1960s saw its apotheosis. The serene reign of Victor Pasmore, Henry Moore, and Barbara Hepworth had given way—alas!—to the graphic provocations of Patrick Caulfield and Bridget Riley. The Festival of Britain, held on London's South Bank in 1951, had popularised modern architecture and art as a matter of national prestige, and as the sixties arrived the Smithsons and Archigram were agitating for more radical, utopian, and continental attitudes. The BBC's Third Programme—engaged in a noble struggle against mediocrity and mass values—played serialist and even electronic music. Town planners were able to demolish Victorian architecture without the preservationist restrictions that would later inhibit them, replacing sooted slum terraces with Corbusian structures in *béton brut*. In founding, with Roland Penrose, the Institute of Contemporary Arts, I also hoped to advance these values. Crafts and even styles of home decoration were experiencing a similar evolution. Terence Conran opened his first Habitat shop in 1964, hoping to bring modern interior design within the reach of ordinary, open-minded people. Everywhere one felt the influence of Scandinavia—even in Edinburgh, where Jo and Bill Currie had been deeply influenced by their friend Rita Lockhart, the elegant Danish wife of an Ayrshire lawyer. A somewhat Scandinavian interior in Edinburgh in those days was easily achieved: all you had to do was paint the walls of your dingy flat white, sand the floorboards (sanding machines, which made an awful racket and filled the air with the dust of centuries, could be rented by the day), varnish the raw pine, and hang Japanese paper lampshades. One could then find furniture at Norway House on Shandwick Place, fabrics at Town Choice in Stockbridge, stainless steel cutlery at the Royal Mile Boutique run by Swiss expatriate Otto Hartmann, and brightly coloured paper and plastic knickknacks at Studio One. One would then have created a perfect setting in which to float about in a Marimekko dress. The great thing about Scandinavian furniture was that its puritan simplicity allowed it to mix perfectly with preindustrial and rustic items: a round-framed wicker chair, a basketwork stool, even a button-back sofa in olive green velvet. Hang a print of a Paul Klee watercolour on the wall, range a few copies of *House & Garden* magazine about the place, and you could have a pennywise version of what would now be called Midcentury Modern. As for the esoteric and spiritual dimensions of modernism, these could find their presence in nearby books of poetry, or perhaps a copy of my allegorical romance *The Green Child*.

Françoise Sagan: Jo had been an au pair girl in Paris in the mid-1950s, and adored everything French, including of course my novel *Bonjour Tristesse*, which was taking Paris by storm. We were actually close neighbours on the Rue de Grenelle. Jo was keen to inculcate a sense of the proximity and superiority of French culture in her children. And family holidays in France did indeed confirm to N that France was superior. French bread smelled wonderful in a bakery, French lemonade was delicious, and you could get toroid lifebuoys advertising French milk: *Buvez le bon lait!* When they got back to Edinburgh N was sent to extracurricular French lessons at the French Institute on Randolph Crescent. He sat in an upstairs room, velvet-dark, watching audio-synchronised slide presentations of stylised, superior French lifestyles: *Pierre is at the boulangerie. Marie drinks a glass of lemonade. Jean-Claude has a plastic torch.* But the biggest French influence on N came from a Chinese lodger called Olly Kwan. When Olly—a law student from Hong Kong— left Ainslie Place he abandoned a pristine collection of bilingual Françoise Hardy 45s on Vogue Records. The plaintive simplicity of Hardy's songs, the universality of her themes, and the beauty of her face were irresistible. Much later, when he lived in Paris himself and wrote French-style pop songs for Japanese singers, N would never forget that an Asian lodger had kindled his love for francophone pop.

Wayne C. Booth: As I pointed out in *The Rhetoric of Fiction* (1961), to be an unreliable narrator is not merely to be ironic or mendacious, but rather to issue the salient warning *caveat lector*: may the reader beware. It was in this helpful spirit that N lied to his little brother in ways that were designed to undermine his own authority. For example, playing in the Doune Gardens one day Mark found a clump of fungus sprouting from a chopped tree stump and wanted immediately to kick it. But N didn't like the idea, and devised a deliberately absurd "Just Acos story" to explain, unreliably, why Mark should refrain. If Mark kicked the fungus, said N, poison would coat the tips of his shoes, which would need to be thrown out. Dustmen would then pick up the toxic items and find their hands irreversibly compromised. At some global meeting of refuse collectors—a grand banquet, perhaps, or international conference— much shaking of hands would spread the fungal infection so widely that all the dustmen in the world would die. The conclusion was Kiplingesque: "And all just acos you kicked the fungus!" With the prospect of mass manslaughter opening up before him, Mark refrained from kicking the mushrooms, which in point of fact were probably quite harmless. Our hyperbolic yet self-deprecatingly unreliable narrator also had a ready answer when Mark came to him one day asking if it was indeed true that everybody died. Mostly, said N, they did. But if one could make it to the age of ninety-nine and eat a little piece of cheese, one could live forever. Like the various world religions that have promised eternal life, N was no doubt trying to allay his brother's anxieties. But since this was such a transparently foolish—self-destroying rather than self-deprecating— lie, it had the opposite effect: Mark was at first comforted, but later terrified. We all erect screens to place around the horrific prospect of our own mortality, but the one N had provided to his brother was broken. When it comes to the concealment of a death-bed, an unreliable screen is the last thing you want.

Yukio Mishima: N must have been six or seven when he dreamed that he was in a school classroom with girls, and that one came up to him and thrust a spear through his chest. He was aston-ished, and gasped: "Why did you do that?" The girl replied: "It's the spear of love!" Suddenly all the pain was transformed to pleasure. The dream seems to have been inspired by a trip with Jo to the National Gallery of Scotland on the Mound. This pillared building displayed classical paintings, including an image of Saint Sebastian shot through with arrows. Just as it had in me, this scene inspired a mixture of awe and erotic wonder in N. He could understand, just by looking at the bloody scene with its aestheticized suffering, the pleasures of both victimhood and aggression, and the sexual connotations of any act of penetration, any violation of a young and beautiful body, even an act of slaughter. Sensing the private shame-fulness of all this, N refused to answer when Jo asked him which had been his favourite painting.

Miroslav Šašek: In 1961 I published *This Is Edinburgh*, the fifth in my series of quirky city guides for children. The Curries had a copy, along with *This Is Paris*. It took me three months to paint the book. I was at the peak of my success—I made *This Is Munich* and *This Is Venice* that same year. The sprinkling Edinburgh rain was my constant foe as I drew the Scottish capital. I depicted—in an amusing style akin to that of Saul Steinberg in America, or Ryohei Yanagihara in Japan—Highland terriers, bagpipe players, or a man flying up the windy steps from Waverley Station to Princes Street. In this way the young Curries came to see their own city through the eyes of a Czech émigré. That was not unprecedented: there was already a fascinating book on their shelves called *The Silent Traveller in Edinburgh*. Chiang Yee, its author and illustrator, was a Chinese citizen exiled from his homeland in 1933. He made everywhere he visited look like China. So Princes Street Gardens, in his rendering, looks like a blossoming oriental mountain. Swivel round in your library seat and you might see my double-page rendering of the shop façades of Princes Street, which would later influence Sylvain Chomet in his animated film *The Illusionist*. In 1981 the existentialist Edinburgh beat group Josef K would trace my panorama and render it in black and gold on the cover of their debut album *The Only Fun in Town*. Together we almost managed to persuade N that Edinburgh was elsewhere.

T. S. Eliot: When N's parents started dating, Bill would often carry my *Collected Essays* pinched beneath his arm. It showed his essential seriousness, and was guaranteed to impress Jo, a university librarian. With the marriage established on these foundations, the children were given *Old Possum's Book of Practical Cats* as a matter of course. N's favourite cat was the Rum Tum Tugger, the perverse beast who always wants to be out when he's in and in when he's out. N was becoming an animal of this type. As evidence I will simply cite a visit to the Stockbridge Toyshop in 1966. Jo tells N that he can have anything he wants. Certainly, gazing up at the window, he had wanted almost everything. But now that he must pick one thing, he cannot decide. A Corgi car or a Matchbox? An India rubber hooter for his Tri-ang tricycle? A model aircraft made of balsa wood? He is taking too long, and the offer is rescinded. N is oddly relieved. An austere and ascetic sense of self-denial sets in, and it is much more delightful than the pleasures of ownership. Like the stubborn Tugger, he only values what he finds for himself.

François Truffaut: In the late 1960s N was a pupil at the Edinburgh Academy prep school. He had to take the bus—in the company of his sensible friend John Thomson, who grew up to be a lawyer, but was essentially already one at seven—from the nineteenth-century crescents of the New Town to this more sub-urban dimension beyond the Botanical Gardens. It felt like time travel, for out there at Inverleith everything was newly built. Imagine a mildly dystopian gated complex like the conformist world you see in my film *Fahrenheit 451*. The prep school has a brick clock tower that surveys a turning circle. There's a house for the head-master, rugby pitches, large classroom wings left and right, an entry atrium that feels like a provincial theatre lobby, a tuck shop where you can buy sweets, an assembly room full of small chairs. Behind that stand various music and art workshops and a gymnasium that smells of rubber mats and squeaks with plimsolls. Corridors lead to more classroom blocks, overlooking a wooded area and the squat spire of a church. A huge new dining hall is being constructed out there for the boarders. N is small for his age, but full of energy. He never walks when he can run. He has no interest in the school's otherworldly sport ("hails," it's called, and you play it with a wooden "clacken"), but likes to imagine he's piloting a futuristic vehicle—his own body—using a stainless steel rudder. He generally tops his English class and nears the bottom for everything else. He's good at drawing and can differentiate proximal microtones better than anyone in his class, but academically he's indolent when subjects don't interest him, and actually gets demoted from the B to the C stream. The extraterrestrial clacken becomes a weapon: N is beaten for being lazy. His guitar teacher keeps telling him to stop improvis-ing. He shudders when people use Americanisms they've picked up from TV, like greeting each other with "Hi!" He hates homework, but enjoys preparing neat reports, like the account he makes—gluing black-and-white photos into a jotter—of the family's 1967 visit to Eire, where the tent blows away in a storm and N falls for a bowl-haired, freckly Irish girl called Christine. There are unfortunately no girls at the Edinburgh Academy. The most impressive thing he sees at prep school is the opening sequence of a film projected in the assembly hall: a red Lamborghini Miura is threading its way through the Alps to the strains of a Quincy Jones arrangement, with Matt Monro crooning in rather synthetic Italian: *Questi giorni, quando viene il bel sole . . .* The film is called *The Italian Job*, and it encodes a Mediterranean sensuality and grandeur—the mountains, the music, the sunshine. All this points to N's own future, which will lie, for the next year or so, far south, beyond the Alps.

Gerald Durrell: In 1969 Bill takes a job with the British Council and is posted to Athens. The living room at 6 Ainslie Place resounds with Greek phrases as Bill learns the language from records: *Κλείσε την πόρτα: Close the door.* There's a description at the beginning of *My Family and Other Animals*—my account of my own family's relocation to Greece, thirty years before—in which I describe my brother Larry's casual suggestion to our mother that we should head to Corfu: "'Why do we stand this bloody climate?' he asked suddenly, making a gesture towards the rain-distorted window . . . 'Why don't we pack up and go to Greece?'" Mother, to our surprise, agrees, and we are soon living on an enchanted isle where I can assemble my own personal menagerie of baby scorpions and ancient tortoises, and Larry can entertain visiting bohemians. The Greece experienced by the Curries is closer to the world Larry describes in his book about working on Cyprus as an English teacher and press attaché, *Bitter Lemons*. Bill drives out first in the family car, a black three-litre Rover P5, which is soon equipped with *corps diplomatique* plates. He rents the upper floor of a house in Psychiko, a district not far from the residence of the military dictator, Georgios Papadopoulos. The rest of the family arrives in September

1969. Each day Bill drives the black Rover down Kifisias Avenue to the British Council's headquarters on Kolonaki Square, while the children walk to St. Catherine's British Embassy School, just a few blocks north of the flat, along gently curving streets punctuated with orange, peach, and pine trees which ring in the summer months with the cheerful sound of cicadas.

1970–1980

Being a man means never being oneself.

—Witold Gombrowicz, *Pornografia*

George Orwell: It is, of course, the first time N has lived under a totalitarian regime. How does such a political arrangement make itself known to the consciousness of a child? N sees a cinema where the weapons on the posters are blacked out, just as the title and author are blacked out on the latest Penguin edition of my novel *Nineteen Eighty-Four*. This is apparently so that paramilitary groups can't carve model weapons out of soap bars and stage some sort of *coup de théâtre*. N notices the little billboards punctuating country roads, showing the junta's symbol: a rising phoenix, the silhouette of a soldier holding a machine gun (with just enough detail to be recognised as a weapon, but not enough to be copied), and the date of the military coup: April 21, 1967. He talks with the secret service men who stand on side streets along the route the dictator's limousine takes home from the city centre. Sometimes these men are friendly, and pinch the cheek of a blond child, as all Greeks tend to do. But they are there to intercept assassins. N learns that when people sing the song "O Giorgos ine poniros"—apparently an innocent story of an untrustworthy husband—it contains a double sense, a hidden meaning, something to do with the Greek king and his relationship with the regime. It plants in N's mind the idea that songs can mean more than they seem to say.

Norman Hunter: N is charmed by the hot weather in Athens, the lemon, pine, and palm trees around the ramshackle building that serves as the British Embassy School. There are regular explosions from the hidden quarries atop Tourkovounia, the "Turkish mountain," which tips the whole area forty-five degrees. Huge shiny flying beetles guzzle the fruit on the peach trees at the bottom of the spiral staircase connecting the kitchen to the flat roof above and garden below. If you step on one it crushes with a horrible crunch. N is given his own personal lemon tree, from which he picks and sucks the fruit. Rose's Lime Juice Cordial from the British Embassy shop can be mixed with cold water from the fridge to slake thirst as one gazes out at the marble-topped mountains of Attica, sometimes obscured by dust storms. A bread man cycles past the house daily, crying: *"Psomi, psomi!"* The kids in the Greek school opposite chant: *"Scholeío, Athína, Psychikó!"* I am N's favourite writer in 1970, for Puffin has just published *The Peculiar Triumph of Professor Branestawm.* Eccentricity and inventiveness can win, that's my message! My book is displayed quite prominently in the St. Catherine's library; the school itself is somewhat eccentric. N loves the fact that you can wear what you like there, and grow your hair to any length. He likes the school's symbol, the owl of Minerva, and its art classroom, where people make wavy abstractions based on Victor Vasarely's paintings. And he particularly appreciates the fact that this institution—unlike the Edinburgh Academy—is mixed. There are women teachers, like the plump Miss Bath or the elegant Miss Porter. And girl pupils. Maria is a Greek girl who wears fashionable miniskirts and high boots. Rupa is an Indian assigned as his Scottish Country Dancing partner. And Kirsti is a serious Norwegian with bobbed blond hair. One day, pressed back in his seat by the seamless acceleration of the luxurious automatic car that transports smooth, handsome American Paul to school, N hears Kirsti describing the midnight sun in Norway. He decides in that moment that he loves her, and begins inking her name on pencil cases and scented erasers. This soon gets back to Kirsti, and one day during lunch she approaches N as he nibbles at a cucumber sandwich and slaps his back to prove to Alex (marine buzz cut, beady eyes, a wiry American friend of her brother) that she doesn't reciprocate these too-much-protested feelings. There's worse humiliation when, during a school coach trip to Delphi, Paul and Kirsti sit together. Paul casually swivels round and asks N whether he knows how babies are made. N has no idea. "The man puts his thing into the woman's," says Paul in the silky voice of Robert Vaughn. Kirsti—neither confirming nor denying this—casts a thin-lipped glance back through the seat-gap. N's face is a sight to see. Can such a thing really be possible? It sounds undignified, uncivilised, and uncomfortable. Even after the coach has parked, the idea—a real-life brainstorm predicting a newly outlandish future—quite overshadows the ruins. N can't stop thinking about it as he climbs the Sacred Way to the Temple of Apollo.

Jesper Jensen: Along with Søren Hansen, who is still in the land of the living, I wrote *The Little Red Schoolbook* in 1969. It was a radical handbook for kids, physically modelled on Chairman Mao's Little Red Book. We were two Danish hippies, teachers who wanted to tell children not to be cowed—or overly controlled—by adults. Adults are paper tigers, that's how we put it. What our book said about sex and religion caused a moral panic in the Vatican, in Britain, and elsewhere. It was banned in France and Italy, bowdlerised in Britain. This panic, needless to say, did not hurt sales; we got lots of free publicity. N read an article about *The Little Red Schoolbook* in a copy of *The Times Literary Supplement* in 1970. It must have been about Mary Whitehouse's campaign against the book, or the pope's, or Margaret Thatcher's. There were so many attacks, it was easy to lose track. Intrigued—and still remembering the humiliation of the school trip to Delphi—N immediately asked his parents to get him a copy. Perhaps relieved that they wouldn't have to explain the facts of life, they ordered one, with a matching copy for his brother Mark. "If anybody tells you it's harmful to masturbate," Søren and I say in the book, "they're lying. If anybody tells you you mustn't do it too much, they're lying too, because you can't do it too much. Ask them how often you ought to do it. They'll usually shut up then." This was a timely message for N, because 1970 was the year in which he first had an orgasm. It happened during siesta time. That in itself was a novelty, for northern Europeans don't generally go to bed in the afternoon. N had his own small room—a former box room—at the front of the house, overlooking "Narcissus Street." Taped to the wall was a calendar featuring drawings of girls in purple maxi skirts. N had pocketed it when it slipped out of an Italian fashion magazine in the Alpha Beta department store. Beyond the shuttered window stood an aromatic pine tree in which cicadas chafed and chirred. During siesta N was lying on his tummy, not thinking of anything in particular, when suddenly a dry spasm filled him with an extraordinary stab of pleasure. Something about it reminded him of the games he played with soap bubbles in the little bathroom across the corridor: catching the light, blown between finger and thumb, each soap bubble swirled with colour then filled with sick brown whorls before popping with a tiny detergent splash. It was something like that, something physical and chemical happening in the middle of his body, and—liberated from any sense of guilt or shame by our handbook—N knew that the bubble would keep popping.

Gerome Ragni: I wrote the American tribal rock opera *Hair* with James Rado and Galt MacDermot. I was mostly responsible for the lyrics. In the Athens apartment, our original Broadway recording of *Hair* was an important presence. There were only four LPs in the

N

I

C

H

E

apartment: a spoken-word comedy record called *The Frost Report on Everything*, an Everly Brothers compilation, *Abbey Road* by the Beatles, and *Hair*, with its cover featuring my red and green solarized Afro. The song that made the most impression on the ten-year-old N was called "Sodomy." My lyric was pithy: "Sodomy, fellatio, cunnilingus, pederasty: Father, why do these words sound so nasty? Masturbation can be fun, join the holy orgy Kama Sutra everyone." There was also one 45 rpm single in the house, bought by Helen, the Scottish live-in nanny. It was "Mony Mony" by Tommy James and the Shondells. N played it in Helen's room, circling around her portable record player getting increasingly ecstatic. "You make me feel (*Mony Mony*) so (*Mony Mony*) good (*Mony Mony*) yeah!" As N moved around the room the music moved too, and as N sang and clapped along to the thumping beat he got higher and higher as the oxygen flowing to his brain thinned out. He became a tribe of one. What other art form could make you feel like this?

Jean Webster: Along with Gerald Durrell and Norman Hunter, I was one of the authors N favored in Athens. Oh, he certainly admired the orange and yellow op art cover of Nikos Kazantzakis's modern sequel to *The Odyssey*, which sat—apparently spinning, a miniaturized Bridget Riley—on the bookshelf in the living room, but he was never going to read its 33,333 seventeen-syllable verses. Good grief! My 1912 epistolary novel *Daddy-Long-Legs* was much more suitable then—though it may be less so now, with its tale of a teenage orphan corresponding with (and then marrying) an anonymous trustee over a decade her senior. N's copy, carefully protected by a cover made from an olive-green bag from the Giant D supermarket, was inscribed with his mother's maiden name and address: "Joyce Hood, Monaliadh, Blanefield, 24/12/51." Joyce changed her name to Jo, just as Jerusha in my novel changes hers to Judy. The novel is about the self-creation of a lively-minded person whose past is as unclear as her future. Both her parents and her future spouse—the trustee she's writing to, who has pledged not to write back—are mute, shrouded in mystery. Yet Judy's vivacity and charm allow her to make a niche for herself. In a sense she writes herself into existence.

Michelangelo Antonioni: N rides a traditional bicycle around the streets of Psychiko. To make it more exciting he removes the mudguards and paints the machine mustard yellow. Sometimes he even rigs up a piece of cardboard so that it clacks and whirrs in the spokes like a motorbike engine. The avenues of Psychiko are mostly tranquil, but sometimes young Greeks race brightly coloured BMW and Alfa Romeo cars. They too are trying to make as much noise as possible. There are also Lancias, and occasionally you can see a Ferrari or a Lamborghini. I imagine all this in long shot, with a wild Farfisa organ on the soundtrack. Sometimes his brother, Mark, is with N, and they ride up to the ridge of Tourkovounia and speed home by "the fast route." Or they head along Narkissou to the bakery, with its World War II machine-gun turrets. One day N cycles past Platea Efkalipton (with its kiosk selling bars of pink-blossoming ION almond chocolate), past the Bluebell Café (where they serve a glass of cold water with every drink), past St. Catherine's school, past the pine-shaded playground to the mysterious hedged roundabout that contains the open-air cinema screen. Peeking through a gap in the hedge, N sees the famous explosion scene in my *Zabriskie Point*. The blast is in slow motion, filmed from every possible angle, and the Pink Floyd music is somehow spiritual, transforming destruction into beauty. Pucci dresses, colour televisions, refrigerators, meat, it all cascades slowly up into the sky and then down again as the real estate developer's desert house is destroyed over and over again. The music turns savage and atonal, punctuated by screams. This consumerist critique, this time-shifting, this revenge, this fantasia of destruction, this philosophical pornography is just what films do, and films like this are what adults watch behind closed doors, and children can only glimpse through a hedge.

Edward Lear:
A cassette tape recorder's a curious thing
On which you can store sonic stuff
A cassette tape resembles a square ball of string
But it's quite as addictive as snuff

If you sing through a tube like the nose of a mole
Some ballad of old bric-a-brac
Like an echo, a mirror, a will-o'-the-wisp
The contraption will sing the thing back

If a globular vat in a cellar of wine
May at last the term "vintage" deserve
So rotting sound, with the passage of time
May become a delicious preserve

So keep these cassettes, these hootings of owls
And brush them to clear out the sand
For, besides a parade of most cretinous howls
Each one is also a land

Johann Wolfgang von Goethe: I would like to make an intervention, if I may, through my translator, from this place where, I am glad to say, I have an upright desk commanding an excellent view from a high window, to mention the title of one of my novels, *Elective Affinities*, and say that, although I was influenced, with that phrase, primarily by my amateur experiments with chemistry, the wider implication is that there exists in the universe a set of extra-geographical, extra-sanguinary connections, or potential connections, between things, and that it is up to us, as sentient and sensible creatures making our way through the world, to find the affinities that will most fruitfully structure our lives. At certain times and places it is believed that only ties of family and place—race and soil—matter, but I value those extraordinary moments when perspectives widen and possibilities for discovery seem infinite, for this eternal openness to what is distant and tenuous is truly what is meant by the term "enlightenment": it is an *Aufklarung*, or clarification. The German title of *Elective Affinities* is *Die Wahlverwandtschaften*: *wahl* means "choice" and *verwandtschaft* is "relationship," so this phrase presents the idea that "chosen relationships" might transcend given or fated bonds. One English translator called the novel *Kindred by Choice*. There is an implied distinction here between the first family, the one we are born into, which we cannot choose, and the second, the one we elect to form with someone we love. On the social level there is the implication of a transition from a feudal order of obligation to a democratic order of choice. And there is a contrast between the fatalistic oriental idea of "tasting one's fate" and the Western individualistic dream of "overcoming one's fate." For a child who is whipped out of one context, one city or nation, and dropped into another, it immediately becomes apparent that other ways of living, thinking, and acting exist—etiquettes, inventions, traditions, and customs that one may think better, or worse, than the life one knows, or, more likely, which may appear to be a mixture of improvements and degradations, from which, perhaps, one may feel free to pick and choose. What is essential is the disappearance of the taken-for-grantedness of one's former, local existence. As the experiences of difference in the life on an individual multiply, they encourage not only what philosophers have come to call, in the centuries following my life span, "cultural relativism," but also a beneficial kind of cultural dilettantism, a fragmented mosaic-like approach to life in which one might, for example, enjoy music as the Italians do, build like an ancient Greek, and reason like Leibniz, Wolff, or Lessing—in other words, like a German. From here at my high death-desk I have witnessed successive waves of the expansion and contraction of possibilities in the lives of individuals, which, it seems to me, are microcosmic representations of the possibilities and restrictions in the scope and reach of humanity itself. The move to Greece—albeit Greece in its worst political moment—was to introduce to the mind of young N a theme of great importance in his future life: the idea that there are always alternative orders, and that one may, by election, which is to say by informed and conscious choice, and by selection, which is to say by travel—by the willed movement toward an ideal—overcome alienation by discovering people and ways of life that fit one's own affinities better than whatever is immediately presented by chance and the mere vagaries of circumstance. N's father, at the British Council in Athens, may have been charged professionally with the spread of British values and the English language, but the effect on his own family was precisely the opposite: now, for the first time, came the possibility of a porosity, an exposure to other values than British ones, and other languages than English. In Greece N began to compile, in his mind, a private encyclopaedia of elective possibilities that was, in a sense, a charter for all his future freedoms.

David Niven: Did I mention that *The Moon's a Balloon*, my 1971 memoir, sold over five million copies worldwide? Oh, are we on? I'm here to recount an anecdote about the Hoods, Jo's parents. I've been chosen because I look a bit like David Hood. Obviously we also share a Christian name. And we were born at about the same time. Like me, David was a bit of a ladies' man, a dapper sort in flannels and blazers, with a receding hairline, monolids, and a pencil moustache. He'd been a regional tennis champion in his youth, and kept a certain debonair charm into late middle age. The contrast with William, the paternal grandfather, could not have been more extreme. David drove a French car—a creamy Renault Dauphine—and flirted in a louche but acceptable way (by the standards of the day, anyway) with the village shopgirls. He liked to tease Granny Jan (a rather serious English teacher) by making caricatures of her as the Giles Grandma from the *Daily Express* cartoons. The Hoods lived in half a house in Blanefield, set just above the Glasgow Road, with the Campsie Hills rising behind. David sold aeronautical parts, a job that kept him close to the Prestwick Aerodrome (as it was then known) during the war. So Bill and Jo first glimpsed each other at Prestwick High School. A visit to Blanefield mostly involved leg-pulling humour: David would teach N to sing "Ye cannae push yer Granny off a bus"—while Jan twinkled and grumbled in the background—or the Glasgow way to say "police" (*po-lis*, with a gormless rising intonation). Meanwhile Jan would make Mark speak a series of spelled-out Scottish surnames, then trip him up with the pronunciation of "M-A-C-H-I-N-E," which of course is not MacHine but *machine*. Mostly, though, my namesake seemed content to watch John Wayne films on the colour telly, which stood beside the fireplace, banging away next to a framed 1950s reproduction of Notre-Dame cathedral seen from the back. Up the garden there was a rhubarb patch and a summer house containing—to N's fascination—a wind-up phonograph and a stack of 78 rpm shellac disks. One of them featured a song called "Yodeling Bill," which might have been a satirical wink in the direction of Jo's beau, except that it must have been made and bought twenty years before they met at Glasgow University. There are photos of the Hoods' visit to Athens in 1971, and they somehow look completely out of place under the brilliantly coloured sun-brollies on the Psychiko terrace: pallid, cigarette-puffing Scots who might think of visiting the Mediterranean on holiday (they'd been to Rome, probably inspired by Peck and Hepburn) but would never actually move there. Personally, I prefer Hollywood. Athens may have the climate, but it just ain't got the roles, old sport.

Wilhelm Reich: Just as N's sexuality is coming to life in shuttered rooms during siesta, he begins to notice anomalies in Psychiko, things that can only be explained by the universal sexual energy I have called "orgone." Why, for instance, does a Jaguar creep along behind Scottish Helen, the buxom, ginger-haired family nanny, when she picks the children up from school? You may call a Jaguar a car, but is it not in these circumstances—infused with accumulations of the orgastic life force—a sort of metal cat? This creature, tawny-colored and stealthy, its bottom wagging as a cat's hindparts do before it pounces, is a car-cat, a sexual jaguar stalking prey. There is no more running now, no more driving; all the creature's instincts are directed toward predation. The driver—the jaguar's brain—is processing the motile algorithms of Helen's bottom, the science of her curves. He forgets his separation from the metal thing around him. He is no longer driving, but driven, no longer a Greek human but now the brain of this prowling, growling beast of prey. Like something transformed by the gods, the metal animal begins to breathe quickly, to yowl and pant, gripped by its deepest instincts—those we have lost in these armor-plated days of repressed little men. The animal grows tense, tight on its chassis. The woman knows, and trembles. She is considered plain in her native land, but here she is rare and beautiful. She is self-conscious about her weight, but now, under the pitiless Attic sun, with nowhere to hide, and two innocent children to guide, her curves inspire the lust they have always wished to provoke. The woman—for now she is an archetype—is both appalled and proud. She doesn't tell the children to pay no attention, because that would draw attention to the stalking. Don't look back! Keep walking! Perhaps this beast will never strike! Perhaps nothing unusual is happening after all! Perhaps it is not a cat, just a car moving—slowly—up the street.

D. H. Lawrence: All islands have something bare and primal, a primal wild force of rock and wave, wind and water, with everything swept and cleaned by the wind, and washed by the water rushing to the shore and sweeping across the shingle like some living thing. In 1970 there's a family holiday on the island of Andros, where the friendly Villiers family are holed up in a big house with a Ping-Pong table, dominated by the twins Sisi and Lala. Somehow the bare-hilled Greek islands recall the Hebrides; you could be on Spetses when you were on Colonsay, and on Colonsay when you were on Spetses, and always the bare and primal liquid force of wind and wave and rock would be there, sweeping over you and making you smooth and inorganic, like ancient rock or water. N remembers a trip inland, and a visit to an old crone who offered too-sweet, honey-dripping Greek sweets—fanouropita, or melomakarona, or portokalopita—and sour Greek marmalade. "The word 'marmalade' comes from the Greek word *melimelon*, which is an apple grafted onto a quince," says Bill, instructively. Out on the hillside, full of marmalade, N runs ahead of the party of adults. He rushes ahead like a young goat, full of the ecstasy of life. What he wants, more than anything else, is for someone to say: "Look, he runs like a goat, as nimble as a young buck! See how nimbly, how goatily, he keeps to the path!" But nobody says it, nobody notices, and that is because I, Lawrence, am not on Spetses, to notice things with my fierce and glittering eyes and speak them out frankly, into the rushing island wind, to utter and issue them from my fiercely truthful bearded face, in that place of wind and water and curves and rocks.

Edward Stratemeyer: Although I put my name to them, I didn't write the Hardy Boys mysteries myself. They were a franchise ghostwritten by employees of my book packaging company, Stratemeyer Syndicate. Frank and Joe Hardy were decent middle-class American kids who doubled as detectives, turning hard-working blue-collar criminals over to the police. They were little fascists, little finks, but you didn't hear it from me. N wasn't really into this stuff, but a big house farther along Narkissou reminded him of one of the covers, the original jacket for *The Tower Treasure*. A rich American boy lived there in the lap of luxury. His nickname was Monster, because he had that kind of screwed-up Jerry Lewis type of face, and liked to goof around. Well, Monster had an out-house set up for band rehearsals. There were amps in there, basses, guitars, a drum kit. Monster and his friends practiced often, so loud you could hear them from the street. One day N was passing and stopped to listen, and Monster caught sight of him and beckoned him in. Could he sing? Now, N loved to sing. He could make the *White Horses* TV show theme ring around the pale staircase of his entrance lobby, with its marbled reverb. So he stepped up to the mic. Monster asked what he'd like to sing, and N said "Hey Jude." Like in a movie, the band just knew it, knew the key and everything, and launched straight in. That's how N remembers it, anyway. There he was at a mic, on a hot afternoon in Athens, with a band of rich kids backing him. A vocalist! It was a heck of a lot better than being a fink.

Paul Gallico: Apparently the gods have decreed that N's life in Athens cannot last. The British Embassy School is not best equipped to get him through all the exams he will need, and to be a success in life one needs, above all, exam results. So in September of 1970 Jo accompanies N from Athens to London on a vehicle called the Europabus. They stay overnight behind the Iron Curtain, in a hotel in Belgrade with an extraordinary mural made of orange and yellow felt. N spends most of the journey with a hand mirror pressed to the window, tilted at forty-five degrees so that the scenery seems to be rushing toward a futuristic vehicle that he is piloting and pointing off-road. Perhaps this represents a wish to be going anywhere other than in the direction of Scotland, with its cold rain and sooty buildings. Jo and N take the train from London to Edinburgh and N is kitted out with a trunk and all the required items of a school uniform. It is frightening and rather Dickensian; N feels like an orphan in the making. As a conciliatory gesture, to soften the imminent parting, Jo takes him to the Bauermeister Bookshop, where he can choose whatever he wants. Among the books he picks are two of my novellas, *The Snow Goose* and *Flowers for Mrs. Harris* (known in America as *Mrs. 'Arris Goes to Paris*). N is as much attracted by the Penguin covers—designed by Tony Meeuwissen—as the promise of a moving avian tale and a light comedy about a char lady who longs for a Dior dress. Both tales will make him cry, but at boarding school he will already be crying quite enough.

Edgar Allan Poe: In the course of a muffled and dim Saturday, with the low clouds almost stifling them, N and his mother arrived by taxi at a particularly dreary cul-de-sac in northern Edinburgh, and soon found themselves, as the final evening of N's freedom hastened on with a terrible inevitability, within sight of the melancholy House of Mackenzie. How to explain that from the first sight of the Victorian building an unbearable sense of dread descended on N? I say unbearable, for there was no admixture of emotional excitement, nothing of the permission to exaggerate that a young dramatist might squeeze from the promise of a terrible or tragic experience. The future seemed to stand in stone: lapidary, drear, cold, and hopeless. N stared up at the craggy eaves of that silhouette on Kinnear Road—the Gothic shard surrounded by glum stalactites of deadened hedge and the beetle-infested trunks of damp trees, its southern aspect confronting an endless hell of rugby pitches—and he could already sense the dormitories within, the rules and punishments, the surveillance, the threats of obloquy, the lack of privacy, the bullying, austerity, and routine to come. All were promised by the skull-like façade that now gazed down with hollow, proprietorial eyes, bespeaking nothing but bleak suffering, filling N to every particle and extremity of his being with a sense of quiescent futility, as some kind of powerful veterinary drug that rushes through a horse, numbing and stunning as it goes. No charm could save him now, and no magic phrase postpone this division from his mother, who delivered him to the unctuous, buzzing, bluebottle-fingered housemaster, trunk and all, before fleeing in shame and haste, in order, perhaps, to conceal her own tears, for it must have been palpable to all—how could it be otherwise?—the pungent and poisonous atmosphere of horror that crept, like fog or a regulation plaid bedspread of suffocating fustian, across the façade of that bleak and ghastly mansion, that desolate and pitiless jail, that hideous specter rising from a keening charnel ground, the House of Mackenzie.

Anthony Burgess: And now, my droogies, life takes a turn to the strack. Little N has been sent to the stripey hole which is boarding skolliwoll, where the boorjoyce malchicks all blub until they're bolnoy. It is indeed a kick in the yarblockos, for there his voloss is chopped off, and into regulation platties and toofles is he tolchocked. Miffi is a lair of ultraviolence, a world of regulations and confiscations, my brats, enforced by a matron most oozhassny. The housemaster is a starry dedoochka called Quack, and the beatings come most frequent. Taken away is *The Little Red Schoolbook*, and taken away the *Hair* songbook. Ruggerby is the only recreation here, my droogies, as frequent and forcible as the Scottish rain. Never is N alone except to dung, and there in the cubicle, where none may viddy, he boohoos, snorting into tissues while, just outside, the boarder bratchnies, cackling and cavorting, wait to vred him up, crunch his litso and rip his cables until out doth spew the red krovvy, all mingled with salties.

Michel Foucault: Let's not exaggerate. While there may be an air of ambient menace in the boarding school, there is little actual violence. The boys provide some knock-around, certainly, some low-level bullying, a lot of teasing. There is the constant threat of an "operation," some kind of initiation ritual in the communal showers, but masterly supervision prevents it from materialising. Control is maintained—as in all such institutions—by carefully calibrated systems of reward and punishment, privilege and deprivation. Mackenzie House is one of the junior residential houses for the Edinburgh Academy, a private school in the British "public school" tradition. Edinburgh Castle looms on the southern horizon, though it's better viewed from the nearby Botanical Gardens. Boarders pass, among the day boys—who outnumber them nine to one—as a kind of class apart, tough and savvy. But actually, within the boarding house itself, surprisingly different values prevail, those of cosmopolitanism and femininity. Soon after learning a boy's name (always the surname), one learns where his family is stationed: Oman, Nigeria, Sierra Leone, Greece . . . Everyone is given a nickname, often a feminine one: Malcolm becomes Molly, Neil Nelly, and so on. For N, different boys try different names: some are jokes about "curry" (Hot Stuff, Stew), some refer to his fashion sense and fondness for singing (Groovy, Humperstinck), some refer to his initials (N.J., pronounced Nidge), one to his quick metabolism and protuberant front teeth (Rabbit) and one to his presumed sexuality (Poof). Nidge and Poof are the names that stick.

Albert Camus: N is in the boot room one day—the ground-floor room where all the shoes are kept. Vurich, handsome and delinquent, is there too. He's teasing N for his patent leather Greek shoes, which N explains allow him to skate the marble pavements of Athens like an ice rink. Attention moves to N's fat watchband. Vurich is preparing some line of attack, so N says, to forestall him: "Hey, wouldn't it be dead funny if Bezzy put his shoes on and found his heels sinking into two little shitey piles of boot polish?" Vurich likes the idea. "Ha ha, that would chiz Bezzy!" So he does the deed, and pollutes the shoes. Bez falls for it but clipes, and the two culprits—brains and muscle—are immediately called to Quack's study. Through the door N hears Quack's duck voice, and then the tawse swooshing and Vurich crying out in pain. When it's his turn, N is confronted with a deal: he can be spared an actual beating if he agrees to become Quack's little helper. He must just report anything he sees, any infringement of any regulation, to the housemaster. He agrees—anything to avoid physical pain! He never actually reports, but does boast about the role in a letter to his father, who replies with alarm: "I hope you are not becoming what we call a little snitch!" N is ashamed. "We" are not people like that. We are not necessarily on the side of crime, but neither do we side with authority. We resist, subtly. We come to moral decisions. We are individuals, but not incapable of solidarity.

Virginia Woolf: If one thing has been widely remarked upon and celebrated, during the posthumous Iliad of my spirit, it is my emphasis on the cardinal importance of a room of one's own. And this is precisely what one does not have at boarding school. N finds some lonely refuge in a boiler room located between the sports changing rooms and a windowless cave dedicated to model-making. Here, in the tropical heat blasted out by a wire-caged gas boiler, he sits on a bare concrete floor next to the mattresses of bed-wetters. The welcome solitude easily outweighs the sharp scent of urine which must be endured in that dim place. N has brought an aquamarine-spined Penguin Modern Classics edition of Alan Paton's *Cry, the Beloved Country*. The book, set in Natal, South Africa, promises both sunshine and sadness. Yet somehow N never seems to progress very far into its dense mass of pages, for his own thoughts rise up and swim before him constantly. He thinks of his other semi-private space, the locker allocated in the glassy corridor directly above. This twelve-inch-square plywood nook is not lockable, and already the housemaster has confiscated several items from it: his *Hair* songbook (apparently subversive), his *Little Red Schoolbook* (definitely immoral), his cassette tape recorder (there is no rule against them because the authorities do not even know what they are, but Quack Mendl takes it anyway), and an American military cap he likes to wear in bed. One book is snatched from him after he is discovered reading it by torchlight under the blankets at night. It is not pornography, but a copy of *Roget's Thesaurus*: N loves to surprise words in their natural habitat as they assemble at dusk across the savannah of creamy pages, but his safari is interrupted and the book is withheld for a week. Soon the visits to the boiler room cease too: Matron discovers him there one day and exclaims, "That's disgusting!" He is banned from his urethral fiefdom forthwith. Matron never specifies what she thinks he has been doing in that stifling chamber, but she seems to believe that a room of one's own has only one likely purpose, and it is a disgusting one.

Henry Darger: I am—well, I was—Henry Darger. When I was twelve they diagnosed "masturbation" and put me in the Lincoln County Asylum for Feeble-Minded Children. I escaped and grew up to be a vulcanologist, a janitor, a hospital dishwasher, a writer, and a drawing-tracing painter. With my neighbor William Schloeder I also formed the Children's Protective Society, because it has always been abhorrent to me that children should be hurt in any way.

N
I
C
H
E

In my novel *The Story of the Vivian Girls, in What Is Known as the Realms of the Unreal, of the Glandeco-Angelinian War Storm Caused by the Child Slave Rebellion* I picture the dearest flowers of all the world—those seven valiant crusading Vivian Girls—being chopped up, broken, and shattered in every conceivable way by the Glandelinians and their evil slave-trading machinery of death. I am sorry to report that the Edinburgh Academy was also in the stranglehold of the Glandelinians when N was a pupil there. When he was ten his mathematics teacher, General Manley, would call boys up to his desk to explain some problem to them, and touch their little penises and testicles by running his hands up the inside of their shorts. Manley was certainly a looker, almost an idol of the Robert Redford school, and he was married with children of his own. But appearances are not everything, and that was a most awfully wrong thing to do. A boy called Kim told his parents, and they told the headmaster, and General Manley was court-martialed and frog-marched out of the Academy in disgrace. They should have tied the general to a maple tree surrounded by purple foxgloves, on a day of lightning flashing from towering cumulonimbus configurations, and shot him by firing squad directly through his waistcoat. Instead, imagine N's surprise on learning that Manley had simply been re-hired immediately by a rival Edinburgh private school! For it appeared that other institutions were also in the hands of the Glandelinians.

Geoffrey Willans: One of the privileges at Miffi is membership of the Senior Common Room, up at the very top of the building, among the chimneys—only a dozen boys are allowed to use this attic room, which boasts a small shelf of titles by Kipling, Agatha Christie, L. P. Hartley, G. K. Chesterton, and myself, Geoffrey Willans. The late Geoffrey Willans, I should say, for I died in 1958, long before the events I am about to recount. Best known for phrases like "as any fule kno," I'm the writer who invented Nigel Molesworth, the St. Custard's schoolboy. You may have seen Ronald Searle's illustrations. Anyway, I was describing the Miffi Senior Common Room, which is visible to me, even after my death, from the vantage point of my book *Down with Skool!* I can see—or, rather, my book can see—a table covered with model soldiers, a pile of comics filled with Spitfires and Achtungs, an oblique view of the spire of Fettes College, and—in pride of place—a portable record player. N is a bit of a Fotherington-Tomas, so the housemaster has no doubt sent him to the Senior Common Room to keep him out of the range of bullies. Among the regulars up here amidst the chimney pots there's a handsome boy called Boyce whose family is stationed in Ghana. Boyce is nicknamed Bug; he in turn refers to N as Poof. One day N, the swot, is writing a self-pitying text on his wedge of school block, the standard-issue writing pad. It begins: "I am an outcast, wandering on the sands of time . . ." What sissy rot! Bug farts, and immediately cries "Saved!" If you shout "Saved!" before someone can call "Sixes!" you're spared the six thumps a fart earns, by schoolboy decree. (If you fail to say "Saved!" your only refuge is denial: you can claim that "he who smelt it dealt it," and hope that confusion will prevail.) Suddenly Bug lunges for the block and rips the top sheet off. Sissy-swot N is mortified, and before anyone can read his lonely poetry he grabs the page back and tosses it through the open window. Bug shrugs and pulls David Bowie's *The Man Who Sold the World* from its dark RCA sleeve. Now, I, Willans, know nothing about Bowie; when I died he was eleven and still strumming his guitar in Mr. Frampton's classroom at the Bromley Tech art block. But apparently he's the big cheese here in 1972. Bug has been singing the bridge from a song called "Ziggy Stardust" all week: "So where were the Spiders / while the fly tried to break our balls?" Dead blue! The kind of twaddle best confined to the rugger pitch, or the dorms of St. Trinian's. Bug's sister has lent him four David Bowie albums—*Space Oddity, The Man Who Sold the World, Hunky Dory,* and *Ziggy Stardust* (which has a much longer title, but I can't read it from here)—and these become a sort of refuge for N, who is suffered to listen, lyric sheet in hand. *The Man Who Sold the World* has the desolate feel of Eliot's *Waste Land,* so it suits Miffi's atmosphere quite well. There are bleak songs like "All the Madmen," which deal with exactly the kind of dreary British institution into which the boys have been plonked by their parents: "Day after day they take some brain away . . ." I prefer the boarding-house song, though, which sums up the tyranny exerted by Gassy, the matron:

> *Come to Miffi, come to Miffi, for a life of misery*
> *There's a notice on the doorstep saying welcome unto thee*
> *Don't believe it, don't believe it, it's a pack of ruddy lies*
> *If it wasn't for the Gasbomb we would live in paradise*

Ironically, this Bowie chap—antidote and antithesis to all the horrors of Scottish boarding schools—will end up sending his own son to Gordonstoun, perhaps the rottenest there is.

James Thurber: Even armies have entertainment divisions, and Miffi was not without amusements. There was an end-of-term concert at which N was urged to pick up a guitar and lead the house in an increasingly hesitant rendition of "She'll Be Coming 'Round the Mountain" as, verse by verse, the boys lost track of what the promissory maiden would be doing. Wearing silk pajamas? Singing hallelujah? And? Nobody quite knew. There was also a publication of sorts, the *Miffi Mag,* run off in lurid lilac typescript on the school Gestetner machine, which scented the stapled sheets with a heady mixture of methanol and isopropyl. If the fumes rising from the pages didn't make you dream, perhaps N's imaginary animal the Kangorilla Bloge (pronounced "bloggy") would: this unsettling hybrid was covered entirely in tartan fabric. Neither kangaroo nor gorilla, it chugged through the world at a constant velocity of two miles per hour, which it verified using a speedometer suspended between waving antennae. Its favorite food was dismembered schoolboy. This Bellocian invention promised a cautionary bestiary which never arrived. Perhaps, though, the Kangorilla is seen to best effect standing proud and alone: multicultural, confused, murderous, and quite unknown to zoos.

Aleksandr Solzhenitsyn: On Sundays the boys are allowed to walk—still dressed in their uniforms, but unsupervised—in the nearby Botanical Gardens. The sun is shining and N takes a copy of the Penguin edition of *Matryona's House and Other Stories* to the fragrant park. He's chosen my book for two reasons. The cover is the first. My surname towers above the powerful image of a fist gripping a sickle over an open tome containing two stalks of corn. The red background makes the drawing look radically communist—and communism excites N, as all forbidden things do. In fact mine is a thoroughly anti-Soviet book (the Soviet sickle on the cover is actually being compared to the reaper's scythe). The second reason is that much of my writing is about living under intolerable conditions in "the gulag archipelago," and reading about the dreadful suffering of characters like Ivan Denisovich makes N feel better about his own life. At least Mackenzie House isn't located in Siberia! In the Botanical Gardens there is no frost, no snow, no tundra. In fact, today the weather is very pleasant. N is lying in the grass near Inverleith House—which is an art gallery standing between ponds and an ice cream hatch—and he's reading about the selfless Matryona and her life with the math teacher, but he keeps getting distracted. First by a butterfly, then a light aircraft, then a girl who is walking by with her family and seems to give him a lingering look. An idea begins to hatch in N's head: He will tell the boys, when he gets back, that he has met a girl. He will say her name was Julie Reed. He will look up the phone book and find the number for a Reed in Pilton, the working-class area just to the north. Then he'll write this number on his hand in biro as proof that Julie has given him her number, and that he has a girlfriend. This will help convince the boys in the Senior Common Room that he is not a homosexual. He returns to the boarding house and executes the plan. All goes well: he is believed. In fact, so successful is his lie that N almost begins to believe it himself. Julie Reed becomes a real presence in his imagination: a quiet, proletarian girl with the pointed face of a mouse. N recalls how, in his first miserable weeks at Miffi, he had in fact made a tiny mouse out of bunched-up silver paper and kept it in his pocket. When he felt the world was against him, he just had to touch this mouse, lending a little of the warmth of his finger to its metallic body, and everything seemed better. Julie Reed was a scaled-up, sexualised version of that mouse, and his need for her almost brought her into existence.

Marguerite Duras: N's first year at boarding school is spent in C dorm. It is a relatively innocent time: the dorm is filled with jovial Highlanders—the Macrae cousins, Sandy and Molly, from Kyle of Lochalsh—and decent, conscientious fellows like Colin Mercer, who will become a doctor, and Nelly Smith, whose people are oil workers in Oman. N tries to teach the boys how to masturbate, facedown on the mattress, twisting and grinding against the flat of the hand, but they express, or feign, incomprehension. At one point he experiments with thrusting his member into approximations of a female sex made, origami style, from paper. The process is inherently unsatisfying, and makes a crackling sound after lights out. So when "Han," a rather delicate boy with oriental features, seduces N one day up in the Senior Common Room, it marks an important step towards a fully adult sexuality, albeit a homosexual one. Han simply climbs on top of N, fully clothed, and stays there for some minutes. When he rolls off, Han says: "Next time, if you want to do that without clothes, tell me." The boys develop a friendship, swinging on tree-tied ropes out over the Water of Leith and visiting the shops of Goldenacre together. One spring day N tells his shocked friend Mercer, "I think my sex hormones have quadrupled overnight!" He now feels ready for the more intimate encounter—the less clothed one—with his Asian friend, but makes the mistake of confessing this within earshot of other boys. "I don't know what you're talking about," says Han. Prelapsarian, N has not yet fathomed our society's hypocritical need for secrecy.

Mary Whitehouse: In 1970s Britain, I was a beacon of light, an inveterate letter-writer and crusader against filth, permissiveness, and sex on television. I had less control over the telephone, although, as a public monopoly run by the post office, that technology was of course also subject to stringent government regulations forbidding obscenity. This did not prevent the boys of Mackenzie House from looking up in the telephone directory a certain Mrs. Dora Noyce, widely reputed in Edinburgh to be the madam of a brothel on Danube Street, and placing a brief, sniggering call in which that lady was most regrettably asked: "Do you do blow jobs?" To which Mrs. Noyce, with admirable calmness, replied: "Why don't you come down here and find out?" She might have added: ". . . after your unmentionables have descended, boys!" For the squeakily excited, well-spoken male voice on the line was clearly prepubescent. Disgusting!

James Joyce: From the boarding school library he has quaffed and guzzled the heady fermented apples of Laurie Lee's *Cider* *with Rosie,* and from his own locker supply of Bauermeister paperbacks—chosen as much for their fetching covers as any literary merit, and purchased with parting guilt by his mother—there is of course the tear-jerking lacework of Paul Gallico, and *Miss Clare Remembers* by Miss Read, but these are pastel-shaded memoirs, for the most part hidebound and anodyne. Such books propose no chrysalid premonition, no hint at the principles of flight. Between the columns and porticos of the Upper School still lie, even at fifty years' distance, the battlefields of Siegfried Sassoon the fox-hunting man, bluff and compelling yet somehow also lumpen: a realm of spiritual phlegm, dull bugles, and the thunder of hooves. No, it is upon the shelves of Bob Stirling, the first inspirational English teacher to appear in this narrative—and oh, it is a wonderful race, that tribe of enlightened instructors, even if they be mere lenders of books!—that N discovers *A Portrait of the Artist as a Young Man,* by myself, Sunny Jim, or Herr Satan, as you wish. Bob Stirling, a rapscallious quartermaster in his black gown, sends him out with the old orange and cream paperback wrapped in its cover of boatered dandies and Dublin rascals, and N heads past the dusk-swept rugby field, his fingers bitten by firthwind and the back of his school coat lashed by fleeting eructations of hail—polka dots that hiss softly as they melt upon the dark twill—to a tree beside the tennis courts. Here he settles down to read my lines, my account of the coming to life of Stephen Dedalus. Hours pass, yet he does not feel the cold. It is a heady experience, an initiation. Where is innocence now? For this is not mere cider, and knowing is always impure: it scorches the throat, as all spirits must. N reads my pages, and from his soul bursts forth a silent utterance of profane joy. To fly, to approach the sun, one must simply become an artist. And so was it said, and so done.

Gabriele D'Annunzio: I flew in 1908 with Wilbur Wright, bombarded Vienna with propaganda from a biplane, and lost the use of my right eye after a crash landing. But by 1971 flying has come on a long way; even children can do it as "unaccompanied minors." The British Council flies N out to Athens every school holiday. There, for a month or so, he can grow his hair, tan, ride his yellow bicycle in the warm Mediterranean sunshine, and feel, temporarily, that all is right with the world. Sometimes the BEA flights involve a transfer at Rome, and N—wandering through the terminal at Leonardo da Vinci Airport—marvels at the elegance of Italian men in crisply tailored purple herringbone suits. Even the elderly here dress well, with aestheticism and self-respect. Too soon, though, these glimpses of Italian dignity and beauty end, and N is once again overflying the Alps with a jigsaw puzzle on the tray table, on his way back to prison. At London the Trident 3 jet becomes a throbbing Vickers Vanguard prop plane, scudding through the eternally low-hanging clouds. N is delivered back to grey, benighted Edinburgh, and the boarding house. "Your hair is looking untidy," mutters Quack in greeting. "Get it seen to!" Narcissus is dispatched to a barber's shop in Goldenacre to have his golden locks snipped and shaved into a military-style crew cut. Sitting there, gazing at his glum and pudgy face in the puzzled barber's mirror, his hair parted on the wrong side (a trick: when cut this way then combed the other, the hair will look slightly longer), N weeps silently. He writes in protest to his mother in Athens, who sends the housemaster a brittle and pretentious letter of instruction: N may only have his hair cut in London, Paris, or Rome. Quack offers a compromise: the barber's shop at Forsyth's on Princes Street. And so N is sent up to Edinburgh's most conservative department store to receive, for twice the price—and a hail of boorish mockery from his peers—exactly the same crew cut.

N
I
C
H
E

Lou Reed: Don't you think I'm sad as fuck to be contributing to this book? It means I'm dead, and I can't tell you how bad being dead makes me feel. My week beats your year. Who said that? It was me, in the sleeve notes for *Metal Machine Music*. I was talking about rock critics, who for me are the scum of the earth. I lived seventy-one years, but a rock critic would have to live 3,692 of his shitty years to experience the kind of intensity I did. Okay, so I'm being called to the witness stand here to testify to the transformative power of my album *Transformer*. Of course it was transformative. That's what art is. I can see this guy listening to it now. The dead can see everything; that's the upside. I spy with my little eye. He's in Jerry's suite of rooms, on the next landing down from the Senior Common Room. Upstairs, that's where he listens to David copying me in songs like "Queen Bitch." Downstairs is where he listens to the real thing, with David on backing vocals. *Vicious! You hit me with a flower!* Jerry is a young master with a crew cut, a classical scholar from Cambridge. He's a soft guy, when he whacks you there's no force in it. They all whack you at that school. A lot of slippers whooshing down on young ass. At least they don't connect you up to electricity. That's what happened to me when I got institutionalized. But *Transformer*, now, that's a shot of electricity in itself. "Walk on the Wild Side," "Satellite of Love," "New York Telephone Conversation." If you could have turned New York attitude—Andy, the Factory, the queens, the drag, the drugs—into a stage show you could watch in your head, that record would be it. So I can only imagine what that would do to the head of a boy of twelve at a Scottish boarding school. It certainly didn't make him braver: twice—much later—he was in the same room as me, and he didn't dare say a word. Once at the Royal Festival Hall in London, in some VIP lounge. And once at Lincoln Center in New York. There was a Bob Wilson opera, something about ancient Egypt. I love Bob, but it seemed to go on forever. I fell asleep, and Laurie had to wake me up to clap. I turned around and saw that guy, N, staring at me. It distracted me momentarily, and I dropped something under my seat. Later, out on the street, I realized I'd lost my reading glasses, and Laurie and I went back, trying to look nonchalant as we faced the whole crowd of people coming out, including this guy. Embarrassing. He just looked at me, probably thinking: "Hey, Grandpa, didn't you use to be Lou Reed?" They called Andy *Grandma*, you know, when he was that age. We all become Grandpas and Grandmas in the end. Before we become angels with mullets, like Bruno Ganz in *Wings of Desire*. We pass among you unseen, but not unremembered. What would *you* say, if you could sense me in a room? Thank you? It's taken as given. Dante, Shakespeare, Poe, Melville, me. We made your life better, and we keep on doing it.

L. P. Hartley: "The past is a foreign country; they do things differently there." That's my most famous single sentence—so famous, indeed, that N half quotes it in a song on his first album, *Circus Maximus*. I'm not sure he knew he was borrowing from the prologue of *The Go-Between*, my 1953 novel. But N was a go-between himself at the age of twelve—the same age as the young Leo Colston, the protagonist of my novel. The events I am about to recount take place in 1972, the year of my death, and the year after *The Go-Between* has been filmed by Joseph Losey. At Mackenzie House there's a pale blond boy called Chris Yule. His sister Debbie is at Houldsworth House, the boarding house for St. George's, which is the sister school to the Academy. N's mentor and tormentor Bug has fallen for Debbie. The first approaches are clumsy: one Saturday N and Bug ride up to Ravelston Dykes on matching Sun racing bikes and hover outside Houldsworth House. Not much is happening. "I dare you to go up to the door and ask for a spanner," says Bug. N is reluctant at first. "I'll give you a pound! No, five pounds!" N has heard this kind of talk before—the pounds usually turn out to be delivered with a fist. "Not that kind of pound," insists Bug, "real ones! Tell you what, I'll give you ten quid." At this price,

N is sorely tempted. As he opens the gate, Bug, in a surge of generosity, increases the reward to fourteen pounds. N knocks at the boarding-house door and asks about the spanner. The matron is not unfriendly, but says they don't have such a thing. On returning, N is handed a jagged pebble Bug has picked up from the ground: "Fourteen pounds makes one stone, I've kept my word." But skirmishes like these will get Bug nowhere: his pursuit of Debbie Yule now becomes epistolary. Again, N serves as go-between, for he is eloquent. Letters are soon flying back and forth between the boarding houses, the Mackenzie House ones all written by N. So much of himself does he pour into this ghostwriting that soon N begins to feel that he too longs for Debbie. But Bug tells him that, after a few dates, the relationship has turned sour: Debbie has noticed the difference between his brusque excitement in person and the romantic tone of his letters. Bug warns N to shut up about Debbie "or I'll never speak to you again." A year later N is sitting in a New York restaurant with the Yules. The Curries are emigrating to Canada and have just driven their new automatic Volvo off the car deck of the SS *France*. Since Mark is friendly with Chris Yule, a dinner has been arranged with the family at a Long Island restaurant. N sits opposite Debbie, but is much too shy to speak to her; letters and life happen in quite different dimensions. Eventually the pretty blonde—she looks like a thirteen-year-old Mia Farrow—leans across and asks: "Do you know a boy called Boyce?" N blushes and stammers: "Intimately." Debbie never addresses him again, and neither does Bug.

Euripides: Before the Currie family leaves Greece, N is taken by his parents to the ancient theatre of Epidaurus to see my play *The Bacchae*. I wish my parents Cleito and Mnesarchus had been so enlightened! But they were just village shopkeepers, not people who drove big black cars and worked for the government. And *The Bacchae* didn't exist then, of course, because I hadn't written it. My play is performed in the curved marble arena under a clear night sky, in ancient Greek, with a full chorus commenting on the action as it unfolds. Of course, we didn't use the word "ancient" for either the theatre or the language, and we called that place Epidavros. It was a sort of health spa, dedicated to Asclepius, the god of medicine, so the theatre was a diversion for sick people: tragedy helped put their woes into perspective. "You think you've got it bad? Be happy Dionysus is not sending earthquakes and fire!" N understood nothing—there was no simultaneous translation, of course—but he was impressed by the sinister oddity of the black-clad chorus. Somehow it suggested not just another kind of theatre, but another kind of world. By the way, let me use this opportunity to get something clear. If you ever hear people say I lived in a cave, and had two disastrous marriages to women who cheated on me left, right, and centre, disregard them: they're probably rumours hatched in the parodies that comic writers came up with in our time to ridicule serious ones. In fact, don't even trust what I'm saying right now: these lines too are probably the work of a parodist. If you're the author of this squib—yes, I'm talking to you, scribe!—hang your head in shame. Really. Commandeering my voice to make people laugh? You're just jealous of the gravitas, darling. Are people going to remember you twenty-five hundred years from now? Really? I know that facts are thin on the ground, and that nature abhors a vacuum (as Aristotle will say in about a century), but come on.

Denton Welch: In 1971 the Currie family leaves Greece and moves to Constable country, the verdant and anodyne tract where the Stour divides Essex from Suffolk. The family makes the trip back across Europe packed into Bill's black Rover three-litre, still sporting its *corps diplomatique* plates. One of the stops is Venice, where the brothers are bought matching pairs of brown velvet flares, soon to be the cause of much trouble. N sleeps in a cot at the foot of the parental bed in Venice, beneath a rather glorious pink Murano chandelier. He wakes early in the morning and is furtively masturbating under the covers when his father suddenly seizes his foot, like a bear scooping up a fish. Bill has been offered the directorate of the Colchester English Study Centre, a school set up to test language-learning publications issued by the Oxford University Press. The family is to live at Willow House, a large, boxy 1930s mansion eight miles north of Colchester. The house—not particularly handsome in itself—stands in a big garden overlooking a valley studded with poplars. Mark is sent to join N as a boarder at the Academy, and one day they're on a school outing at Hillend ski slope when some boys N's age pick on Mark for wearing the fancy Venetian pantaloons. There's a scuffle, and Mark is pushed into a ditch. N—quite incapable of fighting—affects indifference; his little brother will have to hold his own against the school toughs. One need not believe in a teleological universe to find something karmic in a symmetrical episode: on holiday in Dedham with his Edinburgh friend John, N is hailed by some village thugs who—seeing these same brown velvet trousers—start an insulting tirade: "Those are poofy pants, ain't they?" N, standing astride his bicycle, attempts the defence of a milquetoast relativism: "I suppose they might look that way to you." This fails to satisfy the sartorial arbiters, who lead N and John to a leafy footpath and proceed to swing fists in the vicinity of their heads. The two boys offer no resistance, and eventually cycle home, punished and crying. At a village fête behind Dedham church a few days later N recognises the assailants and points them out to Bill, who—just as N had done when his brother was attacked—shrugs the whole thing off; it is not his job to intervene in these shabby battles. The velvet flares are soon mothballed, but the damage has been done.

Frank Harris: I hated boarding school too, you know, but had the good sense to run away. N lacks my mettle. During the summer of 1972 we find him, dressed in a round-collared denim suit, working obediently at his father's language college in Colchester, collating course materials, photocopying and stapling. All sorts of paper stuff fascinates N. He buys *The Times* for its austere look and traces advertisements from magazines, learning the names of all the fonts in the Letraset catalog. His most prized possession is a Cacharel bag made of glossy green card featuring a grainy Sarah Moon photograph of a dreaming girl—the kind of silly goose I take great delight in seducing after a hard day's cattle rustling. (The best book of Moon's photographs, by the way, is entitled *Improbable Memories,* an umbrella term I might well have used for my memoirs.) Flush with cash from his summer job, N is driven one afternoon into central Colchester by his mother, who is rather bored by country life and longs for bookish excitement. She parks her lurid green Mini GT and leads N past stalls selling rainbow-hued tank tops to a bookshop where she selects a thick and frisky memoir marked, prominently, with the words "candid" and "unexpurgated." On the cover twinkles a foxy-looking gentleman with a twirly mustache: it is myself, and I have made another conquest. *My Life and Loves* is the intimate autobiography of an erotomaniac Irishman abroad in the Wild West and elsewhere. The enormous book is profligate in its invention, and tells the truth, as Max Beerbohm cattily remarked, only when the fiction flags. N also makes a propitious discovery that afternoon: lured by the glamour of displays featuring the debut release of an art school group called Roxy Music, he emerges from the High Street branch of W. H. Smith with something else: a T. Rex compilation on the Music for Pleasure label entitled *Ride a White Swan.* This cut-price album in a dark-blue-and-pink sunburst sleeve is the first LP he has bought with his own money. Marc Bolan's childish yet sexually charged songs actually make quite a good complement to my own boastful memories: in Willow House, in 1972, the sap is rising. Later N will augment his collection with *The Slider*, also by T. Rex. Its black-and-white sleeve image of Bolan as a frizzy-haired dandy in an outsized top hat could almost be by Sarah Moon, so the record gets propped up in N's window next to the Cacharel bag. Alas, the sun shines through the willow tree and, magnified by the leaded panes of the bedroom window, warps *The Slider*. Forthwith it will sound like music being played in a shipwreck, or a woozy dance through the ballrooms of Mars. *My Life and Loves*, on the other hand, can stand all the sunshine you may throw.

Samuel Beckett: Consciousness, quoth Spinoza, but I forget the rest. N is in Dedham, in the big house. All is dark and quiet. Moles, voles, hedgehogs, and badgers creep and rustle no doubt in hedgerows, going about their various businesses and trades, if animals can be said to have trades. Earlier and earlier does N creep to bed, during the twilit hours in which badgers no doubt do their business, if badgers can be said to have business, and earlier and earlier does he rise in the morning, creeping and rustling downstairs to the kitchen, where he sits by the fire, at three or four in the morning, in the even glow of the Aga, drinking his tea and listening to the overwhelming nothing out in the garden, the creep and rustle of a nothing lit by dead stars. Consciousness, quoth Spinoza, but I forget the rest, no doubt, I quote, but the rest escapes me, insofar as the mind has clear and direct ideas, but the rest escapes me, indefinite duration, striving, mind and body, quoth he, Spinoza, no doubt, but the rest escapes me. It is a pleasure to fart in an empty kitchen, that at least is certain. And so at two or three in the morning N creeps and rustles down the stairs from sleeping quarters to farting quarters, and boils up his tea, and gazes out at the garden, all dead, no doubt, yet rustling, and lit by stars. His is the only consciousness, in that hugeness of morning, the only human consciousness, at any rate, for the moles, voles, hedgehogs, and badgers are also awake and at work, no doubt, if animals can be said to work, in hedgerows lit by dead stars. And the night is a drug of sorts, and soon there comes a craving in N for its utter solitude, which is never enough, and the even milky light of its pallor, never pale enough, and so he creeps down, candle in hand, at midnight, no doubt, to catch the morning at its most pure, and his own consciousness at its most clear and direct, as Spinoza puts it somewhere, but exactly where escapes me. Horror, however, lifts in N, early one morning, when he comes upon the sound of intelligent conversation. Intelligence, that great deadener! It is the earliest possible of all early possible mornings, and he has crept down, candle in hand, nightcap upon head, farting in his long shift, wrapped from head to foot in winding sheets and antique dress-and-gown, conscious of the silver frost lying upon the garden like a hand mirror lit by dead stars—but there is intelligent conversation drifting from the living room, as if living, waking, breathing people were sitting there, conversing! Is it not appalling to encounter life where one least expects it? He creeps and rustles along the corridor in his winding sheet, farting like a corpse, dragging his chain—did I not mention the chain?—to witness there in the lamplight of the living room the figures of his parents, Pater and Mater, sitting there fully dressed, fully awake, and apparently living, conversing with gin and tonic in hand, waxy as cadavers. He has risen so early—as the dead are said to rise, but do not—that it is still the night before! *O soins tardifs et superflus! Inutile tendresse!* Back up to bed, says his father, and back up to bed, says his mother, and take off those winding sheets at once, and stow that chain, and put down that filthy chamberpot, and extinguish that candle! And back he creeps to bed, to sleep for the prescribed duration, to wait for the probable arrival of morning, to rustle and fart, no doubt, lying there—and this at least is certain—lit by dead stars.

Jeff Nuttall: The ecstatic permissiveness I describe in my book about the 1960s, *Bomb Culture*, opened a Pandora's box of vices. The counterculture of the time was prodded on by a stick, a bad cop—the shadow of the Bomb, and the threat of instant annihilation—but also lured by a carrot, a good cop: sex. In the seventies the context darkened. Since the ugly scenes at the Rolling Stones' concert at Altamont the counterculture had realised that the energies it had released were not always going to be kind or enlightened ones. Sex and violence were still spreading like ripples through the mainstream, which had grown its hair and was keen to share some of the sugar, some of the electricity. But the backdrop against which this was happening was much less utopian. Instead of psychedelics, naked happenings, and love-ins, there was an oil crisis, a three-day week, strikes. Burgess's *Clockwork Orange*—and Kubrick's film of it—brought something called Ultraviolence into fashion, and Richard Allen's *Skinhead* rode the bloody tide. Even a gentlemen's school like the Edinburgh Academy was awash with rumours of everyday street violence: a girl had been raped on Inverleith Road, the boys whispered, and her tits had been sprayed silver—you could still see traces of glittery paint on the holly leaves. Even within the walls of the institution things were sexually a little odd. There was the maths teacher who tickled your testicles as he explained set theory, and there was the housemaster who punished the boys humorously by a system called Reminders. If you did something wrong, Doey—that was his nickname—would intone: "Remind me, Currie!" (he pronounced it "remained me"). At bedtime the reminding ones had to be lying facedown on their tartan blankets, ready to be slippered on the bum by Doey as he made his dorm rounds. These whacks didn't hurt much, and were delivered affectionately, even ironically, with a genial huff, grunt, and twinkle. "One for you, grommit!" More serious infractions were punished by a sort of assignation: you were to meet Doey at dusk down in the basement—in the model-making room, or the changing room—and he would crush you to his chest in a bear hug and whisper to you like a lover. If this was raised with Matron she simply explained that, since Doey had only girls in his family, he liked to express affection to boys in this way. Much later all this exploded into the public domain as "allegations of historical abuse at the Edinburgh Academy in the early 1970s" after the actor Iain Glen spoke out about it in interviews, and Kim Wolfe Murray, scion of the Canongate publishing family, made accusations which led to the sacking of the infamous groping maths teacher. You can see the results of this sexual oddity in subsequent songs by N himself, and in the visionary diagrams of Scottish artist Chad McCail, another "survivor."

Charles Dickens: It was a sad time and a bad time for N, the most difficult time of his brief existence. For in Mackenzie House he felt abandoned by all those he loved, and whom he had formerly imagined must love him. Was the firstborn, who imagined himself the little favourite of his dear mama, to be so cruelly cast aside? Were warm female kisses to be exchanged for the cold blows of unfeeling boys? His heart must surely rend itself in two at this reversal of fortune. During the melancholy vigils of late evening, in the dorm after lights out, with tears staining the pillow, N entertained schemes of self-destruction. Then another idea rushed in upon him: He would run away! He would catch a train somewhere, anywhere! But then it was as if the affronted and anxious faces of his dear family became visible in that half-darkness, swimming before him mad with grief and self-reproach. How could he hurt them, even though they had hurt him? He would sooner eat his own head. By and by there came to him a plan: He settled to starve himself, as revolutionary hot-bloods are wont to do in prison, as a public protest against wrongful incarceration. He would drink only milk, and eat no solid food, and write to his parents telling them this, and then see what would happen. Surely it must pluck at the cords of their hearts? Surely they must relent, and let him return to that charming school in Athens where he had been so happy? The very next day the fast began, and at first N stuck to his plan, and drank only a little milk each day, or a cup of tea. Idly he wondered how long he could last. A week? Two? A month, even? What would be the exact sensation as the end approached, and consciousness sank into weary oblivion, and his time came to die so far from home, so remote from love? I can see the ladies in the audience dabbing handkerchiefs at the corners of their eyes even as I recite this, and I must admit that I too am deeply moved, so that I might cry myself! And yet what follows is coloured with the motley of comedy: Little N, hungry as of course he must be, joins the tuck queue one day, planning to nibble on a chocolate biscuit, and it is in that compromised gesture that he is caught and confronted by the housemaster, and taken to the privacy of his office. "I have received a telegram—a TELEGRAM—" (for of course telegrams cost the earth, and are used only in situations of the utmost urgency) "from your mother," says Doey. "She tells me you are on hunger strike, and yet here you are in the tuck queue." There can be no course of action but to admit—whether it be true or no—that the whole thing has been a sham. What began in sincerity has ended as apparent ruse, a misconception to which N now capitulates. He diverts his unhappiness into private neurotic symptoms, like standing at the bathroom sink soaping and rubbing his hands for hours, until they are covered with a smooth white cream, strange mitts of foam. But a few months later, when he skips tea for quite a different reason—he has hidden in the music room to hear David Bowie's new single "Drive-in Saturday" played on the radio—Doey catches him and, thinking he is again embarking upon a hunger strike, suspends N's one great privilege, his membership of the Senior Common Room, the only place where he can hear Bowie's records. He is banished from that attic for several weeks, and the severity of the punishment is calibrated, not to the relatively minor offence of missing a single meal, but to the programmatic—one might even say political—use he has made of starvation in the past. When it comes to food, then (but to more than food), the cry always rising to our poor wee hero's lips is quite the opposite of the famous request uttered by that healthy orphan, Oliver Twist. He is saying, effectively: "Please, sir, I want less!"

Evelyn Waugh: There is alleged to be some sort of connection between my *Vile Bodies* and a perfectly beastly record album called *Aladdin Sane* by a latter-day music hall entertainer known as David Bowie. Followers of the variety stage tell me that this slender vaudevillian brought a copy of my novel along with him on a transatlantic crossing and found my themes of fragmentation and chaos compelling evidence of some congruence between the ghastliness of the 1920s and the even greater abomination of the 1970s. Having raised my ear trumpet to the gramophone record in question I must agree that he has at least reproduced the aspect of chaos with a grim accuracy: the piano which dominates proceedings sounds as if it has fallen into the hands of a shell-shocked flamingo, if those unfortunate birds could be said to have hands. Mr. Bowie strings an entirely ungrammatical series of sentences over this piece of gratuitous musical cruelty like fairy lights over a barroom brawl: I distinguished some nonsense about Paris, Japanese rice wine, and war, which I gather this young decadent is against. *Harumph*. N, the protagonist of this memoir—and I shall be phantom-writing to *The Daily Telegraph* in protest against my inclusion in it—familiarised himself with the album's title song down in the model-making room of his boarding house, where he might better have employed his time gluing together plastic Messerschmitts. He could also claim some misguided adherence to my ideas, since I'm told he had in his locker a Penguin paper-covered edition of *Decline and Fall* (apparently it was that book's cover, drawn by a group of doodlers called Bentley, Farrell & Burnett, which provided the book's main point of appeal). As for the pantomimic record's cover, I shall forebear to comment, except to observe that it folds out into an image of a sort of monstrous Aubrey Beardsley—on the condition that the unfortunate aesthete had been forced to dance to *Prélude à l'après-midi d'un faune* stark naked, his body painted from head to toe with melted tin, his face riven by a garish thunderbolt. Quite what this has to do with my satire I cannot for the life of me divine. Which is an unfortunate expression, for there is in fact no life left in me. Should this freakish faun also be here amongst the shades, dancing to the strains of a diabolical flute I am thankfully too deaf to hear—which, may God forbid!—I can only pray that the respective chambers of hell to which we have been allocated stand several leagues apart.

Saint Paul the Apostle:

1. Paul, a messenger of Jesus Christ, by God's will, to the readers of this book.

2. Blessings be upon you, and peace, from God the Father, and from Jesus his son.

3. This epistle, the Epistle to the Memoir Readers, concerns N's life in E dorm in the year of our Lord 1973.

4. E dorm huddles beneath the craggy, crenellated eaves of Mackenzie House, and in it there are six beds.

5. The beds contain Bezzy, Boyce, Vurich, Currie, Cameron-Jones, and Mercer.

6. Bezzy is a freckled boy from the Antipodes, indeed an aboriginal, or partly so.

7. Boyce and Vurich are the wild boys in the dorm, much given to jumping into each other's arms after lights out to demonstrate "what I do with my girlfriend back in Africa." (Boyce's family is stationed in Ghana, Vurich's in Kenya.)

8. Currie, Cameron-Jones, and Mercer are the dorm weaklings. They never jump into bed with each other, although Currie sometimes gets Cameron-Jones to stroke his arm.

9. Currie and Mercer are actually members of the Scripture Union, the evangelical group, and each night they use biro to answer questions in the official Scripture Union Bible Study brochure.

10. Currie mainly does this because he likes the orange logo depicting a stylized oil lamp. But it's possible that he simply has a taste for what we might call "didactic style" or "the aesthetics of goodness."

11. At the Henderson Row Upper School N devises advertising campaigns for Scripture Union meetings not from any religious conviction but because he enjoys the idea of promoting religion as a product like any other.

12. Posters N has drawn for the SU are placed on the school notice board next to the library, or run off on the school Gestetner machine and pinned up in classrooms.

13. A typical poster, in faded lavender ink that smells of methylated spirits, has a traced headline in Franklin Gothic Condensed: "Solomon and the Baby-Cutting Trick."

14. It tells the story of the Judgment of Solomon (Kings 3:16).

15. Rotary flatbed stencil duplicators, mimeographs, or—yea and hosanna!—hectographs are spirit duplicating machines.

16. N is therefore using the school Gestetner to duplicate the Holy Spirit.

17. He is, if you will, "gestetnering" God. And yet perhaps he has put Gestetner in the place of God, for the Lord Almighty is, for him, a mere means of access to that most holy object, the school duplicating machine.

18. Nevertheless, shall we condemn him, when he is spreading the word of God?

19. Is he not, in his way, trying to offset by lithography the moral abominations that happen nightly in E dorm, and indeed throughout that entire school—an institution that ought to be cast forthwith into the deepest sulphur pits of hell?

20. With this rhetorical question I end my Epistle to the Memoir Readers; in the name of God the highest and most holy, amen.

Fyodor Dostoyevsky: Every exile comes to an end eventually, and although three years of rigorous abjection in a boarding school may feel like thirty to an intelligent person—the man of our times, acute in sensitivity, over-alert—yet this apparent eternity, too, must draw to a close. As we have seen, N's hunger strike—which he did not even have the dignity to honour—has come to nothing. His parents and the authorities, while continuing to monitor this hot-house flower with some concern, have concluded that all was bluff. He continues to attend classes at the Edinburgh Academy Upper School—where he is known as a "geit," a sprat of the first year—and is even set to work, like a prison inmate, carving foolish lamps and bookcases in woodwork classes held beneath the gymnasium with its inscription of Horace's line about the beauty of dying for your country. He takes violin lessons in the master's lodge with dour Mr. Stewart, who is actually only interested in rugby. What an exquisite instrument of torture is a violin! It scratches and squeals like a mur-dered polecat, and cannot play chords, and stiffens one's frail shoul-der, no matter how much cloth one props it up with! But if there is one thing that can be said for violins, gentlemen, it is that while playing them one is not playing rugby! In the view of Mr Stewart, this is clearly a matter of regret. For this mediocrity every moment away from the sidelines is time wasted. His irritability is blatantly obvious when, one day, he seizes a scrap of pencilled-in music paper from N's violin case, props it on the piano, and plonks out—with malign satirical emphasis and mocking insensitivity—a nonsensical tune. The message is clear: So you think, pale weed, that you can express yourself with music? And yet your mastery of the basics is laughably inadequate. You will never amount to much, for you fail to practise your scales and are never seen on the rugby field, unless skulking near the touch line like a malingerer, shunning the scrums and hoping the action will stay up at the other end, for fear that your puny little body will be damaged. You will master neither pitch! Do not think of bringing your "compositions" near me! After this humiliation N stops showing up at violin lessons, although his parents continue to be billed for them. Eventually the head of the music department writes to his mother informing her that N has missed every single violin lesson of the summer term. A letter of saddening ferocity arrives from Jo. It has been written in the heat of a rage that only passionate redheaded people can reach. "This is your first betrayal," it declares. It is not just the rugby team that has been let down, nor the violin teacher, nor indeed the violin section of the school's second orchestra, of which N has become leader, if only because he will never be good enough for the school's first orchestra, and is able only to improvise wildly while watching the other violinists—those who can actually read music—and copying their bow positions. Queen, team, country, family, all have been let down! Nobody was fooled by your hunger strike, N, nor your foolish attempts to write music on manuscript paper, nor your feigning on the rugby field, under the face-stinging grey bars of Scottish rain! And yet—did I spell this out clearly enough in my *Notes from Underground*?—the sensitive and intelligent man of our times may draw a peculiar satisfaction, a particle of relief, from disgrace. Yes, N was abject and dishonourable. Yes, he was a coward and—no doubt, where his own brother was concerned—a minor bully of the worst kind. He was, not to put too fine a point upon it, vermin, deserving of no respect from the respectable, nor friendship from the friendly. He was in fact a Judas, liable to betray anyone at any point. And this meant that he could be relied upon for nothing, ever again. His responsibility was diminished by his bad character. A life of miserable solitude awaited, filled with the awful silence that reigns when one's schoolmates "send one to Coventry," and act as if one isn't there. And yet there was something delightful in this, even as N squirmed at the shame of it all. Yes, gentlemen, even abjection can be something delightful! A "first betrayal" implied a whole series of betrayals yet to come, and this license was now presented to N like a fresh book of cheques from the Bank of Betrayal. Who could say what liberties, what debaucheries, he could not now purchase? A career in crime—filled with strategic misdemeanours so microscopic they were almost imperceptible—was clearly awaiting N, our microbial Raskolnikov.

Jean de Brunhoff: In September 1973 the five elephants—three small ones, two big—packed their possessions into boxes, squeezed into their new blue Volvo estate and left Dedham forever. The shiny new car sported the registration number OGO 20L, which made people who saw it laugh, because they thought it meant "Oh go to hell!" (Oddly enough, the Rover it replaced had the registration number TSG 666.) Hell was not the elephant family's destination, however: they intended to emigrate to Montréal in Canada, which is a very cold place, not a hot one. And so Daddy Elephant drove the Volvo to Southampton, where the SS *France* was berthed. The night before boarding, the elephants stayed in a hotel, and at midnight there was an evacuation. Someone claiming to be from the Provisional Irish Republican Army had phoned up to say there was a bomb in the hotel, so the police came to search while the elephants stood outside with all the other animal guests, shivering. As a result, the next day boarding the *paquebot France* felt like getting into a life raft to escape a sinking liner: the United Kingdom herself, which was just on the verge of introducing a three-day week and power cuts. The crossing took five days, during which the small elephant Mark vomited whenever waves rocked the ship even slightly. The family was lodged in a cabin below the surface of the water, without windows. This might have been claustrophobic had the boat not been so enormous— more like a floating town than a liner. The young elephants explored the metal citadel from top to bottom. Its uppermost deck was dominated by two gigantic funnels which looked like huge red pachyderms, their black ears flying freely in the wind. Below, there were swimming pools and sundecks at which one would be served *bouillon*, a warming beef soup. Indoors there was a dining hall where wine flowed copiously. There were shops and bars, an amusement arcade, and a cinema in which the boys watched *Live and Let Die* twice, because it was free. As the SS *France* chugged into New York Harbour the two young male elephants were photographed on deck wearing sports jackets, mimicking the stance of the Statue of Liberty. Behind them soared the twin towers of the World Trade Center, which had only just opened. Twenty-eight years later, on just such a fine September day, N would watch these two enormous towers crumple and disappear into an intense cloud of smoke, dust, and debris. They collapsed like the two front legs of a great elephant felled by hunters.

Mordecai Richler: Bill Currie arrived in Montréal just as the language wars were swinging into gear. Bill 101 would pass in 1977, making French the official language of a province in which 78 percent of the population are francophone and Catholic. Many English speakers would desert the province at that point, heading for Toronto and Ottawa. My views on this, as a Jew, were withering: the Québécois nationalists were ridiculous bigots, with a murky history of anti-Semitism. They would lose two independence referenda, the first in 1980, but these would be battles lost in a war largely won:

French would prevail. Bellow and Cohen got the hell out, I stayed, but I was not well-liked. Almost nobody writes research papers on me these days in Canadian universities, despite *Duddy Kravitz*; my provocations turned both the French speakers and my own Jewish community against me. Bill's job was right there on the front line of Québec's cultural battle: he'd arrived to run the English language department at Sir George Williams University, which had originated as a YMCA organization offering night classes for English speakers. In 1974 it merged with Loyola to become Concordia University, but the place was never noted for concord. In 1969 black student radicals had occupied the Henry F. Hall Building's computer department, inflicting two million dollars' worth of damage on the equipment after a dispute with a racist biology professor. The police ended up smoking them out and jailing the ringleaders; no charges were laid against the prof. After camping in a single room in a lodging house run by a certain Madame Vallois, the Curries moved into a large bungalow in the English-speaking suburb of Beaconsfield, and sent their male children to Macdonald High School (Emma was put into French immersion). The boys were both considered educationally ahead of their peers at Mac High: Mark was advanced two years, N one. Their ranch-style bungalow faced Lake Saint-Louis, which was iced over all winter, thick with feet of snow. Bill came home on the commuter train every evening with icicles dangling from his newly grown mustache. N went downtown on Saturdays for an art class at the university, but it was all a far cry from my inner-city experience growing up on Rue St. Urbain, or Cohen's in Mount Royal. What the hell kind of stories come out of the suburbs?

Jacques Brel: At around the time the Beatles were giving up concerts in the anglophone countries, I was doing the same in the francophone ones. The Beatles cited the screaming that drowned out their music; I could have cited vomiting: my own. Every appearance I made was preceded by such terror, such intensity that I was physically sick. Of course, they turned out to be great shows, but I was beginning to tire of the whole rigmarole. I didn't want to become "an industrialist of song." I had an acting career by now, strong side interests in flying and yachting, and even thought I might have a novel in me. I took the role of Don Quixote in a musical called *Man of La Mancha*, then more or less retired to French Polynesia with my new love, Maddly Bamy. I was following in the footsteps of Gauguin, if you like, but a Gauguin who piloted his own light aircraft. While all this was happening, English-speaking people were beginning to find out about my music through a stage musical called *Jacques Brel Is Alive and Well and Living in Paris*, featuring translations by Mort Shuman. David Bowie saw it several times in London in 1968. Later, when he got famous with songs clearly indebted to mine, including covers of "Amsterdam" and "La Mort," he tried to organise a meeting with me, but I responded coldly: "Why would I want to meet that faggot?" (You've got to remember that he dressed as a woman, or a Martian, or both, at the time.) Anyway, Bowie apparently loved Mort's version of "Au Suivant," "Next," which admittedly I do sing in a slurred, faggy voice, just to make the satire more piquant. In the mid-seventies I got a surprise hit in the English-speaking world when Terry Jacks covered my song "Le Moribond" as "Seasons in the Sun." At about the same time the Brel stage show became a film produced by Ely Landau, and I made a short cameo for it singing "Ne Me Quitte Pas." To be honest the film is a stinker—the cast, like Bowie, camps things up way too much, prancing around in scarves and curls as if they've just failed an audition for *Hair*. The translations are bijou and impressionistic—sugary flurries of decorative language rather than my stark satirical takes on existential issues. Anyway, retirement is a bit like being dead: you just have to sit back and watch the ripples of your influence spread in whichever way they can, with whatever effects they end up having. The ripples reached N and Jo in Montréal. The American Film Theater was a series of low-budget but high-prestige films based on theatrical productions. The idea was that you bought a season ticket and came regularly to see a selection of productions of filmed theatre. It was a kind of lucky dip, a smorgasbord of cheap masterpieces from artists like Ionesco, Pinter, Chekhov, Brecht. N and his mother, although sparks do fly between them, are really similar: they share some kind of intellectual hunger, a thirst for beauty and novelty, a strong interest in all things French. So Jo drove the Volvo to Mac High on Wednesday afternoons, collected N, and took him to this half-empty cinema in Dorval, where they saw this dialogue-free film of my songs. The stuff about death disturbed the hell out of a fourteen-year-old just starting to sense the full meaning of his own mortality. But something about the songs—and particularly my performance, the long zoom into my tear-blurred eyes as I sing about loss and grief, insecurity and love—really hooked N. After I died of cancer—just when everything was going so well, and all my bitterness was finally turning into sweetness—N transformed himself into Momus and sang some of my songs in English, exactly as his hero Bowie did. And Scott Walker. And Marc Almond. More ripples, more faggots, when men should be turning themselves into gods! And one day I really believe they will.

Irving Layton: I am Irving Layton, born Israel Pincu Lazarovitch in Romania. I moved—I was moved—to Montréal as a baby. The Curries are much newer immigrants, and much more suburban than I was. Their life is made up of trips to Roy's Drug Store or the Fairview shopping center in the Volvo. It's N getting chewing gum stuck in his hair by Robert Ferrari, a Tom Petty–faced bully, on the yellow school bus. It's chasing a hockey puck around a skating track you have to sweep into being on the lake. It's skiing in the Laurentian Mountains in a brown snowsuit and boots, with yellow, red, and orange flashes across your woolly hat. It's hot buttered toast while watching a cartoon about Hercules, the blather of free local phone calls, earning nickels and dimes babysitting the little Scottish Canadians who live next door. It's the frog chorus down at the landing stage in summer, a supermarket called Steinberg where you can buy a powdered orange juice called Tang invented for astronauts. It's trips downtown to catch a lecture by my old friend Saul Bellow at McGill, or a quick run with Jo to the Beaconsfield library—where the air is so dry that you get a hard static shock when you touch the door handle—to borrow my 1974 collection, *The Pole-Vaulter*, with its bold orange and purple cover. And it's the self-conscious purchase of an austere paperback entitled *The Making of Modern Poetry in Canada*, edited by Dudek and Gnarowski, simply because one rather likes the idea of making modern poetry in Canada.

Don Marquis: It seems to us likely that the cockroach Archy, whose adventures N reads in the overheated basement of the Montréal house, would have found it a lot easier to dance out his poems on the sensitive electric typewriters of 1974 than the mechanical ones of 1927. At Mac High, having not a single friend, N often heads during break time to the typewriting room, which features row upon row of Smith Coronas, and types something just for the joy of hearing the clacking sound of a literary tap dance. Imagine the love poems Archy could have written to the cat Mehitabel on those taut, sprung machines! (Assuming, that is, that they had been left switched on and stocked with paper.) N also has a romantic interest in typewriters: he likes the fact that the typing room mostly attracts girls, for secretaries are still—in the age of Virginia Slim cigarettes and "You've come a long way, baby"—mostly women. At home there is an even finer specimen, a red IBM Selectric on which Jo writes

journalism intended for *The New Yorker*. Retrieving a used IBM
ribbon from the wastepaper basket next to the picture window, N
is able to piece together from the punched-out letters the following
poem, which Archy has dedicated to his dear immortal cat:

> boss these jumpy keys take some getting used to and where
>   is the
> return oh there it goes
> damn thing banjaxed me
> even after i learned to work it
>
> my vers libre can now be freer still
> although i feel as if i am rattling a machinegun
> operating this device and if i were indeed
> rattling a gatling
> i would like to be cutting down that punk
> freddy the rat
> my mortal enemy
> ratatattat o boy ratatattat
>
> boss there are no other creepycrawlies in this joint
> except when the mayflies hatch out on the lake
> swarm inland and cover the clapperboard
> where the jerks shed their skins disgustingly
> and so begin their transmigration
> into other forms or souls
> like we all did
>
> those nymphs give me the creeps boss
> because deep down i am not like them
> i was born a poet as you know
> and mehitabel was cleopatra

well boss i would love to work this thing all night
but must instead
head to the pine cupboard
where the furs hang limp like lines
in a poem by e e cummings
and there i will find some glue to guzzle
while i puzzle up a few new metaphors

i hope you like internal rhymes

archy

J. P. Donleavy: The Canadian winter gives way to a Canadian spring, the oil trucks stop coming to pump oil into the basement storage tanks, and the snow shrivels. N's Siberian paper round, delivering *The Montreal Star* at five in the morning through snowdrifts five feet deep, comes to a happy end also. There is still sledging at Thomson Point, where one afternoon quiet, sexy Debbie Léger flings herself into the snow with her legs and arms spread wide and N thinks of flinging himself on top of her, nylon against nylon, wool on wool, but instead sharply barks (but how he regrets it later, replaying the scene in his mind accompanied by the Tyrannosaurus Rex song "Debora," *duggery duggery duggery duggry-dug!*): "Get up, you lazy girl!" For consolation there is Yvonne Kulker, skulking with her brother in the concealed bungalow next door, sleek with the eyes of a wolf behind the lozenge lunettes of a pharmacist. For Yvonne, N takes his Rotring pen and draws a desert scene, precise as an architect's technical drawing, with the two of them hand in hand progressing towards a setting sun, all carefully coloured in with Windsor & Newton inks. He never sends the valentine. When the warm weather returns the family makes a trip to the Blue Ridge Mountains and comes back with bold blue sweatshirts proclaim-

N
I
C
H
E

ing that "Virginia is for lovers!" But what exactly are lovers? For the answer N has to rifle furtively through the pages of my *Beastly Beatitudes of Balthazar B*, in which there is a scene of initiation by a nanny, crowned by the ejaculation: "O Bella o Bella please it's coming out of me, it's coming out of me, hold me please." In the bathroom of the Beaconsfield bungalow N also finds something new coming out of him, some creamy trickle of human essence, which, with guilty haste, he flushes away in the bathroom at the end of the corridor, between the bedroom belonging to his sister and the more private one where his parents lie. There are other initiations, other debuts. My prose has made its mark with its free, sensual, Joycean lilt, and—emboldened by it, and perhaps also by the howling doggerel of David Bowie's *Sprechgesang* in "Future Legend," "ripping and rewrapping mink and shining silver fox"—N composes a pretentious prose poem that begins: "Chalk click, Latin, ablatives, A-stems and guilt . . ." It is mailed to the *Canadian Forum* magazine, and in due course the fourteen-year-old genius receives a polite letter of rejection from that coven of leftist intellectual aesthetes, who nevertheless request him not to stop sending such things in. He desists immediately.

Isaac Asimov: Mac High represents a moment of culture shock for N. He's been advanced a year, and is already small for his age, so he's surrounded by suburban Canadians who all seem to be called Mike, excel at ice hockey and American football, and attract sluts called Vicky who are cheerleaders. Despite being thrown in with kids who are older, bigger, and further through puberty than he is, N finds it hard to score anything less than top marks in every class, and the merit certificates come whooshing through the mail at regular intervals, accumulating uselessly on the living room desk like holiday pesetas. There's one wonderful teacher, the bearded and playful Mr. Robertson, who guides the North American literature class humorously through readings of *Death of a Salesman*, *The Yearling*, *A Bell for Adano*, *The Skin of Our Teeth*, *The Emperor Jones*, *The Teahouse of the August Moon*, *Our Town*, and *The Glass Menagerie*. But among his classmates N makes no friends, preferring to spend his free time in the school library reading calculator magazines. Calculators are the closest thing 1974 has to robots and computers, even if their vocabulary is limited to two words: SHELLOIL and HELLO, which you have to write upside down by punching in the numbers 71077345 and 0.7734. N finds the Sinclair models the most pleasing, aesthetically; their clean lines and well-chosen typography (perhaps influenced by the elegantly pale products Dieter Rams is designing for Braun) make them the precursors of Apple computers. There's no question of actually owning one, though. Radio Shack at the Laval shopping center may sell kits that kids clever with screwdrivers and solder can build for less than a hundred dollars, but N is not interested in actual calculators. He's interested in the idea that humanity is on the verge of creating artificial, mechanical life. One of the things he can do in the library is dream of a future world in which everyone has a calculator, a computer, a robot. He can do that by borrowing my book of short stories *I, Robot*, and perhaps combining that with Shaw's *Pygmalion* and a biography of Mao Tse-Tung. Somehow, those three books, plus a calculator magazine, prefigure the future rather well. For a more immersive experience N travels to the underground shopping arcades of downtown Montréal, built to allow shoppers to cross the city twenty feet beneath the snow. He rides the escalators to the glass corridors of the Place Bonaventure, a wholesale mall without a single shopper. Near the station he can also play a coin-operated racing car game with jaggy hieroglyphics representing—if you really strain at the raked screen behind the steering wheel—a car and track seen from above. Speed Race is only the second computer simulation N has experienced: the first was an incredibly dull lunar landing game on a mainframe at the King's Buildings, part of Edinburgh University, where a friend's brother was studying computer science. You "played" this by entering numbers controlling fuel burn and speed of descent, but it was about as exciting as a spreadsheet. For darker visions of the future N relies on the sexily dystopian visions of Bowie's *Diamond Dogs* album, which he finds quite unexpectedly one day in the record racks at Eaton's department store at Fairview:

> *And in the death, as the last few corpses lay rotting on the*
> *slimy thoroughfare . . .*

Bill is appalled by the dog howl with which this tone poem begins. Bowie's accompanying tour actually starts in Montréal, but N is forbidden to go when a local news report shows the freaks lining up for tickets. In the totalitarian dystopia of his family N will never be allowed to dress in silver foil, dye his hair, or shave his eyebrows. Meanwhile at school he has to put up with the sight of bragging jocks standing at their lockers, flashing their Bowie tickets like ice skate blades. It's hard to believe that this delicate, ambiguous British singer—the foxy, balletic Jeremiah that N is somehow surprised *not* to see reflected back from the Mac High bathroom mirrors—can belong to just anyone.

Robert Hughes: Modern art has always had as its first task its own remaking—the primal horde must rise up against the tribal father, in Freud's brutal language. Never has that axiom been more true than during the rambunctious, rollicking 1970s, when it seemed as if anything went, from neon tubes to piles of bricks, from bed-ins to soiled diapers. Nothing was too radical: if George Maciunas, the eccentric Lithuanian immigrant who founded Fluxus, determined that it should be so, even the copy of *Time* magazine you are now holding could become a work of art. It was all in the power of designation: Maciunas only needed to say "Let there be art!" and there it was, a latter-day Duchampian clutter of brochures, bowler hats, and bicycle wheels. So when N went downtown to attend his art classes at Concordia University, but ended up playing with the photocopiers in his father's office instead, who's to say that the zines he created weren't better art, more artful art, than the sketches, sculptures, and paintings he was assigned to make in class? The result of this tinkering with a reproduction machine as expensive as a family car was an in-house magazine with a circulation of just five: *Curreview*. Its logo, stylised down to the simplest of geometrical shapes, showed a head hovering above the chevron of an open book. Inside, under headlines in typefaces traced from dry transfer lettering catalogues, you could read articles about the difference between cars and automobiles, descriptions of maple syrup tasting at the Morgan Arboretum, and images of silhouettes chasing hockey pucks around frozen lakes. There were reviews of a new sitcom called *Rhoda* and bleak satire on a quiz game called *Truth or Consequences*. There was a celebrity profile of a five-year-old girl called Tammy Lang, the youngest member of the transplanted Scottish family who lived next door. There was even a parody of an eighteenth-century revolutionary squib calling on readers to rise up against that imperial abomination, N's long-suffering little sister. As with Fluxus, form and style mattered just as much as content: the author of this almanac was just as fascinated by the return of a 1940s typeface called Thrills as he was by the 1970s technology that allowed him to reproduce it. There's a bittersweet irony in the fact that Fluxus papers now find themselves in museum vitrines, for such publications were never intended to last—like *Curreview* they were supposed to flutter for

a moment in the glorious ticker tape parade of pure ephemerality,
before disappearing forever.

E. E. Cummings:
it is the revenant summer of 1974, and
n hangs from a wrought-iron palmette balcony four
stories above alva street. the red maple leaf of air
canada has brought four-fifths of the family home
and all is cheerful. n is an escapee from both
his dreary montréal suburb and his former edinburgh prison,
the draconian boarding house a few miles north.
in one hand he holds a glass of shloer apple juice
and in the other exactly 108 dry lentils which it is his intention
to rattle down upon the heads of hoi polloi *en passant*.
blazoned on the horizon stands edinburgh castle,
where a gun thunders at one and fireworks sear at night
above the coppergreen bulge of st. george's church.
far below, between rankins and law & forrest,
mr. christie the grocer can be seen serving sticky
dried figs to the original mrs. doubtfire, annabella coutts, owner
of half a dozen cats and a jumble shop on south east circus place.
n hears the voice of paul allen introducing the afternoon
repeat of *kaleidoscope*, the arts review program on radio 4.
paul is talking about dan flavin, whose neon lights—humming
mysteriously in pinks and chilly greens—one might see at the
arts council gallery over on charlotte square, dressed
in one's obligatory *pattes d'éléphant*, beige-tan negative-heel earth
  shoes
and a light blue plastic jacket with backstripe in red.
alternatively, one might schlep along to hell, subcultural
den of music on thistle street, or virgin, or henderson's
salad table, or the king hero coffee bar, where some

broken-voiced schoolboys in uniform might recognize one from
the long-ago summer term of 1973 and ask "are you in the
academy?"
(mishearing and mysterious, one must now reply: "no, i'm nick
currie!")

Mary Tyler Moore: I'm not sure, because I'm not really her, but
there probably were weekend afternoons when Mary Richards just
sat at home reading the poetry of Charles Simic in her yellow chair
by the window of her apartment, the first one, the one in the old
house. Styrofoam snow would be falling softly across the mocked-up
backdrop of the city of Minneapolis, and for the first time in, gosh, I
don't know how long, there'd be no Rhoda bursting in with a cheery
"Hey kid!," no Mr. Grant ringing the bell to chew over some new
crisis in the office, no Ted and Georgette to announce their engage-
ment, no Sue Ann Nivens with ridiculous home tips, no Murray . . .
aw, good old Murr! Mary Richards, played by me, would just be
sitting there in a rare moment of peace, reading the same sentence
of Simic over and over again, not really taking it in:

> It's the silence the teacher loves,
> The taste of the infinite in it.

Mary Richards's face—identical to mine—might well qualify as
the face of the 1970s, at least in N's mind. Of course, David
Bowie's face was right up there too, though you might say that
the constant changes made Bowie's face more of a blur. He could
be whatever you wanted to see: man, woman, soft, hard. There
were even times when Bowie and Mary looked surprisingly similar. Maybe Mary had thinned her eyebrows so much that they
almost disappeared, and Bowie had shaved his off. Maybe their
hair was being done by the same Hollywood hairdresser, and fea-

tured the same rich golden-brown streaks. Maybe they both wore something with boxy shoulders. Mary also conceivably reminded N of his mother—and perhaps 1970s David Bowie did too, for they were both volatile, both redheads. Anyhow, *The Mary Tyler Moore Show* lasted until 1977, the year David Bowie peaked with his albums *Low* and *"Heroes,"* which were both just—and this is a very Mary adjective—terrific. The Currie family ended their North American adventure in 1975, just after the release of the *Young Americans* album and right before the episode in which Mary Richards moves to a new high-rise apartment. That move was a mistake, we thought later, but going back to Scotland wasn't a mistake for the Curries. The language wars in Québec were making Bill's job difficult and the whole family just felt more European than Canadian, more urban than suburban. So they bought a town house in Edinburgh at 9 Drummond Place, where Bill started a language school, the Edinburgh Language Foundation. It soon became quite successful, and expanded into a huge building in Haddington called Templedean Hall. And you know what? There was a lot of continuity. N could still buy David Bowie's records, of course, and the family could still watch my show, as well as Valerie in her spinoff show *Rhoda*: "I went to art school; my entrance exam was on a book of matches." They watched on a cream-colored plastic cube called a Sony Trinitron KV-1340UB, this time in color. Can you believe they'd only had black-and-white sets up until then? I think it was a deliberate thing, something a bit Shaker-Quaker: in order to keep television weak, you'd kept it watery and gray-looking. Well, in 1975 we were finally allowed to burst into color, but the Curries still kept us weak by keeping us small. From a seat just a few feet away—where Bill was probably dozing after a hard day with the Vietnamese or the Venezuelans—we were nothing more than goldfish swimming in a bowl, prismatic splashes on a Japanese sugar lump.

Richard Adams: When the family returned to Scotland, Mark was sent to Loretto, a school for gentlemen farmers in the nearby town of Musselburgh, where he'd won a scholarship. N was slotted back into his old class at the Edinburgh Academy, but the two years he'd been away had quite transformed his classmates—their frames were a good foot taller now, their voices an octave lower. N remained small for his age, and light of voice. He walked down the hill every morning—it took seven minutes at a good clip—from Drummond Place to Henderson Row, where the Upper School building stood, with the line "*Η ΠΑΙΔΕΙΑ ΚΑΙ ΤΗΣ ΣΟΦΙΑΣ ΚΑΙ ΤΗΣ ΑΡΕΤΗΣ ΜΗΤΗΡ*" blazoned along its capital in Greek: "Education is the mother of learning and virtue." No longer a boarding-school hardcase, he fell in with a little band of undemanding day-boy nerds: John Thomson, David Ogden, and Stuart Wylie. John—the Wing Commander—was intelligent but uncool, tiny David twee, camp, and insinuating, and Stuart a plump-fingered electronics whiz who'd already started his own mail-order business. N had terrible trouble with the science subjects—all he remembered from biology, for instance, was a single haiku:

> *fertilisation:*
> *the fusion of two gametes*
> *to form a zygote*

One afternoon N had a sad reunion with Boyce—the taunting boarding-school friend who had called him Rabbit (because of his big front teeth and twitching nose) and borrowed his eloquence at boarding school to impress Debbie Yule. While N had stayed lagomorphic, Bug was now a hulking brute like a rugby player. He cast a withering glance at N. They were the only two pupils in a reading period classroom, and funnily enough they were both carrying nov-

els of mine. N had *Shardik* (my own favourite of my books), Bug
had *Watership Down*. They sat there in total silence for an hour,
absorbed by my animal epics, and then, when the bell went, they
separated without a word, like a bear and a rabbit from separate
books, incommensurable worlds.

William Carlos Williams:
kites

your essay on scott
wins the prize
so choose a book
whatever you like

you like kites
and dream
of flying a red one
late at night
above the town

the penguin book of kites
lacks gravitas
what to do?
the oxford anthology of english literature
volume II
has more class

cap-
tured in that paper cage
kermode, hollander, bloom, price,
trapp and trilling

may flap
but can't pull off the trick
of flying
(perhaps
they are unwilling)

Ivor Cutler: The sky grows dark and hail begins to rattle on the
roof of the pea-green Volvo. "Let us go for a spin," says Father, "and
I will teach you how to drive." We take the Linlithgow road, but
soon—defeated by the bracing Scottish weather—we pull off the
grim highway and enter the car park of some ruined shed. "Who is
McOnomy?" I ask naively, seeing the name picked out in white and
blue. "Don't be foolish, son," retorts Father, "McOnomy is just a
name they made up for a cut-price electrical goods warehouse. Everything here is cheap, and that is much appreciated by the Scots."
We enter, pass the tea urn with its metal teats, and stand side by side
at the urinal. Father hoists open the flies of his tweed plus fours,
purchased at John Dickson and Son, gunmaker of Frederick Street.
"Once our bladders are empty," Father proposes, his eyes fixed on
the wall ahead, "we can fill them again with tea." This done, we pe-
ruse the ranks of washing machines, hair dryers, mixers, and video
game consoles. "Would you like Pong?" demands Father. "Is it a
bad smell?" I ask. Father does not know, but thinks the price quite
a good bargain. "You attach it to the TV," he bluffs, "and it takes the
programmes away." We find a shopping trolley and put in one box
of Pong. "Which of these long-playing records would your mother
like?" asks Father, as we approach the brightly coloured racks. They
are all attractively priced at 99p. I select Paul Simon's *Still Crazy
After All These Years*, Peter Skellern's *Holding My Own*, a Stevie
Wonder double album, and *Jammy Smears* by Ivor Cutler. "Aren't
the discounts at Comet magnificent?" Father marvels. "I thought
we were at McOnomy?" But a look around confirms my mistake:

now everything is red and the signs say "COMET." Father is in raptures: he is proposing to buy twenty-seven sheepskin coats to match the thirteen he brought home last week from the Ingleston Sunday Market. "But Father," I splutter, "your wardrobe already bulges with sheepskin!" Father is, for once, equanimous. "Never you mind that, son," he replies kindly. "We shall build new cupboards, with louvered slatted doors. We shall need them for all the things we can now afford, thanks to my prospering business and the significant reductions on offer at the A1 Cash & Carry. We shall soon have all the Club biscuits, Smiths Salt 'n' Shake crisps and Liebfraumilch we could desire." I protest: "But Father, are we to become gluttons and drunkards? Is it not a cardinal sin?" Father will have none of it. "Do you want your driving lesson or not?" he snaps. "Come into the sleet and learn the rudiments of the three-point turn. With luck we will be playing Pong by dusk."

Dorothy L. Sayers: "Come near, I pray thee, that I may feel thee, my son, whether thou be my very son Esau or not," as Isaac sayeth unto Jacob. As a begetter of characters—I shall example my most famous creation, Lord Peter Death Bredon Wimsey—one watches with uncommon apprehension as they fall into the hands of actors, interlopers, and sundry other epigones. One's own death does not lessen by one whit one's interest in the destiny of this wanton progeny: have they fallen to Sheol or Gehenna? I am somewhat in favour of Peter Carmichael as the 1970s television Wimsey, but bridle at N's silly cartoon parody of same, entitled *Lord James, Private Eye and Handsome Man*. A single sheet of A4 survives from 1975, hand-coloured in pencil. The jowly Lord James sports a centre parting, monocle, yellow bow tie, smoking jacket, and riding crop, which he holds behind his back as if concealing a weapon. The first frames show the dilettante aristocrat at a party, speaking to a lady who exclaims: "Oh, you're the famous private eye and handsome man

Lord James?" The suave detective is about to offer his card when a character off-screen shrills: "My jewels!" Lord James is duly led to the empty box, produces a magnifying glass, glances at the clues, and concludes, with unseemly haste: "The thief was a tall man wearing a blue jacket." I ask you! There should be sixteen chapters in that, with Wimsey eventually kicking himself for being such a dashed contemptible chump! Instead, smug Lord James leaves the building, and we immediately see the culprit outside a butcher's shop, standing in a bus queue. He is two feet taller than everyone else, the only figure in blue. Our dunderheaded detective, however, is all cloud, no witness: he slides into his green Rolls and drives off. Suddenly—hell and all the harrowing thereof!—a tire bursts. And that is where the squib fizzles, for its author's concentration has turned to something else—he is inserting furniture screws into a perfectly good piano, probably. In fact, this irksome scamp is even now mocking me in an autobiography composed entirely of the parodic and the spasmodic. "Yea, a soft answer turneth away wrath: but grievous words stir up anger!"

Witold Gombrowicz: It must have been sheer indolence that prevented N from leaving school at sixteen to learn some honest trade like onion selling or canary breeding. Instead of becoming a useful member of society, multiplying birds or hawking bulbs, he lingered on, or rather malingered, in the Edinburgh Academy's seventh block, where he mostly played push-penny with a small group of like-minded wastrels, sitting useless exams from time to time and editing the school arts magazine *Focus*, which meant letting budding satirists mock him by submitting punk lyrics as if they were their own poems. Editor N foolishly published "Belsen Was a Gas" as if it were the original work of a boy who later became a distinguished professor at Birkbeck College rather than a song performed at the final Sex Pistols concert. And oh how they laughed and sneered, the clever boys in the other classroom, the ones who listened to Bob Dylan records rather than wasting precious time playing push-penny and sending each other into paroxysms of throttled giggles by impersonating Ivor Cutler! N's feckless little band of nerds—Puckle, Glen, the Wing Commander, the Brown twins—met up in Cramond lounges and New Town basements to play through *The Beatles Songbook* and drink Strongbow cider, but N was painfully aware of the gaucherie of this band (Tower Volts and the Generators, they called themselves). He had, after all, written an essay entitled "The Most Important Person Alive Today" about that paradigmatic hysterical singer, the ginger extraterrestrial who had recently moved to Berlin and was going to swim with dolphins, if only he could find any there. Unsure of what to do with the possibilities offered by freedom, N stayed on too long at school and got, frankly, bored. Bored, bored, bored! He opted out of a horrible Monday afternoon ritual called Corps, which involved boys dressing as sailors, soldiers, or airmen and marching up and down the school yards shouting things. Instead, posing as an anti-militarist conscientious objector, N was permitted to do something called Social Services, which meant that he was sent to an old people's home in Stockbridge to chat with semi-centenarians, or detailed to assist the office staff at Oxfam, just off Leith Walk. There he sat with a buxom and alkaline secretary with flour-smelling hair, helping feebly with the filing and photocopying. One afternoon, when she had gone to the toilet, N leaned forward and dipped the tip of his tongue into the girl's tepid cup of tea. Absurd! Why pollute a perfectly good hot drink that way? Belonging to a secretary? In the office of a charitable institution? It made no sense! The girl came back and—*mine de rien!*—took a sip from the saliva-polluted chalice for all the world as if this were still a normal office, the nerve centre of a charitable organisation in an important provincial capital. When, as we know, it was now something else: the site of an audacious and successful sexual crime.

Dr. Alex Comfort: N's walk home from school in 1977 takes him up Silvermills Lane (a cobbled street of warehouses later obliterated by ugly residential buildings), past the dentist's surgery he somehow always associates with Pink Floyd's *Animals* album, and on up the hill to the family town house at 9 Drummond Place. Secretaries are no longer working in the ground-floor dining room; Nora and Elizabeth, who run the office for the Edinburgh Language Foundation, have been relocated to a building just off Charlotte Square. It's just as well, because their presence tends to make N feel frisky after school, during those dangerous hours when he's alone, and hasn't yet felt the need to unpack Racine's *Phèdre* from his briefcase and start his homework. Some small stimulus—the passing of a bosomy dental assistant on the narrow pavement across the road, a glimpse of the gauzy nymphs in the David Hamilton posters on the wall—can make N hungry for the keen private pangs of surreptitious orgasm. But what will provide the stimulus? He has no actual pornography, being too shy to buy the stuff over the counter. Well, I'm proud to say that N's first impulse is to scurry down to his parents' bedroom, where a copy of my bestseller *The Joy of Sex* lies inexpertly hidden under the bed. It has probably been left there by N's parents as a gesture towards sex education. Sex as a topic has never been officially broached, and "the talk" has never come. My book—hiding in plain view between carpet and mattress—helps fill in the gaps. Inside, drawings—critics have scoffed that they depict members of Abba or bearded sociology professors at redbrick universities—help to explain all the possible positions for intercourse, but they prove less than stimulating to N. He stuffs the book back into its hiding place and heads instead to the sitting room, where his mother keeps a pile of recent editions of *Vogue*. Three or four copies will do the job. Upstairs in his room N arranges himself tummy-down on his bed, his chin balanced on the mattress edge, one hand down his slim-cut school trousers. With the other he flips the pages of the *Vogue*s piled on the floor, creating an exciting sequence of editorial and advertising images of voluptuous women in expensive clothes. Despite the fact that no single model is completely naked, the suggestion of luxurious sensuality on each glossy page is enough to inch orgasm closer, and a thrusting, grinding motion completes the process within a few minutes. Containing the wriggling results neatly in his foreskin, N runs along the town house landing—the situation, three floors up, is vertiginous, a bannistered ledge cantilevered between skylight and staircase—to the children's bathroom, where he cleans up then hastens back to return the *Vogue*s to their pile under the marble-topped table in the living room below, all the time listening for the click of the glass door on the ground floor and the return of the first family member. It's easy to say that my book would have given him a more educational orgasm, but perhaps we should allow the schoolboy some component of aesthetic pleasure as he engineers his heady rush. *The Joy of Sex* may offer solid clinical advice, but the art direction in *Vogue* puts up, well, stiff competition.

Franz Boas: If you know me at all it is as the founder of an influential school of cultural relativism in anthropology: in the Germany of my birth and the America of my adoption I promoted the idea that cultures don't progress through fixed stages on a path toward something like European civilization, but are all on divergent yet equally valid paths of their own. But I doubt that you *have* heard of me, for your twenty-first-century ethnography museums lie empty and your anthropology departments rot. Your semi-populist governments rail against the idea of multiculturalism and force immigrants to assimilate to European standards—even to profess, in absurd tests and attestations, to endorse them. Never has Rousseau's idea of the noble savage—as an exemplar, a paradigm, someone one might study and learn from—been less fashionable. And yet paradoxically you have never been more tribal, and thus you have never been, yourselves, more explicable by the terms and tools of anthropology. Take young N as an example: at the age of seventeen he is learning to drive the family Volvo, and this is very much a rite of initiation into adult life. A firsthand report from N would contain testimony to the sense of power he gets driving his father's car alone, a sense of potency that manifests itself quite literally as an erection.

He passes his driving test and is put to work in a sort of apprenticeship to the Edinburgh Language Foundation, ferrying students out to the college's Haddington campus and taking them on afternoon expeditions around the city. So we must speak of an extended clan structure: at this stage it looks as though N could be drawn into the family business, which would become, as it were, ELF & Sons. On the other hand, in terms of his potential for mate selection—the passage from a family of origin to a family of foundation—N seems deeply impoverished. He is still attending an all-male school— although the Edinburgh Academy has made the decision to admit girls, it currently has only six females among six hundred male pupils. His friends seem to be uniformly sisterless. His sister's peers are an unpromising source of potential mates: these St. George's girls prefer N's hunky brother Mark, and N mostly ignores them. Among the "theoretically possibles" is Sophie Eveling, the daughter of acerbic playwright Stanley Eveling (but N would probably get on better with Stanley, whose television column in *The Scotsman* he reads); another is Kirsteen Morrison, a beautiful, petite, and dark-haired girl who later becomes a commodities trader in Singapore. Kirsteen comes along on a family holiday to the island of Colonsay, where N drives her around in his mother's red MGB and pushes her on a rubber tire swing. But he's shy and utterly inexperienced with girls. With his lantern chin and myopic gaze, N comes across as gawky, judgmental, and standoffish. His main problem is a cultural one: he is not at home in his home environment. He dreams of art school, and of Europe. Soon he will meet a European art school girl, and begin to long for her, or for a kind of life that will contain people like her.

Juan Goytisolo: Our bittersweet protagonist—who, as we have established in our various fictional voices, is a nervous virgin, an exile in the midst of his own kith, a tumbling weed on the sands of time—first sees his future Beatrice sitting on the steps of number 10 George Square, where the "language foundation" his father runs has rented classrooms from the university. Beatrice is working during the summer as a monitor. Like N she has been hired by ELF to speak English to foreign students and take them on undemanding afternoon expeditions: Edinburgh Castle, the zoo, Bruntsfield Links. She mostly ends up, naughtily, speaking Spanish to the Spanish-speakers. Sitting there among the students on George Square, Beatrice is a sort of Juliette Gréco, pale and frail, dark, owlish and arty, asthenic of shoulder. Her face is oriental in its handsome roundness, her eyes black and vivid, her hair chopped simply like Louise Brooks's in *Pandora's Box*. Beatrice incarnates perfection for N, despite being slightly bandy about the legs and walking like a young Alicante widow in shoes as flat as her chest. Beatrice, reserved and somewhat self-absorbed, radiates a defiant cool that speaks of the Mediterranean and art school. She's an artist already, exactly the kind of creature N wants to become. An air of existential tragedy hangs over her: she fully believes she will be dead by thirty. As they head towards the student-centre refectory Beatrice's face breaks occasionally into a smile that tightens her cheekbones and reveals a wide row of tiny mammalian teeth. N already knows her older sister—big-breasted, generous, and pragmatic.

The girls couldn't be more different. They live in a high, sunny corner flat up at Bruntsfield, a few minutes' walk from the university. Beatrice is studying painting. From the first glimpse of her, N is smitten; a moon-eyed process of longing is kindled within him. He's the son of the boss of the company she works for; surely he has a chance? Actually, he doesn't, but his futile battle to impress her, to date her, to correspond with her, and even to transform himself into her will serve him later in countless songs of longing and loss and, finally, bemused resignation—for when a songwriter loses, he wins; songs of loss resonate more than songs of success. When Beatrice tells him—on a bench in Princes Street Gardens, after an awkward date at the Fruitmarket Gallery—that she isn't interested in a physical relationship, N will climb Calton Hill and weep as the sun sets behind the unfinished ruin of the National Monument. Nevertheless they continue to meet every day, to chat earnestly and steer their wards from site to site. By osmosis as much as design, Beatrice influences N artistically, helping him to appreciate Brecht, Paul Klee, Leonard Cohen, Nicolas de Staël. When N finally sees David Bowie perform—at the Glasgow Apollo, with the *Stage* tour—Beatrice will be by his side. She will be his Felice Bauer, his Milena Jesenská, almost his Constance Dowling. On that first day, hunched behind her perpetual cigarette, Beatrice represents all that our bittersweet protagonist desires. She removes her gold-rimmed National Health Service spectacles and greets him with a certain reserve, a conspiratorial sarcasm. On their dates—on snowy nights, when N has been able to borrow his mother's red MG, and to whisk Beatrice to Henderson's Salad Table and then back to her door—she will reward him with a dry and cursory kiss flavoured with smoke. She will write him letters from art school, and send abstracted, carelessly punctuated cards from Paris or San Gimigniano: "Helo Uncle Peter . . ." In this way Beatrice will gorgeously ruin N's summers and cause him to turn in desperation to the "melancholy science" of Adorno and Benjamin. Everything deepens and ripens. Rilke has said all there is to say about unrequited love; can we ever feel vividly enough the pain of Gaspara Stampa?

Bruno Munari: Design is art in the age of the mass—it adds quality to quantity. Given the opportunity to visit my rooftop apartment overlooking Milan, N might have discovered didactic inventions delightful in their judicious, playful use of colour and form. I could have showed him my bonsai garden, including plants over half a century old, or demonstrated my Rube Goldberg–like machines, primed to tick in waltz time and flicker with colours just as artistically as do the mobiles of Alexander Calder. We could have flipped together through books made of origami or die-cut holes, my joyfully didactic books showing how to draw a tree or the sun. Had I come, in turn, to visit N's high room in Edinburgh—a room capable of catching the evening sunlight while Eno's *Discreet Music* played in a Philips cassette machine—I would have encouraged his project to make small paper models of his furniture, and then to move them around on an outline of his room until he arrived at the perfect organisation of space. Granted, probably he would keep the piano in front of the blocked-up door connecting his room to the bigger one his brother occupied (for the ghost of a seamstress had been documented in *The British Journal of Parapsychology* trying to cross that threshold, rattling that handle). The fireplace would of course have to remain blocked up, and the John Lewis curtains with their 1970s take on Art Deco motifs would still drape the high Georgian window. In the end all that could really be moved would be the yellow table itself, with its small black-shaded gilt lamp (a florid nineteenth-century accessory poised, with postmodern abandon, on an aseptic structure worthy of Le Corbusier). Nevertheless, it's the principle of freedom that would matter, the paper "map" serving to illustrate the perpetual possibility of altering one's surroundings, in this case through design. Furniture is too heavy to drag around speculatively, but with cut-out shapes one pushes it here and there with the tip of a finger.

Theodor Adorno: *Scintille, diamant, tourne, ô miroir!* That the son of a successful Edinburgh businessman should profit by, for instance, being gifted with a company charge card allowing him to acquire an unlimited supply of free books at James Thin's, the university bookseller on South Bridge, should surprise no one. Nor would the vigilant observer be astonished to learn that this scion—the beneficiary, after all, of an unwarranted privilege of which he is all too painfully aware—should gravitate to the philosophy section overlooking Infirmary Street and there, held rapt by the seductive ecstasies of class guilt, should select—as one selects fine wines in a vintner's shop—paperbacks from the Verso imprint's English translations of works written by myself, Benjamin, Horkheimer, and others of the Frankfurt School. N's favourite volume is my "reflections from damaged life," *Minima Moralia*. My most personal and subtle work, *Minima Moralia* is a sort of diary of my thoughts during the war years. N writes in his own diary that reading it "saddens any subsequent walk," and yet this sadness is also a sort of communion, and therefore a consolation. Our young protagonist is, or aspires to be, a cultural critic who presses intellectual subtleties into the service of the working classes. The fact that Marx was unambiguous about the function of the intelligentsia does not make its status any less paradoxical: this class is free to place itself at the disposal of the proletariat by hammering together a sturdy *kulturkritik* that must include a comprehensive criticism, precisely, of its own class privilege—which is to say, of the very conditions that make critique itself possible. For what is a world-historical view without that melancholy science, the ability to reflect—an ability which history itself has denied the proletariat? The aporia calls to mind Offenbach's

Tales of Hoffmann: in Act III, Giulietta feels nothing for Hoffmann, but Captain Dapertutto has promised her a diamond if she can steal the poet's reflection from the mirror. When she succeeds—for Hoffmann loves her, and gives his reflection willingly—the captain prepares a chalice of poison for Hoffmann's accomplice Nicklausse, but Giulietta drinks it by mistake and dies in the poet's arms. And so it is with the proletarian Weltanschauung, which must wither upon contact with the self-hating embrace of the intellectuals. Having put their reflections into the service of another class only to find the love unrequited, the poets, no longer able to find themselves in the now-empty mirror, can offer only a view from nowhere—one that slays precisely that which it wishes to serve.

Andy Warhol: One day I guess N is at home reading a copy of my book *The Philosophy of Andy Warhol (From A to B & Back Again)*, which isn't really something I wrote but a paste job put together by Pat Hackett out of taped conversations I had with Bob and Brigid. I'm A, you see, and Bob and Brigid are both B. The book was easy to write; I just had to talk. And even what I'm saying now isn't necessarily anything I actually wrote, or even said, but something I might say, put together by N, using my voice. Which, you know, I think is great, because it means less work for me. And work is harder when you're dead. Not that I think that famous people are really ever dead—probably we're working just as hard as we ever did. I mean, if I'm talking now I can't be dead, even if it's N who's really talking. The important thing isn't whether you're alive or dead, but whether you're famous. I don't even know about that, these days. "In the future everybody will be famous for fifteen people," as N likes to say. So anyway, N is sitting at his yellow table on the third floor of their town house one day in 1979 when his father runs in excitedly from his Volvo and yells to N to put on Radio 3, because there's something he's going to like very much. It turns out to be a documentary about Paul Klee. It's been made by Edward Lucie-Smith, who interviewed me once for a similar show the BBC was doing. He called me Granny, because he heard that everybody calls me that. Which they do—that thing about Dracula and Cinderella is just Lou. Anyway, this Klee show is really well put together by this pretty famous producer Piers Plowright, with electronic music by Malcolm Clarke of the BBC Radiophonic Workshop, kind of computer Arabic music. There's an interview with the British artist Tom Phillips, and Ed's own poems about Klee's cat Bimbo. You know, there's a photo of Klee with Bimbo standing on his shoulder, and he looks exactly like Truman Capote! I mean Klee, not Bimbo. But Truman looks like a cat too. Anyway, do you know what's best, for me, about this show? It's when they go to Tunisia, and Klee just falls in love with the colors, and he watches a little girl dancing next to a donkey. He totally forgets that he's Swiss. But the music is a European version of Tunisian music, like something you'd hear in Looney Tunes or Merrie Melodies. There's crazy reverberation that could make you jump if you weren't prepared for it. "If only I survive, a saucy voice cries in me!" That cuts through so loud, with the reverb! As soon as he hears that, N knows this is something he needs to tape. Like me, he always has a blank cassette ready, because you never know what you're going to hear. Maybe he plans to start something like *Interview* magazine one day. Or put together a book made up of other people talking. Bill—that's N's father—likes to tease him, saying: "All you do is fiddle around with disks and tapes all day!" But actually he doesn't mind that, because N has given him cassettes of things like Brian Eno's ambient music, which Bill plays in the car. And although fiddling around with disks and tapes might not look like hard work, it really is. Like being dead, or being an artist.

Max Weber: As 1979 begins N makes a giant leap in self-development: he buys a new Letts diary with A5-sized pages, across whose printed lines he writes a two-hundred-word account of each day. Previously he's been in charge of a five-year family diary, which notes in a few words what each of the five Curries has been doing. This new, more expansive and individualistic approach moves diary-keeping from something communitarian towards a more expressive activity, a sort of laboratory of emerging selfhood. Of course, N is not oblivious to the fact that this recapitulates the historical outline I make in my book *The Protestant Ethic and the Spirit of Capitalism*, which N has bought with his blue account card up at Thin's bookshop. There I detail—in ways that N finds an absolute revelation—how Protestant northern European cultures developed, side by side, the religious mind-set in which giving a private account of oneself as an individual to a personal God is paramount, and the commercial habit of rendering financial transactions in the form of double-column account books. The resulting cluster of cultural values—individualism, guilt, the making of narratives in the form of prayers, diaries, and spreadsheets—is a fascinating one, and shows N for the first time the unexpected and yet perfectly credible connections between his family's culture (a secularised version of Scottish Calvinism) and a long and flourishing strand of European history: the secret parallelism of religion and commerce. One makes an account of oneself in business via accountancy, in religion via prayer, and as an individual via the narrative of a diary. These seemingly disparate forms are intertwined, in the history of the West, much more closely than we generally imagine: business is a form of culture, prayer is a kind of narrative, and diary-keeping is a sort of semantic accountancy. Suddenly N understands why his father (raised very strictly as a member of a fundamentalist Protestant sect called the Plymouth Brethren) asked him to letter a sign declaring 1976 an *"annus mirabilis"* for his business: outwardly, this sign was simply something to hang on the wall of the Edinburgh Language Foundation's first office, to raise morale and bring good luck. It may also have referred to John Dryden's poem about the miraculous year 1666 (although in fact 1666 was a disastrous year in which most of London burned down). But it also referred to the Calvinist idea that success in business might be an outward sign of membership of God's elect—in other words of predestination. The destiny of an individual might simultaneously have both worldly and cosmic dimensions. The thread of narcissism in this—for the doctrine of election is about the salvation of individuals, not groups—is evident, and the strange concatenation of worldliness with asceticism (a religious-style holding back from the world combined with a commercial involvement in it) became a sort of template for the relation of father to son: thenceforth, N would write often to his father giving accounts of educational or financial successes on the understanding that, between the lines, and in an entirely secularised way, this would signal not only that he was "prospering" out in the world, but crucially that these outward successes were signs of something celestial: possible membership of God's elect. But of course—and James Hogg's *Private Memoirs and Confessions of a Justified Sinner* is based on this ambiguity—a Protestant never quite knows what it signifies to prosper in a worldly way. It might be a sign of God's favor, but don't the Psalms also say that the wicked "spread themselves like the green bay tree"?

J. P. Guilford: In the early postwar period I begin to research the psychometric dimensions of creativity—the personality correlates of highly creative individuals. Are they introverts or extroverts, leaders or followers, flexible or rigid? In the context of the Cold War, I argue, we need new ways to recognize and nurture inventiveness if we aren't to fall behind. N encounters my 1959 essay "Traits of Creativity" in a 1970 Penguin anthology put together by Professor P. E. Vernon of Calgary University. On its cover the book features a

Stubbs etching showing a baby apparently punching its way out of the womb. N at this point wants to go to art school to study either industrial or graphic design, and his foxy aunt Barbara—a Glasgow librarian with access to all the prospectuses—helps him choose the Central School in London. But at the last moment N—a nervous eighteen-year-old—backs out and signs up instead for an English literature M.A. at the University of Aberdeen. In his first year he's also studying psychology and sociology, and when Betty Fraser, the psychology lecturer, arrives at the big Brutalist slab of the Arts Lecture Theatre one afternoon to address the topic of inventiveness, N feels his ears burning. Highly creative people are fluent, says Fraser, somewhat introverted, subtly dominant, desurgent, divergent in their thinking style, humorous, notably original, and even eccentric in their self-presentation. They have an "internal locus of evaluation," which means that they measure success or failure by their own standards, not the prevalent norms. They're playful and tend, at school, to mock the authoritarians and conformists who appeal to teachers. Reading up on this in the white Penguin volume with the rebellious fetus on the cover N recognizes—or thinks he does, for there's a horoscopic aspect to all this—the personality profile of heroes of his, from Kafka to Beckett and Bowie. Most of all, though, he recognizes his own idealized self. It comes as a pleasant surprise to know that scientists are working—using questionnaires and correlations if not actually Bunsen burners and microscopes—to isolate and analyze something as volatile and evasive as talent. From this moment on whenever N gets depressed or self-hating at university he immerses himself in the creativity section of the psychology library and reads dust-dry studies of the traits of creative people, shamelessly identifying with every clumsy word and drawing a sense of secret validation from the pen sketches we've assembled. In short, he begins a campaign to persuade himself that he is an artist.

Malcolm Bradbury: Despite Herbert Read, despite Eliot and Pound and the rest of them, modernism hits Britain late, like the report of dull thunder on the eastern horizon. By the time N reads my book on the subject it's a spent force, already glossed over and edged out by this new, playfully regressive attitude called the postmodern. But N somehow finds the austere, elitist, progressive ideas of modernism unbearably exciting. He sits at the pine table in the breakfast room—with its expensive faux-rustic cabinets from Heidi's—reading the fat green paperback I've edited on the topic: *Modernism: A Guide to European Literature 1890–1930.* It's a sort of prospectus of musty excitements, decorated with a blown-up detail of an Art Deco railway poster: *Etoile du Nord, Pullman, Antwerp à Bruxelles.* This combination of the retro and the streamlined calls to mind the games Kraftwerk have recently been playing on their *Trans-Europe Express* album. The symbolism is both fresh and ancient, a sort of futuristic antiquity taking place in a Europe that is at once close and far away. Modernism, in my book, becomes an unbuffered rush from one continental city to the next. Its accent is on innovation, originality, freshness, even a certain savagery: Freud's Primal Horde is constantly rising up against the stodgy potted plants, pianofortes, and salons of the nineteenth century. The rebellion is mostly intact; you can quite easily—as N is doing while he reads—be recording a Public Image Limited session to tape as you're reading, easily squaring the shocking newness, the bracing atonality of a song like "Careering" with the Poundian injunction to "make it new." Is pop music pastiching modernism, or belatedly coming to terms with its requirements? Can modernism survive commercialisation, or is its accommodation inevitably its terminus? "A face is raining across the border," Lydon sings in a voice both lilting and terrible, and what you hear is a very modernist sense of difficulty as a hieratic calling, largely unrewarded in the marketplace. Later, in the 1980s, popular culture will not be like this—there will be pastiche, *passéisme,* the collapse of high and low, a faux-Motown backbeat everywhere, shrill synth trumpets, a pervasive Warholian amoralism, a darkening convergence of critical judgment and commercial fortune. This will happen, to be precise, somewhere between parts one and two of Bowie's "It's No Game," though I, Malcolm Bradbury—busy supervising Ian McEwan's early fictions at the University of East Anglia's new creative writing program—cannot really be expected to know this. Modernism's mandarin austerity will become something abandoned, something to be found, should one seek it, in the thoughts of a dwindling tribe of ancients. N will befriend one such, a queer fish named Ron Bailey. This tiny, wiry, amused man has spent his life dressing windows at Patrick Thomson, the department store on the North Bridge. An art student of the 1920s, he has furnished his bare flat with discarded mannequins. He is the closest thing Edinburgh has to a Tzara or a Ball, a Bellmer or a Richter. One day, on a skip-diving expedition, N earnestly asks the old queen whether he would call himself a modernist. "Oh yes," smiles Bailey, "of course! My generation had the luxury of knowing that to be modern and to be modernist were one and the same thing." It's a certainty—a sense of artistic direction, progress, and purpose—that N will always lack, for his generation will make no distinction between forward and back.

Hermann Hesse: Herr N—while not unsympathetic as a character—is a half-man, half-wolf amalgam, prowling through the upper parts of the family house under the bright skylight. His family has given him the use of a bedroom equipped with a piano, and from that room they hear strange muffled noises emerging constantly; he is apparently snorting and puffing and dragging things into place with his pointed snout, and then comes the sound of guitars, pianos, and tape recorders modified with tissues and furniture screws, and the dreadful moon-howling common to the whole lupine pack. He shares the upper bathroom with a ginger hamster, and the toilet doubles as a photographic darkroom in which he installs an orange lamp and a pale green Russian enlarger, a Zenith. At such times a unique smell hovers above the bathroom's blue carpet, as alkaline clouds of hydroquinone gather around the pediment of the basin and grey images creep across blank paper. One afternoon the idiotic kitten climbs up into the rafters and the wolf called Mark has to be pushed up through a hatch with a torch to search for him; they both emerge sooty and sheepish. During the reading of my novel *Steppenwolf*, to get into the spirit of the thing, N buys a bottle of red wine and slowly drinks his way through it, one glass per chapter. He becomes more wolfish with every page. Nietzsche begins to appear in his thoughts; the particular superman he follows is singing about ash while walking with stately poise along a beach in a world with an ink-black sky. The animal's mother has recently returned from China bringing the gift of a heavy padded military coat in army blue trimmed with synthetic fur. In this garment the steppe dog lopes through the streets of Edinburgh, a ripped-off Raskolnikov. When he turns eighteen he visits a disreputable cinema called the Classic and sees a remarkable Italian soft-core porn film entitled *Velluto Nero*, set in Egypt and featuring languid Laura Gemser. The calm oscillating synth motif by Dario Baldan Bembo impresses him enormously: in his shabby cinema seat he fights the urge to howl along. At home the news anchor is reporting on the sugar-lump-shaped Sony Trinitron that Pierrot has stolen rubies from a royal coffin, lit by the brilliance of gold and flickering candlelight. The wolf's father, half asleep in a low-slung white chair, fills in the missing details: a pale laundry maid has washed a bucket-load of faded clothes and sinister moths have blotted out the sun. The wolf clicks up the stairs to his high retreat to listen to Schoenberg.

Albert Einstein: It must have been during this period that N discovered two formulae for the definition of success in his life: the first was the imperative to increase the ratio of meaning to time, the second was to cram as many events—outward, or merely mental—into each second as was possible in any context (this he measured by a unit he named the "event/second"). The alert reader will understand that these formulae correspond with our conventional and existing measures of quality and quantity. Insofar as life presented itself to young N as a problem to be solved, the problem was not a lack of material things, for these were abundantly provided. It was, rather, an existential deficit, a lack of human meaning. The things to fear were those states of boredom, blankness, alienation, and depression in which we teeter on the edge of an abyss of sheer insignificance. If time could be enriched—by reading books, say, or simply indulging a fulfilling daydream—it would never feel wasted. And if more events could be packed into smaller units of time—as subjectively happens when we travel between cities on a fast train, or when densely packed events, at an art biennial, for instance, are matched to an eager and responsive mind—then a life could be stretched almost to infinity. As for that universal human problem, the fear of death, N liked to refer to something I remarked when my good friend Michele Besso died: "That means nothing. People like us, who believe in physics, know that the distinction between past, present, and future is only a stubbornly persistent illusion."

Francis Ponge: If I were to pastiche an addendum to my book *The Voice of Things* I might look at a reproduction N has Blu Tacked to the wall of his student room in Aberdeen. Mounted on a sheet of black paper N has bought in an art materials shop, it's a small reproduction of a painting showing a Paris boulevard in the late nineteenth century. But wait, first let me set the scene. Hillhead Halls of Residence is a sort of walled encampment on the top of a hill overlooking the Don River. The buildings are modernist blocks, and the whole thing feels like an African missionary centre, or a Soviet-era apartment block in a Siberian mining town. It's grim but—surrounded by wooded slopes that plunge to Seaton Park and the mercury meander of the river—also beautiful. In each apartment six locked bedrooms are grouped alongside a communal kitchen and bathroom. There's a central building with a refectory, bar, and café, and a series of television lounges scattered across the site, each tuned to a single channel, allowing students to make a sort of "televisual safari" from lounge to lounge. Something in N—some love of austerity and autonomy, of limitation as the hidden face of opportunity—responds to the tiny bedroom he's been allocated in Esslemont House, overlooking the bus-turning circle. There's a desk, a radiator, a bed with a thin orange duvet, a wardrobe. To this N adds the things he's brought up from the family home in Edinburgh: an Akai tape deck with Dolby noise reduction, the radio amp and speakers from the family's old music centre, a guitar, a Smith Corona typewriter, a few clothes. There's an opportunity here to become a new person, but very few materials to hand. In an attempt to connect himself with the glamour of sophistication, N has subscribed to some exotic literary magazines: *Bananas* emerges from far-off Notting Hill Gate and publishes short stories with quirky illustrations; *Gambit* is a journal of avant-garde theatre published by John Calder. *Gambit* 33–34 is a fat double issue on Polish theatre, and for some reason N has two copies. He carefully cuts from one of them images of Tadeusz Kantor's production of *The Dead Class*—grotesque scenes of Polish villagers carrying corpse-like dummies on their backs—and mounts them on the outside of his door, as if to say: "A form of aestheticised insanity is constantly happening in here: be prepared!" Inside, pinned to a propped cork slab, there's a postcard of a Kirchner painting of a circus ring, under which N has mounted a typed meditation by Franz Kafka: "You do not need to leave your room. Remain sitting at your table and listen. Do not even listen, simply wait, be quiet, still and solitary. The world will freely offer itself to you to be unmasked, it has no choice, it will roll in ecstasy at your feet." This reads well when Magazine's song "The Great Beautician in the Sky" is lurching out of the Akai. And then there's the Paris painting, which is *Avenue de l'Opera Rain Effect* by Camille Pissarro, painted in 1898. It's not exactly radical with its Post-Impressionist scene of black barouche and calèche carriages scuttling like beetles across rainy cobbles, but it reassures N with its glimpse of the kind of cosmopolitan nineteenth-century European cities he fancies he will spend his life in. And if you're prepared to make do with a smaller, granite-grey, seagull-flecked and Presbyterian version of this scene, slightly fish-scented, there's always the 20 bus idling outside, waiting to take you to Union Street.

Nathalie Sarraute: It can't be helped . . . One is thrown together with *them* whether one wants it or not . . . I am talking about certain people we all know . . . It's not as if they aren't welcome in their way . . . One might even become sentimental about them a long time after the fact . . . Nobody lives in a vacuum and no man is an island . . . There's the one at the bus stop whose mother wants him to have company every day on the way to school . . . You have so much in common, in your little caps! You're introduced, and thus wedded . . . You're both eight years old . . . Now you're eighteen it's the one next door who listens to Roxy Music and has a neurotic need to be in company so that he can talk about his problems. A cup of Earl Grey, Nick? Lapsang souchong? In this way he extracts you from your room like a beachcomber prising open a clam, or a man coming home to his wife. You were writing your diary, or reading French novels, or listening to quiet music, or pleasuring yourself, but his need is greater . . . The living must take priority over the dead, as reality must hold sway over fantasy, and clamour over silence. And so, drinking smoked tea, he begins his narrative of self, a narcissism of negativity that is nevertheless—it seems to you—an act of self-indulgence. You are being used as a therapist, unpaid. One day this man will have a wife, and she will become familiar with all this, but for now you will have to do. You are the quiet one, and quietness always invites invasion. Quietness is essentially feminine. There is, however, one way out. Your neighbour— a barrel-chested geography student—is endlessly curious about the diary you write in those yellow Chartwell notebooks. He only wants to know one thing: what you *really* think of him. And so, accidentally on purpose, you leave the book open one evening when he is visiting your room. You're playing him a tape of Magazine . . . He's telling you that cynical songs about love repel him . . . You reply that this is odd, since one of his favourite songs concerns a man who builds his dream home around an inflatable doll . . . As you speak, you notice with satisfaction that he is reading over your shoulder a passage in your yellow notebook that reads: "Other people are so mediocre: the way they stand and drone in coherent monotones, sabotaging vitality. I am secretive, but just give me the chance and I'll swagger and shout the thoughts that would turn a listener to stone; quite unnoticed I'll explode." The next-door neighbour twists on the grey heels of his Derby shoes and leaves without a word.

Henry Miller: A Greek communist called Babis—handsome and confident, a radical agitator and possibly a rogue—is standing for election as a class representative in the sociology lecture. For some reason this fellow is deeply unpopular with the other students, do you see, and so when he asks for someone to second his candidacy there's an ominous silence followed by a slow handclap.

N is struck by the pettiness of this reaction and immediately volunteers his support. As a result, Babis invites the spiky and tightly wound N to his room in Dunbar Hall to join a supposed discussion group dedicated to "culture and society." No one else turns up. Well, naturally, you see! But the boys discuss life and politics until dawn, and a lasting friendship begins. It turns out that Babis's parents were fleeing Psychiko shortly before N's parents arrived there: as communists, they were on the Athens junta's hit list. Babis's father was imprisoned, and his mother, Anna, escaped to Rome, where Babis and his sister, Sophia, were educated at St. George's, an English-speaking school. There are affinities, do you see, in outlook if not in temperament. So from 1980 Babis invites N each summer to the big apartment on the Via Giulia his mother shares with Aldo de Iaco, the Italian writer she has made her second husband. N has been to Italy before—with his family, and with his school friend John Thomson—but this is a different experience, something much more immersive. Aldo himself is gruff and reticent, a walking bust of Marx. But his bookshelves heave with Einaudi volumes on the history of the Italian South, and his record collection jumps with radical folk songs. For bedside reading N selects an English copy of my travelogue through 1940s America, *The Air-Conditioned Nightmare*. He identifies strongly with the book's rejection of a bland and moribund conservative homeland, its proposal of Europe as a paradise of artistic and sexual freedom. Both Babis and N fancy themselves as writers at this time: N is writing a Bellow-esque novel called *Pang's Compass* and Babis has started a surreal tale about children who disappear into a television set. Aldo shows no interest in these projects, nor in his stepson's British friend, who would probably like to ask what he thinks of Sam Beckett. Meanwhile Babis and Anna harangue each other in teasing after-dinner arguments more like lovers' spats than the conversations of mother and son. Wild thunderstorms cross Rome, setting off car alarms. Guards stand outside the historic monuments with machine guns chatting up the girls and taunting N as he passes: "*E vero, e vero?*" Is *what* true? Has somebody been spreading rumors? On the Piazza del Popolo the faces are saturnine and sinister, yet the city seems to heal something in N. This Rome excludes but also fascinates him with its European and intellectual ambience, and to be excluded and yet fascinated is something N enjoys: there is some element of forbidden glamour, even of voyeurism at play. Babis introduces him to Buckley, a cheerful homosexual bringing avant-garde music to the British Council. In a Trastevere kitchen a Roman girl with long brown legs emerging from a man's white shirt appraises N with "*E bello!*" but the fierce Scottish virgin pours embarrassed scorn on the idea of his own beauty. Calvinism will do that, even diluted by Italy, do you see? The boys are soon joined by Zoe, a wiry blond French girl Babis has picked up dancing on a Greek beach. The daughter of a dentist, Zoe exudes a vacant sensuality: on their first day together, standing before him on a Roman tram, Zoe fixes N with lazy panda-bear eyes and squeezes her warm rubbery tummy against the hard tip of N's knee. Much later, do you see, they will become lovers, and N will rename her Zoe-Pascale in order to differentiate her from his best friend's girl. The three attend an open-air John Cage concert in the courtyard of the Palazzo Spada, lit by flickering torches—it's a delightfully delicate prepared piano piece called "Daughters of the Lonesome Isle"—and N feels suddenly as if everything in his world has come right: this sexual life of art and radical community in hot weather is everything he's craved to know. "I could well imagine you living in Rome," says Babis, flatteringly. The next night they're under the stars by the Palatine Hill, and David Tudor is rummaging inside a piano with a piezo microphone. As the music plays N entertains mental images of a still damp garden, fires on the hillside, a home in a tunnel, the coming of a train, mute uncomprehending cavemen, the stillness of history, an igloo home that must be remade, toys bought and regularly lost in the crystal-line snow, Beatrice, topaz, the sorry speed of fireflies, the dialogue of the spheres, and a figure swimming, casting endlessly through the legs of the waist-high water-blind crowd. He cries to hear and see this, hmm?

William McIlvanney: I was with N's dad, Bill Currie, on the English course at Glasgow University in the late fifties. I wouldn't say he was well-liked. "There are few more impressive sights in the world than a Scotsman on the make!" is the caption I placed under Bill's photo in the class yearbook. He was, shall we say, a wee bitty full of himself. We all were, I suppose, but he probably disguised the self-regard less expertly. Bill dressed it up in tweeds and plus fours. Didn't he go on to write a lot of books about fly-fishing? You can get on fine with sportswriting—my brother Hugh got famous writing about boxing and horses, for heaven's sake! As for me, well . . . I wrote socialist poetry, and then did a Lawrentian novel about miners, then invented Laidlaw, a Glasgow detective who keeps a copy of Kierkegaard's *Either/Or* in his desk drawer. In the late seventies I was having a dry spell, shall we say, and became writer in residence at Aberdeen University. I had this little office in the Taylor Building, on what they called the Bridge. Dental surgery hours. I'm not quite sure whether teeth were being pulled, or legs. N was this rather effete young man carrying his father's face under a blond quiff. A bit horsey-looking; I have an impression of a pallid stick in padded clothes. He was probably one of the ones to watch in the Creative Writing Group, along with Ian Stephen and Ali Smith. He used to read us mood pieces modelled on the short prose works of Giorgio de Chirico. I thought he might be destined for poetry, but he told me he found it smelly somehow. He brought me the beginnings of a novel in longhand—it was about an alien-ated young man discovering a group of musicians all sharing a flat in the Tollcross area of Edinburgh. Not very good, but it was my job to encourage and enable. The first thing I told N was that I was going to bill him for my optician's fees—he'd made me read this scrawl in longhand! He chuckled. The second thing—and I meant this as praise—was that I could hear Kafka playing like distant music behind several scenes. There was an undercurrent of menace which I enjoyed, something Pinteresque: weasels scuffled beneath the cocktail cabinet. N surprised me when he said he didn't believe in editing. He wanted the writing to have the fresh, improvisational quality of jazz; the mistakes should be left in. "Well, you'll have to change your attitude on that," I told him, because really, the arrogance of it! What publisher is going to let an author just splurge out whatever comes into his head? First thought is decidedly not best thought. Well, watching now from Hades' farther shore I can see to my utter distress that such things do happen: just look at Morrissey's autobiography, for Christ's sake! Penguin puts it out as a "Classic," and yet it's apparently never crossed the desk of an editor, let alone the generations of approving critics required to qualify something as a genuine classic. This is what happens when narcissism runs rampant in the world, and when publishing is in thrall to mere celebrity. Sure, I could have been rich and famous, but I chose a coterie, a niche. Those who half know me know that my Laidlaw book became the popular TV series *Taggart*, and the beginning of the genre they call Tartan Noir. Except that that isn't what happened at all. I often felt that the *Taggart* writers took my scenario and made their own version. I never saw a penny. I talked to lawyers about it, but didn't pursue it. Sean Connery wanted to film *Laidlaw*, but I dawdled with the script—the dry periods got wetter—and it never happened. I died in 2015 without having read the books N finally got around to publishing. If I'd run into him I would have asked, stroking my silver moustache, a twinkle in my eye: "So, you finally let the editors get to you?"

Robert Bresson: Friendship is a mysterious thing; one of my films is about a girl who befriends a donkey. N has a copy of my *Notes on Cinematography*, and enjoys its puritan aesthetic: the idea, for instance, that a director should never overstimulate viewers, but let filmic elements unfold one by one. There's no need to gild a picture with unnecessary music: one should embrace simplicity of means and simplicity of feeling. You can show the bonds between Marie and the donkey Balthazar by concentrating on the eyes. It's as a potential filmmaker that N meets a group of art students from Gray's School of Art, a series of bronze-and-glass cubes sited in bucolic meadows on the other side of town. Unlike N's other friends, the art students are all Scots. Keith and Graham have come to Phoenix, the university film and television society, to borrow video equipment. N likes them immediately: Graham is tall and brisk, Keith a bearded working-class painter with a neurotic blink. Later the circle will be joined by another Keith, a mild and kindly music fan with traces of acne scars on his face. The artists will invite N often to their lodgings in terrace houses, and out to the art school itself. Keith is from Edinburgh, but his Leith tower block might as well stand on a different planet from the UNESCO-protected crescents N knows. Art nevertheless brings them close, that and a shared appreciation of groups like Josef K and the Fall, or the more obscure Wire side projects. Keith teaches N about the painters he loves—Philip Guston, Chaim Soutine, Max Beckmann. With Graham they scout up film locations in Aberdeen's windy corners. Rubbish bins and car parks suddenly fizz with dramatic possibility. All one need do is raise one's hands and hold them in front of one's eyes in a square shape and the world is transformed into potential cinema. The art school itself—which deeply impresses N with its mission to actualise creativity, and its architectural clarity—will serve as the location for a Lynchian film called *The Derelict*, which N will script. It will concern a homeless flasher at the city library, and a cache of bare pink mice hiding behind a shelf. N's girlfriend Fientje will act in it, and Keith will play Lalune, the moon-faced pervert. Scenes will be shot in the art school library at the end of the 1981 summer term, but never edited. A mysterious whine on the soundtrack will render the videotapes unusable.

Erich Fromm: I came from a long line of rabbis, so I confronted a world of modern problems—individual isolation, bourgeois acquisitiveness, the fear of freedom, our automaton conformism—from a place that was essentially medieval. Although I joined the Frankfurt School and worked alongside Marcuse, Benjamin, and Adorno, I was of a more mystical bent, bringing the Torah and Meister Eckhart to bear on my philosophy. For instance, I coined paradoxical axioms like: "The normals are sick, the sick are healthy"—which was actually a simple extension of Freud's view that society is built on neurosis, but could have reflected a mystical asceticism too. It seemed to me that sometimes the great thinkers had left undeveloped the spiritual implications of their ideas: the insights of religion should not be dismissed as "false consciousness," but brushed down and adapted to modern life. I liked this saying of Marx: "The less you are, the more you have; the less you express your own life, the greater is your alienated life—the greater is the store of your estranged being. Everything the economist takes from you in the terms of life and humanity, he restores to you in the form of money and wealth." It's something the Judaic and Christian traditions had been telling us all along: "The more we have, the less we own," as Eckhart put it. So, N was particularly influenced by two of my books, *The Art of Loving* and *To Have or to Be?* These were warnings against the traps and snares of modern life, and it was good to read them in a wintry town at the age of twenty. I recommended to him above all productivity—that one should become the making man, the homo faber that Marx had organized his whole Weltanschauung around, rather than the kind of human being endorsed by the bourgeois consumer societies: someone receptive, conformist, authoritarian, exploitative, robotic, acquisitive, fit only for hoarding and marketing. "Having" and "being" are both verbs, but "having" is a verb freighted with nouns—the objects it feels compelled to pile up. Possession in bourgeois society assumes the character of something fanatical and sacred because private property has become the sole bastion of identity. Take away my property and I have nothing left, for I have developed no inner resources, no being. As for love, it is not something one "falls into" by chance. It requires knowledge, effort, and faith. It is something produced, not something consumed. It is an art, and like all arts requires practice, trial and error, the development of technique. One way to be capable of loving is to develop the ability to be alone, and N is certainly alone while reading *The Art of Loving*. But perhaps he will not remain so for very long.

1980–1990

Because I was very isolated, and not having a

community of artists that I associated with, or

a circle of friends, I tended to go to literature, to

music, to artists dead or alive to find some kind

of bonding . . . It was my community, you know:

predominantly deceased artists.

—David Sylvian, talking to Chris Roberts

Éric Rohmer: My 1980 film is set in Vence, in a big, vulgar villa high on a hill. It's August, and dragonflies bask on the crazy paving by the swimming pool. The house belongs to Dr. Brouard, a dentist, but he's away on holiday with his wife. Evidence of the dentist's taste for the rustic and the industrial is everywhere: besides a quad system and Renoir reproductions there are old beams, bellows, an antique spinning wheel. Four young people have come to stay— the dentist's daughter Zoe, her Greek boyfriend Babis, Zoe's friend Consuela—a Jewish medical student from Central America—and N, a stern young Scot who has just bought a copy of *Closer* by Joy Division and listens to its mournful songs while gazing down at Nice. Consuela has a moon-shaped face and long unfashionable hair, but is attractive in a conservative way. She declares that she would like to write studies of drug-taking or suicide. Babis dominates, joking continually, choosing what to do, amusing the girls with his project to write a zany children's book. One day he takes N and Zoe to a ravine where they follow a stream up between wooded, cliffed slopes. All the ramblers here are naked except shy N, who insists on keeping his clothes on. Babis eventually gets tired and decides to walk back on his own, leaving N with the naked Zoe. They wade back through the cool waters under deep green trees. That evening there's a long debate around the kitchen table, led by Consuela.

Why does Zoe dress so scantily or not at all? Why does Babis find it so difficult to make love with her? Why has Consuela had bulimia nervosa for three years? Why is N so self-sufficient and passive-aggressive? Why does he keep a diary? Babis has made a joke about threesome sex, and Consuela wants to know what's behind it. She teases him: he analyses things too much, he's too serious, he isn't serious enough, he doesn't listen . . . After N has left the villa he learns that the mooted threesome really did take place, but was a dismal disappointment. The others, it seems, were just waiting for him to leave. I'm not quite sure how to end the film. Perhaps there'll be a scene at Ostia, outside Rome. It will feature Babis, N again, and two of Babis's school friends, Paolo and Lawrence. Again everyone will be naked save N. The three school friends will be lying there smoking dope and playing a game of Go. N will head off for a walk, finding a crowded section of beach. He'll return pursued by two policemen who will shout, with pistols drawn, "*Scandalo publico!*" This is apparently the private beach of the Italian president. The naked boys will manage to bury their drugs in the sand and bribe the police with cigarettes. I'm not sure, though—perhaps I'll just end it in Vence with N in the little chapel decorated by Matisse, gazing at the almost-algebraic notations of the Stations of the Cross, with Joy Division's "The Eternal" playing on the soundtrack, if we can get the rights.

Anaïs Nin: Fientje was half-Scottish and half-Belgian. She had been brought up in Africa, where her father was a high-ranking diplomat, but sent to boarding school in the Scottish countryside. She was studying economics and politics, but was also interested in sculpture and poetry. She met N in the Creative Writing Group. Her pale, butter-colored features and twisty eyes recalled the famous *Portrait of a Young Girl* by the Netherlandish painter Petrus Christus, which N happened to have up on his wall, or a Brancusi bronze head: the almond-shaped *Sleeping Muse*, perhaps. Fientje had two characteristic temperamental states: a withering scorn she must have picked up at boarding school, and a twee sentimentality N liked to call "pixieish." She would scorch and excoriate him one moment, speaking callously of their relationship in terms of cost-benefit analysis. Then the next she would stroke the boy's thin face, telling him tenderly that he looked *"triste."* Her beauty, intelligence, and political radicalism appealed to N enormously, for political righteousness is also a form of beauty. So—although she already had a boyfriend, a benign beanpole, an English agricultural student called Tim—N found himself one day in Fientje's room at Skene Square, clasping a bag of butteries from the bakery next door, flipping through sketchpads full of nude self-portraits. Suddenly Fientje insinuated herself into his lap and began kissing him full on the mouth. The warm, liquid invasiveness of the gesture—the first fully sexual kiss of his life, making him momentarily unsure of his ability to breathe—felt to N like a process of gentle drowning. It was May, the month of universal sensuality, when Fien came knocking at his hall of residence door with the second major revelation: her naked intimacy, beneath his orange duvet, in that lonely room with its view of trees and the slope down to the sliding sparkle of the Don River. High up around the room's plain cornice ran a motto N had copied out from a poem by Brecht: "Canalising a river, grafting a fruit tree, educating a person, transforming a state: these are instances of fruitful criticism and at the same time instances of art." Halfway through this first penetration, as N fumbled with a foreskin he barely knew how to retract, came a sleeting squall of criticism from Fientje: "Oh, for Christ's sake, what are you fiddling about for? Just pull it back and push it in!" Somehow the young fruit tree did not wither, and this first act of love—as harsh and beautiful as spring itself—pushed toward its climax.

Ogden Nash:

That precious student we call N
Is being difficult again:
Trapped there in the English village
He takes to reading Ivan Illich
(I don't mean Tolstoy's Russian one,
I'm talking of the Austrian
Whose tracts decry decent sobriety
And scream: "*Let us deschool society!*")

And so N makes a peevish fuss
And bridles at his syllabus
Saying: "Mrs. Gaskell is so dead!
Give me Goethe, please, instead!"
His tutor Mr. Hewison,
Apparently as bored as him,
Surprisingly allows our N
To rip it up and start again.

And so we find N self-prescribing
Books that hardly bear describing:
Young Werther and his tragedy
Flaubert's *Bouvard et Pecuchet*
And Rilke's interesting squib
The Notebooks of Malte Laurids Brigge
They even let our brittle fellow
Study *Herzog* by Saul Bellow

But all this freedom simply makes
N long for more, and so he takes
A year out, then another one
To sing the things that must be sung

N
I
C
H
E

And when at last he's done his worst
Why, back he comes to take a first!
The moral is: Why not be rash?
Yours not-so-truly, Ogden Nash.

Tove Jansson: In the early days there had been such fun for the Scots Family Moomintroll! There was Moominpappa, who could pull the monstrous fish from rivers then smoke the wickedness out of them until they tasted marvellous. There was Moominmamma, running around trying to cater to the needs of all the lodgers— Snuffkin, the tinker who paid his rent by playing the flute; the Hemulens, who came to look after the three young trolls; Little My with her wild tantrums; the Snork Maiden; and of course Moomintroll himself, the grumpy poet. When they had been together it had been so easy to survive disaster! Why, when the flood had swept through the valley it had only separated Moominmamma and Moominpappa temporarily! When the fiery comet had hung overhead the family had survived by hiding in a Greek cave! When they were woken from their hibernation in the bleak Canadian midwinter only to find themselves face-to-face with the Groke herself, the Moomins had escaped back to Edinburgh! Now Moominmamma was at New College studying theology and Moominpappa had a thriving business teaching English. The hall cupboards with their louvered doors hid mountains of Club biscuits and Smiths Salt 'n' Shake crisps. But with success came something unsurvivable: the earthquake that would split the Moomin Family Currie apart forever. Moominpappa had an affair with his secretary, the tooth maiden Norakin. He pretended to be going fishing, but really he was lying in a bed breathing in the intoxicating smoke that spouted from Norakin's beautiful nostrils and curled between her perfect teeth. When Moominmama found out, there was nothing for it— she fled to the western isles and found a lover of her own: a tiny, bald, impossibly rich animal called Gray Ham. Moomintroll had already disappeared off to university, but the unfolding disaster left him very sad inside. What if he were to return to the family home one weekend only to find it empty, the warm old nest bare and cold? What if all that greeted him in Edinburgh were the rumour that the Moomin Family Currie could be glimpsed on a boat somewhere, perhaps quite far away, dimly visible as a speck on the horizon, attempting the long voyage back home? Moomintroll pictured them leaning together for warmth, stock-still on the deck as if cast in stone, braving hail and lightning with a suspicious implacability. What if those beloved figures were not even alive? And what if the boat should never reach haven?

Joseph II, Holy Roman Emperor of Austria: With time, my achievements in reforming and modernising Austria through enlightened despotism have been forgotten, and the one thing people mention now—if they speak of me at all—is my remark to Mozart that his *Marriage of Figaro* contained too many notes. And thus do the artists in time take revenge upon the men of action and power! Now I am called—grandiose in my imperial robes but completely unbriefed by my advisors—to explain things that have happened, or not happened, to insignificant people two hundred years after my death. And I am honestly quite at a loss to explain why N—another musician, how troublesome!—has written precisely no musical notes by the age of twenty. Perhaps he and Mozart, like Jack Spratt and his wife, can form some alliance and even the scores? Oh, certainly, N has tossed off a few compositions as a child, without being anything like as prodigious as Wolfgang Amadeus; musical standards have fallen precipitously between the 1760s and the 1960s, and between Salzburg and Edinburgh. At the age of twenty N is still mostly expressing himself with short stories, which he bangs out on an infernal writing machine called a "typewriter." Much more magical, however, is another device, or series of devices: the tape recorders he borrows from his father's language laboratories, along with all the cassettes he requires. (Fortunately, my advisors have been found and are supplying me with notes at this point.) Although not blank—they are already filled with stuffy English voices reciting the absurd example sentences found only in language learning textbooks—these cassettes invite a sort of filling-in, a cluttering-up, a remaking. (My beloved Austria, although already cluttered with mountains, seemed to bring out the same impulses in me.) A technological peculiarity of the language lab tape recorders helps N: these are two-track machines, designed to give the student a separate track on which to leave answers:

TEACHER: There's an elephant in the garden, and it's trying to come into the house!
STUDENT: Well, don't let it come in!

N uses, or abuses, this facility, developing a simple multitrack recording system by overdubbing, mixing down, then overdubbing again. (I am reading this information directly off cards being handed to me by Wolfgang Adler, my chief advisor, condemned to hold this position through all eternity.) Since this is an analog process, the results get increasingly muffled. They typically feature, for percussion, a metronome, cardboard boxes, and an anglepoise lamp (whose spring supplies cymbal crashes, pseudo-guiro, and reverberation), and for guitar a broken acoustic instrument muffled by tissues and recorded with a condenser mic jammed under broken strings. If the recording is being made in Edinburgh, the old family Bösendorfer is at hand to supply additional piano sounds, mostly of the John Cage prepared variety. (By the way, Adler tells me that Cage agrees with me entirely about Mozart and his damned notes—I shall offer the American a baronetcy if I meet him in hell.) It is a compilation tape of demos made in this way—muffled and scratchy, but popping with urgency—that N hands to guitarist Malcolm Ross in 1981 at what turns out to be the second-to-last concert ever played by an Edinburgh musical ensemble named after a character invented by a writer of the later Hapsburg Empire: Josef K. While Josef K the beat group dies after receiving bad reviews for its debut album, Josef K the Kafka character is stabbed to death in a quarry by two gentlemen in frock coats. And while my Hapsburg Empire withers shortly after the assassination of the Archduke Franz Ferdinand in 1914, the Happy Family—the pop group N forms with Malcolm Ross and other ex-members—fails to extend the legacy of Josef K in the popular imagination. That is a feat which is later achieved by a group called Franz Ferdinand. Adler, you have confused me completely with all these scraps of paper: too many notes!

Kenneth Tynan: I must say I sympathise with the emperor's frustration about being remembered as "the man who told Mozart he used too many notes." I wish the British public remembered me for my theatre and my criticism, but a life's work seems to have been eclipsed in the popular imagination by a single sulphurous epithet: I am "the man who said fuck." It happened in late 1965, during a live BBC television broadcast. Debating Mary McCarthy on the topic of censorship, I said: "I doubt if there are very many rational people in this world to whom the word 'fuck' is particularly diabolical or revolting or totally forbidden." On the morrow (and the morrow of the morrow) came the inevitable tabloid outrage: apparently "millions of viewers" had been shocked by a programme which only a few thousand were watching. Fifteen years later, in 1980, the F-word was still banned by the BBC. N, a literature student who somewhat resembled me, happened to be listening to John Peel's alternative music programme one night. Peel played the new single from the Slits, "In the Beginning There Was Rhythm," but bleeped the line "fucking is rhythm." Wondering why complaints to the BBC came only from pro-censorship activists—and feeling very much that this distorted the whole debate—N dashed off a puckish letter to Peel's producer, John Walters, proclaiming himself offended that the word "fucking" *wasn't* in the broadcast. To his surprise he received a terse typewritten reply from Walters a few days later simply stating that as the word "fuck" was still held generally to be taboo, the BBC couldn't air it. It seems that Peel and Walters had a long memory for correspondence for, five years later, when Peel played the Momus song "Hotel Marquis de Sade"—pretty much the only time he ever played any Momus at all—he apologised in a sarcastic tone "for the appearance of breasts in that lyric."

Max Brod: Both alive and dead I have watched the ripples of my decision to disobey my dear friend Franz Kafka's request to destroy his writings spreading through the cultural history of the twentieth century. Franz's influence reached its first heights in the postwar years, when horror at the Holocaust combined with the popularisation of existentialist themes to sear aspects of my friend's premonitory vision into the work of authors all over the world: Borges, Camus, Beckett, Pinter, Singer, Ionesco, Jocelyn Brooke, Max Frisch, Robbe-Grillet, Barthelme, Gombrowicz, Joe Orton. After my own death in 1968 I continued to observe this process—a vindication both of Franz's work and my decision to save it—as it proceeded to form new generations of writers working in the "magic realist" genre of the 1980s: Angela Carter, Italo Calvino, Gabriel García Márquez. It did not escape my attention that, around 1980, musicians in the popular idiom were also distilling my friend's sensibility into their songs. I feel sure that Franz would have appreciated this in the same spirit in which he delighted in the productions of Löwy's Yiddish theatre troupe from Lemberg. There was a certain David Bowie, dressed as the most beautiful clown in the circus, singing in "Ashes to Ashes": "Want an axe to break the ice" (a paraphrase of Franz's saying that a book must be "the axe for the frozen sea within us"). There was Howard Devoto's "Song from Under the Floorboards," judged by many to be his band Magazine's masterpiece: a song which gives voice to Gregor Samsa, and places him in the landscape Dostoyevsky sketched in *Notes from Underground*. The Edinburgh beat group Josef K took the influence furthest, however, not just in their choice of name, but in the lyrical content of countless songs: "Crazy to Exist," "Sense of Guilt," "Final Request." N began to attend their concerts regularly, muffled in the padded blue army greatcoat his mother had brought back from her trip to China, a Penguin edition of Franz's short stories stuffed into his pocket. Josef K played at the art school, at a so-called Frank Sinatra Evening at Valentino's discotheque, or with Magazine at an old church hall above a rehearsal space called the Moon. The music was a brittle jangle and the group, dressed in shirts buttoned up to their necks, looked genuinely Eastern European—like four tense, neurotic Czech waiters. They released their debut album *The Only Fun in Town* in the summer of 1981. It was a stark and rushed affair recorded in eight days in Brussels—a replacement for a lusher album they'd made at Edinburgh's Castle Sound studios, deleted while it was still at the test pressing stage: it hadn't reflected the chaos and frenzy of their live sound, singer Paul Haig explained. The new Brussels recording came wrapped in a scratchy black and gold sleeve depicting Princes Street with the dome of West Register House in Charlotte Square surrounded by crows. Just down the hill from that dome, in a mezzanine room his father let him use during the university holidays, N listened to this record—both local and glamorously cosmopolitan, with its traces of Prague and Brussels—constantly. It had a frenetic yet oblique edge to it, a sense of brash and reckless vigilance apparently caused by the consumption of too much speed and too many Velvet Underground records. But what do I, Max Brod, know of such things—I who never intoxicated myself with anything stronger than red wine and did not live to see the Velvet Revolution? Observing from beyond the grave Havel's unlikely rise to the Czech presidency, however, I did entertain a fleeting vision, no less absurd: Franz Kafka as the president of Czechoslovakia, a survivor against all the odds, now aged 106 and fully endorsed by Paul Haig from Josef K.

Ari Up: There was a kind of cultural battle going on in 1981, a sea change in the world of post-punk. Art school groups like the Human League and Scritti Politti suddenly started selling their souls to Babylon. There was supposed to be this turn towards "bright yellow shiny pop." Thatcherite bullshit! Everything was suddenly zoot suits, cocktail bars, and the *NME* telling its readers to "dance don't riot." Ambitious go-getters like Spandau Ballet and ABC impressed the influential critics and jelled all too well with corporate values. I used to joke that Martin Fry was actually Michael Heseltine's son. Josef K split up after Paul Morley's disappointed review of *The Only Fun in Town*—"it sounds like the weakest folk music to me," he said—and my group the Slits got dropped from CBS after we put out *Return of the Giant Slits*. I think N was the only person who bought that album! He loved it. Reggae producer Dennis Bovell gave us a gently experimental sound, organic and hesitant and dubby. And there were radical Bristolians all over it—the Pop Group's drummer Bruce Smith, a very young Neneh Cherry, Dick O'Dell from Y Records. N tried to emulate this sound in his home recordings using lots of dub and delay effects, which he just played manually on his little two-track recorder. It wasn't so difficult to copy: we were still quite amateurish in our musical abilities. But the soul was in it! Jah Rastafari! My lyrics, with their bohemian moralism, must have reminded him of writers like Erich Fromm. I sing that avoiding meeting other people's gaze means: "You're one of them and you are safe, sleeping down the street." We three Slits (me, Viv, and Tessa) became a model for N of what girls—not typical girls but rude and unruly art school girls—might be like. If it wasn't for us he'd just have had Pluto paperbacks like Ann Foreman's *Femininity as Alienation* to confuse him with the idea that being a woman was a special case of Marxist processes like reification and alienation. Ha ha! We be real women of flesh and blood, you know what I'm saying? I remember seeing N in the audience at our gig at Raffles in Aberdeen; he was watching me rocking back and forth in my chair to African music before we took the stage. That summer he became—to take the title of another Slits single— the "Man Next Door": he started living next door to his childhood homes. His parents separated and sold the Drummond Place town house, his mother took a basement next door to the old family flat on Great Stuart Street, his father moved in next door to the Ainslie Place warren where they'd spent the second half of the 1960s. N made his scratchy demos in his mother's basement or the mezzanine room his father let him use at 7 Ainslie Place—a space so low you had to walk around hunched up to avoid banging your head, with views out to Fife over the old walled family garden. Fientje— the "wild woman of Waga Waga"—would visit from time to time to bawl at or ball him. It was all fine, the patriarchy deserved it. In August he handed his muffled cassette of demos—*Germs of Gems* by Group of One—to guitarist Malcolm Ross at what turned out to be Josef K's second-to-last concert, at Valentino's in Edinburgh. It was supposed to get passed on to Alan Horne, who ran Postcard Records, but Ross kept it and one day in late August phoned N at his mother's place suggesting he use the now-unemployed musicians of Josef K to record a demo.

Cesare Pavese: N begins the autumn term of 1981 sharing a granite terrace flat in Aberdeen with his European friends Babis and Zoe. But a letter from Josef K bass player Davy Weddell arrives, announcing that 4AD Records want to sign the Happy Family. N negotiates a one-year hiatus with the English department and drives back to Edinburgh in his Wolseley 1300. On a street in central Dundee he spots a rotating Picador bookstand still in its polythene wrapping. It tilts, obviously discarded, against a skip outside a local bookshop, which N whimsically imagines must have been too puritanical to want to display Picador's cosmopolitan titles—mostly modern European literature in translation—face-outward. N immediately bundles the stand into his car and brings it to Edinburgh, where it fits nicely on the short linoleum-covered staircase leading up to the self-contained mezzanine studio his father is letting him live in. It's now a matter of populating the stand with paperbacks, many of which do actually turn out to be Picadors. Among his first purchases are an anthology called *The Existential Imagination from De Sade to Sartre*—which contains my short story "Suicides"—and the Quartet edition of my diaries, entitled *This Business of Living*. On the burgundy cover I'm wearing a scarf and double-breasted suit, caught by the camera in the gesture of lighting a cigarette. I am an Italian, a writer, an existentialist, an antifascist, a poet, a publisher, an intellectual, a diarist . . . and a suicide, for I took my own life in 1950 after an unhappy affair with the American actress Constance Dowling. (What a pity the Quartet edition spells her name "Dawling" on the back!) Diaries of tormented writers are N's favourite form of literature at this time, and indeed he is still keeping his own, seeking to rival the eloquent soul-searching and caustic introspection achieved by Kafka. Mine is one of the more wretched and tormented journals—it ends with the awful line: "Not words. An act. I won't write any more." This ending (which was also the conclusion of my life) gives retrospective weight to all the verbal sighs that have come before it. When he starts writing material for the Happy Family—for N too has come to the end of words and the beginning of deeds—he draws heavily on my journal. The most impressive song on the demo he records with ex-members of Josef K in Palladium studios is called "Innermost Thoughts"—a phrase N lifts wholesale from my first entry, headed "Innermost Thoughts on My Work." This song, with its booming bass line and darkly romantic lyrics about a failed love affair, is the one that has impressed Ivo Watts-Russell at 4AD Records. When he comes to record an album with his group, N will begin one track with a reference to the title of my diary itself, *Il Mestiere di Vivere*:

Now at last I've mastered this business of living

I'm not sure where this need to plunder the dignity of the darkest pages of twentieth-century literature comes from: N is not alone in doing it, for this is the age of "miserabilism," of long raincoats and greeny-grey Penguin Modern Classics. Perhaps this generation feels that rock music needs to be made slower, more sonorous, more serious? Perhaps musicians feel that existentialist literature has a spiritual dignity they can borrow, spreading its darkness and weight through the relatively trivial medium of popular music? Perhaps these pale young men are simply depressed: Ian Curtis has followed me to an early grave, dangling on a rope, his final releases swathed in the imagery of Italian funerary monuments. The decade of the 1980s has not begun well: the Soviets have ratcheted up Cold War tension by invading Afghanistan, and right-wing hawks have swept to power in the U.S. and U.K. A slew of independent labels are meanwhile distinguishing themselves from the majors (some of which, like Thorn-EMI, are industrial conglomerates directly implicated in the arms industries) by expressing bleakness via flanged bass lines, flanged guitars. Flanging is an effect, you see, which makes musical instruments sound afraid.

Tony Wilson: The Happy Family sent out only five tapes of a demo featuring three songs—"Puritans," "Innermost Thoughts," and "My Double"—but the Josef K connection was enough to guarantee attention. N typed up short letters on an IBM typewriter and sent the packages out from his mother's basement flat on Great Stuart Street. One went to Geoff Travis at Rough Trade, one to me at Factory, one to Chris Parry at Fiction, one to Ivo at 4AD, and one to Cherry Red. I don't think the Factory letter said much of consequence, and I didn't bother responding. The letter to Ivo said something about how they'd be proud to be on the same label as the Birthday Party. That did the trick—that and I suppose the boomy, doomy sound of "Innermost Thoughts," which, with its thin film of twinkling autoharps and distant melodicas, was almost the audio equivalent of the famous long pan through shallow water in Tarkovsky's film *Stalker*. I'm talking about the sequence that did so much to influence Nigel Grierson and Vaughan Oliver, the designers who came to define 4AD's visual identity in much the same way as Peter Saville defined ours at Factory. The song "My Double" was a jokey take on Dostoyevsky's *The Double*, which itself leans heavily on Gogol's *The Overcoat*; the track was distinguished by Malcolm Ross's spooky slide guitar, which slithered around on top of a sinister Mellotron line as the narrator hissed: "Why can't my double learn a little decency?" Actually, this dark humour was the direction the group would take, probably to Ivo's chagrin. Does humour belong in pop? I don't know, debate it at the Oxford Union. Did the Situationists use humour? Certainly. "Under the pavement is the beach." That's funny! We independent labels had all defined our house styles by now, and maybe the urge to rebel was starting to take hold in some of our artists. Why not put a whoopee cushion under the aesthetes? By the time they made their debut album, the Happy Family had gone all quirky, chirpy, and Brechtian. They opted out of a 23 Envelope sleeve, preferring to decorate the cover of their concept album with a 1960s pastiche: "Songs from the career of the Dictator Hall—The Man on Your Street—STEREO." I would never have tolerated that on Factory, but Ivo spent a fortune buying the rights to a photo of Earth seen from space. The tape sent to Chris Parry landed them a support slot on the Cure's Eight Appearances Tour in November 1981. So within weeks of their first rehearsals the Happy Family not only had a recording deal but were playing their first two gigs, at Edinburgh's Odeon and Glasgow's Pavilion. At the Edinburgh show Alan Rankine from the Associates hovered backstage—a potential producer, along with Gavin Friday of the Virgin Prunes—and Robert Smith kindly showed N how to use his guitar amp. The group were nervous, loud, and under-rehearsed, with Maisie banging clumsily on a floor tom and N forgetting to turn up the volume on his guitar for half the set. Unfortunately, the *New Musical Express* had assigned a reviewer, who summed things up with pithy cruelty: "The Happy Family are like a horde of invading cockroaches: someone turn the light on!"

Colin MacInnes: It's no longer the 1950s, and N is no longer a teenager. But in the music game he's an absolute beginner: wet behind the ears, a soft Lord Snooty with his public school education and his semi-English accent. The lads from Josef K teach him their own brand of cool, and show him their Edinburgh. There's Maisie, Josef K's driver, with his blue Citroën hatchback and svelte cheekbones. Maisie plays the drums first, then the Fender Jaguar. There's Davy Weddell—he was Josef K's bassist—and soon Ian Stoddart joins on drums. The boys take N to the Royal Mile Café with its cheap coffees and its big window overlooking the Kafkaesque cathedral. They drive him down to the Victoria Café off Leith Walk, the only place in the Edinburgh of 1981 where you can get a proper cappuccino, or to the Tap o' Lauriston pub next to the art school, where members of the Fire Engines hang out with firebrand actor

Tam Dean Burn and the fiercely shy Paul Haig sits with one hand slipped into the half-hidden pocket of his Oxfam suit (oddly, Haig chooses to tuck the jacket into his trousers). There's the retro-styled City Café with its bottles of "pills"—it takes N a while to realise that the boys are actually saying "Pils," which is short for Grolsch Pilsner, an imported beer that comes in bottles with a wired ceramic top. But there are real pills too, the amphetamine capsules so central to Josef K's frenetic sound. N only tries them once: to help him through an all-night Monopoly game up at Malc and Syuzen's flat in Sciennes. The powder introduces an evil fizzle to his nostrils, and no matter how boring the game gets N can't fall asleep. Class is inevitably an issue: the lads are Firrhill boys—that's the state school they all went to in Colinton—but Malc (who puts the Happy Family together but soon leaves to play guitar in Aztec Camera and Orange Juice) is the son of the head of New College, the theological university on the Mound where N's mother has just been immersing herself in Greek and Latin, earning a bachelor of divinity degree. N is particularly taken by Malc's punky wife Syuzen, who grew up in one of the tower blocks in Leith and tells funny stories from a world that might as well be mythological, full of the sort of characters you find in Fall songs. The Happy Family at first rehearse in the same upstairs bedroom that Josef K used, in the Ross family home on the Colinton Road. N trips over his New Romantic waiter-style trousers (grey, baggy, stripe up the side) in his excitement as he rushes up from the Morningside bus stop. Later the group practises in a muffled sub-basement in N's dad's language college, which has Ping-Pong tables and snack machines for breaks. Ian Stoddart contracts Hodgkin's lymphoma and has to be replaced by frenetic Josef K drummer Ronnie Torrance (Ian—a much better drummer—eventually beats the cancer and joins Win). The de facto leader of the group is bassist Davy; he's probably the one with the best working-class credentials, and is rumoured to have been a bit of a housebreaker in his teens. When the windows at the back of the Edinburgh Language Foundation are left open one night and burglars make off with some expensive video equipment, Davy is immediately suspected. He denies everything, and N transmits the denial to his dad, the college principal. His word is accepted, but N secretly thinks that Davy's friends probably did steal the VCRs, and that they had every right to: as a socialist he doesn't really care much about property. The stuff was all insured, anyway. It's also socialism that leads N to split the publishing money he receives from Beggars Banquet Music four ways, although technically he's the only songwriter. This has the unfortunate result of allowing Davy Weddell to trade in his Starburst bass (a cheap instrument from Woolworths with a uniquely rubbery sound) for a more expensive, more professional Fender Jazz bass. The Happy Family stops sounding like Josef K and starts sounding like any other band.

Joyce Cary: The London phone book is so fat it's had to be chopped in two. Swell-bellied jets hang low as they queue into Heathrow. The water has been pumped seven times through your stomach and you've got to share the air with eight million other poor sods. Noted scoundrel and painter Gulley Jimson has just got out of prison after a month at Her Majesty's pleasure—no, that's not right! The Happy Family—Davy, Maisie, N—have come down on the train to meet Ivo, the posh hippy who runs 4AD Records. His office is on the Hogarth Road at Earl's Court, just above the Beggars Banquet shop. Circle and District Line trains rush and rattle an inch from the window. 4AD and Beggars are flush with cash from Gary Numan, the hideous Bowie waxwork who sings about cars and electricity. The first encounter our boys have with label-meister Ivo is somewhat muted. N is wearing his kingfisher-coloured iridescent trousers but probably doesn't look like pop star material with his glaikit chin. Davy is prematurely balding, a waiter in a white shirt. Ivo is a lanky geography teacher crossed with the puppet of a Polish tailor in a Brothers Quay animation. His first eye contact with N fizzles into an apologetic vagueness. He takes the boys to a windowless stockroom, introducing his partner Martin Mills on the way. The business deal he outlines is as halfhearted as his manner: 4AD used to sign bands to multi-album contracts, he explains, but now they just do it record by record. They'll release an EP, see how it goes, then perhaps stretch to an LP in 1982. There'll be a publishing deal with Beggars, for which the grand sum of £750 will be offered. The boys are then ferried in a leased BMW to Ivo's flat in Acton, a suburb of brutal ordinariness. Yet Ivo's place on the first floor of a semi-detached becomes, within, a cavern of refined marvels: lilac walls, mynah birds in cages, a tasteful collection of books and records. Photography tomes by Diane Arbus and Leni Riefenstahl betoken a modish interest in freakery and fascism. That evening Ivo plays N John Cale's *Music for a New Society*, Tim Buckley's *Greetings from L.A.*, and Tom Waits's *Closing Time*—his first exposure to these artists—as well as a cassette of a new record he's about to put out: a fuzzboxed, cathedral-ringing thing called *Garlands* by another Scottish group, the Cocteau Twins. Liz Fraser warbles like one of Ivo's caged birds. The next day, while the others head out for some tourist stuff and Ivo goes to work, N stays home with the eclectic record collection, playing New Order, Rema-Rema, and Gilbert & Lewis. In the early afternoon Ivo explodes through the front door unexpectedly, like a man who's suddenly remembered he's forgotten to hide some awful secret, or—at any rate—like a fellow who doesn't quite trust you to be alone in his flat during the hours of daylight. Well, quite right: Gulley Jimson would have covered your walls with tigers by now.

John Peel: With the best will in the world there are some people who just raise your hackles at a first meeting. Who knows why?

Perhaps they remind you too much of suppressed aspects of yourself: your privileged education, your original accent, some of your less attractive sexual proclivities. I never encouraged groups to drop by Broadcasting House, so I was already somewhat irritable to be called down to the lobby one evening in 1982 to meet the Happy Family, a Scottish group apparently formed around the rhythm section of Josef K, of whom I'd been somewhat supportive. It was made worse by the fact that I'd just been seeing Clare Grogan—the schoolgirlish actress who sang with another fine Scottish group of the day, Altered Images. The Happy Family, alas, had spotted her crossing the lobby. When I emerged seconds later N flashed me a lubricious grin and said: "We just saw Miss Grogan! Ha ha ha!" He all but winked at me in the "say no more" manner of Monty Python's Arthur Nudge. The implication was that although he thought he knew what I'd been up to he'd be willing—in exchange, clearly, for exposure on my programme—to keep it from my beloved wife, the Pig. Well, let me make this perfectly clear: my private life is mine and mine alone, and my intentions toward Miss Grogan were entirely proper. I can't help it if we all find ourselves in the same gene pool and you see me as some kind of indie daddy. Six years later I apparently made halfhearted advances to N's girlfriend, a radio plugger. On a Radio 1 road trip I allegedly blundered my way into this young woman's hotel bedroom and asked whether "if I were ten years younger, ten stone lighter, and about ten inches narrower around the waist," she might be interested? She laughed and told me to go to bed. It does sound like one of my lines, I must admit. But all this should have been kept private. I saw this revelation coming quite a long way off. That's why I kept N as far as possible from my airwaves. Certain infants need to be stifled in the cradle. The Happy Family would wither on the vine, and so would Momus. Altered Images filled countless session slots on my programme with twee, creepy songs like "Happy Birthday" and "Dead Popstars";

Momus, with his watered-down Brel shtick, didn't get one. You'll thank me for this one day, I promise. I must say I worried when, a few years after my death, I heard that N would be interviewed for David Cavanagh's book about me, *Good Night and Good Riddance*. Surprisingly, he turned out to have taken his exclusion—his riddance, I suppose—in very good sort. I was praised to the skies as a benign agronomist: "Like some kind of greenhouse, his nightly programme protected all sorts of delicate plants from the cold winds of commerce, at least until they were big and tough enough to make it on their own." I must say I spluttered into my ghostly burgundy when I read that. I'm certainly no saint, but I can be a sentimental bugger. When even the people who ought to hate you love you, you know you must've done something right.

Alain Robbe-Grillet: A room up by the artificial ski slope. Haig is about to move to Brussels. Haig was the singer in Josef K. The boys have come here in a blue car to say goodbye. The sun is sinking behind the electricity pylons, casting angular shadows across the walls of Haig's neurotically tidy bedroom. His records—from James Brown to Frank Sinatra—seem to be in alphabetical order. To avoid conversation, Haig puts on an electronic pop album called *Penthouse and Pavement* by Heaven 17. The cover features illustrations of young businessmen shaking hands in Sheffield, Edinburgh, and London: "The New Partnership—That's opening doors all over the world." It looks like a shareholder report. This is the order of the day; Lydon is pretending that Public Image Limited is a company, and Haig is doing the same with an imaginary organisation he calls Rhythm of Life. He has told the press that RoL might sell music, or might just tin peaches. Musicians are becoming corporate, and embracing machinery. N is nervous and spiky; he admires Haig, but is convinced that the Slavic-boned singer dislikes him. Haig has dyed his hair lemon white, and now looks like Roy Batty in *Blade Runner*, which happens to be Haig's favourite film. He serves coffee and biscuits, carefully ignoring N. Davy is telling him that the Happy Family will produce music that is "very percussive." Haig takes this as a cue to demonstrate his new Linn Electronics LinnDrum. The machine produces a thumping, dead sound. N wonders whether the drum sound isn't a bit "fascistic" and criticises Haig's solo remake of the Josef K song "Heaven Sent" as "too pentatonic." Haig—possibly interpreting "too pentatonic" as "too black"—continues to avoid eye contact; when N asks him a question he replies in Davy's direction. He disagrees with N's contention that the move to Brussels will be challenging because "so much of Josef K's music was about Edinburgh." Haig is diametrically opposed: his songs were never about Edinburgh in the first place. He will record his debut solo album in New York with machines. Nineteen eighty-two is also the year in which I publish my novel *Djinn*, which recounts—in increasingly complex grammar—how a man called Simon is recruited by a woman called Jean to fight the rise of computers, robots, and automation.

Harold Pinter: It is—or failed to become—one of my early plays. The curtain opens on a couple lying together in bed. I wanted Michael Jayston and Vivien Merchant for the roles. The man would be smoking. White bedsheets, a white room. Possibly they've just woken up from a short postcoital nap. The man is holding a piece of paper, scanning it with a puzzled expression. The woman files her nails.

THE MAN: Darling, do you remember that time . . . We were at a party, or . . . [*to himself*] . . . in a field? A man came up and spoke to us. Do you remember?

THE WOMAN: Hmm? No, I don't. I don't remember that.

THE MAN: Yes, you do, darling. A man came up and spoke to us. [*Pause*]

THE WOMAN: What was he like, this man? Short, tall?

THE MAN: Not short, not tall. Dull, pleasant, medium build.

THE WOMAN: Darling, that could be absolutely anyone!

THE MAN: Don't you remember? I remember. [*Snapping his fingers*] Hall! That was his name, Hall.

THE WOMAN: Hall?

THE MAN: Yes, he said his name was Hall. He's sent us a letter. This letter.

THE WOMAN: That letter? What does it say?

THE MAN: It's quite extraordinary, really. He says he's . . . He *claims* he's won a lottery. He's very rich now. And he doesn't know what to do.

THE WOMAN: [*Sits up in bed*] What do you mean, he doesn't know what to do?

THE MAN: He doesn't know what to do . . . with himself. His days are empty. It says that here, look: "My days are empty. What do you think I should do?" [*Pause*]

THE WOMAN: How funny. Is that all?

THE MAN: No, he wants us to know that he has a yacht now. And a big house. On Lake Geneva. He says that if we hear any rumours about him, we should disregard them. It seems he's launched himself into politics.

THE WOMAN: Into politics? What does this have to do with us, darling? Why has he written? I still don't remember this man. [*Pause*]

THE MAN: [*Puffing out smoke and turning the paper over*] Well, that's the most extraordinary cheek, I must say!

THE WOMAN: What is?

THE MAN: [*Chuckling*] You'll never believe this!

THE WOMAN: What?

THE MAN: He wants us to come. Immediately. To Lake Geneva. He asks for you particularly. He calls you "my doll." He wants you to be his . . . his . . . Darling? [*The Woman has thrown down the nail* *file, wrapped herself in a bedsheet, jumped up, and is opening cupboards, throwing clothes into a suitcase.*] Darling, what are you doing? Where are you going?

THE WOMAN: To Lake Geneva.

Actually, this is the beginning of a concept album released in 1982 by the Happy Family. It's called *The Man on Your Street*, and subtitled *Songs from the Career of the Dictator Hall*. The woman goes to Lake Geneva, abandoning her salesman husband and her teenage son. Hall becomes a neofascist demagogue, a dictator. Sam, the son of the salesman, meets Maria, Hall's estranged and abused daughter. They become lovers, join the Red Brigades, and set out on a mission which culminates in Hall's assassination, one early spring day in Turin. This all unfolds in nine songs. My plays don't have songs in them. That would very much spoil the music of the language, I feel.

Roland Barthes: The Happy Family is named after a line N wrote in one of his sociology assignments, a semiological analysis of a single edition of *The Radio Times*: "Myth thrives by incest, but there's always room for the reader in the happy family." In the group, the relationship between bassist Davy Weddell and Neill Martin, the Happy Family's new synth player, is—to paraphrase Saussure—arbitrary. Neill is clever (he knows the names of chords) but cruel and competitive: he adapts the bass player's surname until the sound-image shifts to "Widdle," which brings with it an unsavoury series of connotations. Davy responds by launching a campaign to cast Neill as an interloper and a neurotic. Up to this point Davy has been—as one review of their album puts it sarcastically—"the group's glittering prize." His sheer inarticulacy has given him the power of proletarian otherness in the eyes of N, who is keen to escape the bourgeois *doxa*. But Neill's intelligence, dark ectomorphic looks, and warm, ingratiating manner are seductive. Visually, he has some of the appeal of the young Paul Haig, whose photo used to appear in the music press above the ironic caption: "Is this man too talented to live?" Neill's story is that he's a classical piano genius whose hands are slowly being crippled by arthritis. He is interested in the near-death research of Elisabeth Kübler-Ross. His girlfriend Gillian is an art student. From the perspective of the other musicians in the group, what makes Neill most dangerous is the fact that he owns machines—a Korg M1 synth, a string machine, a clavinet that used to belong to Midge Ure of Slik, a drum machine—that could make them redundant. Like Paul Haig, the Happy Family could decide overnight to abandon drums and wires and become a "synthpop project." It's not as if the others write anything, and the more the group rehearses the worse—and the louder—the music seems to sound, with Ronnie Torrance bashing away on the floor toms and everyone else turning up to compete. There have been a few concerts—one in Glasgow, for instance, supporting Jah Wobble from PiL—but not enough to feed five hungry mouths. The Happy Family is unsustainable. A family or a pop group is a good example of a syntagm, which can be imagined as a sentence comprising various paradigmatic elements that are notionally in competition with each other. Now imagine someone coming along who can make these interlocking elements redundant by duplicating their functions.

Viv Stanshall: *The Man on Your Street* is recorded out in the East Lothian countryside at Castle Sound, a recording studio in an ancient schoolhouse that has been raised from its resting place at the bottom of a squelchy peat bog. The obscene flags, spikes, and spires of Rawlinson End can be seen flapping and jabbing in the distance, emerging from a rum fog of fart smoke created by Old Scrotum, the family retainer. "May the gods bequeath us a fumigation," grumbles Sir Henry, peering through a telescope at the five boys as they load in their amps, guitars, keyboards, and drums. The studio is run by Calum Malcolm, who whelped Josef K recordings back in the days when his studio tottered on the cliff-edge of Edinburgh Castle, and the ersatz East Europeans spat out a brash jangle worthy of the Velvet Underground. Viscount Ivo Russell-Terrier has sent a letter commanding N to "sing your heart out!" And N complies, but for some reason nobody wants to buy a concept album which mashes up the Red Brigades with *The Sound of Music*. Reviews conclude that the Happy Family are a little too clever for their own good. In desperation N considers transforming the group into a gamelan ensemble. The final straw comes in the summer, when scouts for the BBC audition the Happy Family for a new youth television programme called *One Million Buzzing Poo Flies Landing on Doo-Doo from a Dog* and decide they aren't good enough. Faced with the prospect of making more Happy Family recordings, 4AD shudders like a terrified Pekingese, rolls over, and plays dead. Against the advice of the late Matthew Arnold—who runs the Aberdeen English department under the assumed name of Professor Andrew Rutherford—N takes another year away from the varsity and starts recording songs with Neill and his treacherous machines. The result is prissy spider-dribble that walks like David Sylvian wearing Joni Mitchell's tangled knickers. N spends most of 1983 eating kidney beans and lentils slow-cooked in an electric pot, and I leave it to you to imagine what *that* smells like. He knocks his head on mezzanine beams decorated with postcards featuring the lithographs of expressionist E. L. Kirchner—each bump improves you, lawdylawks—and takes penitent trips to Glasgow to see Giles Havergal and Robert David MacDonald's productions of Jean Genet and Karl Kraus at the Citizens Theatre, where the dead and the unemployed get in for free. Each day N walks up to the Edinburgh University library, where he sits reading *The Spurt of Blood* by Antonin Artaud or working on a doomed novel set on the island of Bali. Arthur's Seat, visible above the trees of the Meadows, hovers like an ambitious volcanic extra, hoping for the part of Gunung Agung. One day—perhaps copying his friend Neill's neuroses, or due to a profound vitamin and orgone deficiency resulting from his vegetarianism—N finds himself suffering from tunnel vision: the world shrinks down to nothing more than the aisles and shelves of the library. "A book tunnel, you say? The fellow's been stuck in one ever since!" Sir Henry Rawlinson—trapped in a book himself—is thinking that aloud, and very loudly indeed.

Alexander Pope: At the threshold of that most awful year, 1984, we find young N employed temporarily in the field of data input, tapping figures into dumb terminals deep in the fundament of an Edinburgh insurance concern. The dullness of this toil—which he has been obliged to accept to ensure continued access to unemployment benefits—crushes his spirit and coaxes N to assay pleasures unknown; when a workmate called Eric, round of spectacle, is assigned to the chair adjacent, N summons within himself a half-hearted homosexual lust for the boy. It passes the time. The musick best able to sweeten his foul distemper is to be found upon a disc entitled *Power, Corruption & Lies* by New Order. The sibylline couplets whispered by Bernard Albrecht, a melancholic Mancunian, seem to heave upon a slow sea of chords better fitted, one may suppose, for the requiem of some hapless regent:

> *You've caught me at a bad time*
> *So why don't you piss off*

By year's end N has returned to Aberdeen and is making a final rush at his English literature degree. This time he inhabits, as though in self-chastisement, a frosty garden shed behind the home of a Torry fishwife. His bunk hole lacks running water but does possess a gas fire, above which he has taped with evident care a sooty photocopy of Sir Godfrey Kneller's portrait of me, Alexander Pope. It is possible that my startled, irascible, ungulate, and papal features—for I am long of nostril and fleshy of lip, with a quizzical and sardonic mien—suggest an amalgam of N's heroes of this era: the Flemish phlegmatic Jacques Brel, and Howard Devoto, whose new solo album *Jerky Versions of the Dream* contains the lines:

> *Stirring the blue-grey waves . . .*
> *My brain's a leaky boat*

Should a new edition of my *Dunciad* be required, I will pass over these poets in silence, for I find myself quite unqualified to judge— and even less condemn—their work.

Jacques Rivette: The year is 1984, and we are in Aberdeen, not Paris. The following scenario refers both to *Alice in Wonderland* and my 1974 film *Céline and Julie Go Boating*. Ali Smith—a literature student who will one day become a famous novelist—is shivering over a book in a park one afternoon when Julie, an attractive blond art student, scurries by like the White Rabbit. The girls become fast friends and soon Ali is shuttling her black and burgundy Citroen 2CV daily between King's College and Gray's School of Art. N is a sort of Mad Hatter, a bearded aesthete dressed in a thick grey sweater a manufacturing error has given a big orange spot on one sleeve ("Out, damned spot!" is Ali's comment when she sees it). Through his art school friends—all called Keith—N hears that A *might* be a lesbian, and that Julie *might* be her lover. This is inconvenient: N has decided that, due to her very evident literary talent, Ali should be his girlfriend. The rumours are half confirmed when a huge canvas appears in a temporary exhibition at the Aberdeen

Art Gallery. Painted by Julie, it clearly depicts Ali in the nude. Ali, however, tells N that Julie used a body double. This is preposterous, but amusing to imagine: "Now Ali, I'm only going to paint your head. I've asked Britt Ekland to pose for the body." N continues, in his naïve way, to try to impress Ali. One day he finds a parking ticket taped to the windscreen of her 2CV. With a semi-sexual thrill he peels it off, takes it to the fines office, and pays. Since they're both in the Creative Writing Group, N finds it easy to set up a literary date with Ali in the Sports Pavilion Café, which is the fashionable student hang that year. As a pretext, N has taken a poem Ali has written about Anne Frank and remade it as a sonnet. She responds with another literary quote: "Tread softly because you tread on my dreams." A poem—it's meant to be a love poem—comparing Ali to the Groke from the Moomin tales somehow fails to advance the courtship, although later Ali will become something of an expert on Tove Jansson's adult fiction. A song on the first Momus album, though, does touch her: "King Solomon's Song and Mine" mentions a "sweet Alison" and elicits a "placative" cassette tape and a warm letter from Ali: "I never realised!" Later she sends him a copy of her first novel, *Like*. It is, according to the dust jacket, the story of "two young girls discovering strong attraction for each other." On the facing page Ali has scribbled: "It is not autobiographical—my head, not my body."

William Shakespeare: Do you doubt, modern people, that I can wrap my tongue around your soapy, anodyne language if I must? I abandoned iambic pentameter long ago. And yet what you call Standard English is a manila envelope fit only for manila thoughts. The greatest escape I can offer you is the density and richness of my Elizabethan lexis with its excess and elegance—its parrots and Barbary apes, its voyages and violence, its callbacks to a classicism you have willfully forgotten, and its spherical background music. The more alien all this may be to you, the more valuable must it become. As in a pop-up book for children, each line in a sonnet of mine can spring into life—if you will just linger in its shade, and promenade beneath its bowers—as a garden filling suddenly with birds and flowers. Each humanist scholar must receive the baptism of a long immersion in my depths, and N is no exception. He may be bored by the history plays, but he appreciates my comedies, my songs, my whimsies—*A Midsummer Night's Dream, As You Like It, The Tempest*—as well as what you epigones, you second Elizabethans, insist on lumping together under the clumsy rubric of "problem plays": *Measure for Measure, Hamlet.* In the late spring of 1984—picture it!—N is sitting his final exams in a gymnasium at Aberdeen University. Outside the Kittybrewster kids are wearing fluorescent socks and "Frankie Says Relax" T-shirts, but in this desk-filled gym N has come up against an unskippable essay question about my play *Timon of Athens.* Actually, even I can barely remember the plot; Middleton wrote a great wedge of it, and much comes from Lucian. Luckily, textbooks are allowed in the exam hall, and N scrambles to get the gist of the play. Students don't necessarily know things, but they know where to source them—as I did with my Plutarch, my Petrarch, my Holinshed. So, glossing Timon's longer speeches in the big green omnibus that his father annotated back in *his* days as an undergraduate, N discovers that the play begins with Timon surrounded by friends and ends with him living in a cave, fulminating against the whole city of Athens, giving all his money to a besieging army intent on razing the place. From this scant knowledge he works up a bungled, fudged essay and hopes that it will pass muster. Convinced that he will just scrape his degree, he arranges to graduate in absentia. On the day the exam results are published N phones the English department from Edinburgh, where he's taken a job as a messenger in a civil service office, determined to save enough money to move to London and become a musician. The departmental secretary on the other end of the phone line sounds triumphant: "Well, Mr. Currie, you've got a master of arts with first-class honours." After the various disruptions and stubbornnesses of N's academic career this is genuinely shocking. "Heavens above!" The secretary confirms the cosmological order: "Yes, the heavens are above." N may never use this degree for any sort of employment—in fact, it will probably count against him, for nobody wants an overqualified troubadour—but he will certainly use his literary education, and his ability to write somewhat in the manner of dead heroes. He will become, in time, a pantaloon: an old humanist scholar surrounded by his books, clucking at the world's avarice and stupidity. A Japanese Prospero, a melancholy Jaques, a kind of Timon.

Stevie Smith: Nineteen eighty-four is the year N moves to London, but in an odd way it's my year too. Of course, I've already been dead for seven years when Glenda Jackson plays me in a film, and thirteen by the time the Morrissey fans start beating a path to Palmers Green to ask me what I think of the Smiths. "What do you mean, what do I think of them—I *was* one!" is about all I can manage, not actually being there. N has already been down to the Smoke once to see his old university friends Babis and Zoe, who are now pretending they're married because it gives them the right to a marvellous student flat overlooking the gardens of Mecklenburgh Square. Babis is at the London School of Economics studying transport planning. "You should move here: inner London is the most left-wing place in Britain," he tells N, describing how Ken Livingstone at the Greater London Council is the city's real leader, completely at odds with Thatcher—that dreadful woad-smeared Boadicea with her unnecessary wars on Argentinians, coal miners, and socialists. And so N drives a van down from Edinburgh loaded with furniture belonging to his friends Malcolm and Syuzen. He lives with them for the first few weeks in a dark ground-floor flat on the Queenstown Road in Battersea, before moving to an over-heated room in Streatham. Nineteen eighty-five rolls around, and there are wonderful parties thrown on the Queenstown Road by the Postcard Records mafia: Edwyn Collins and Roddy Frame lark around pissed, plugging their guitars into plastic musical toys, though N tends to feel more comfortable with their less competi-tive, more kindly wives: the Glaswegian, Grace, and the American, Kathy. Edwyn can be sharp-tongued; one evening he compares N's music to early Genesis, and you can tell it's not meant as praise. At work N is also happy to be in the company of women: he takes a job at J. D. Potter, a nautical bookshop near the Tower of London. The manageress is a plump lady called Jenny and his fellow assistant a lemon-haired slip of a Goth called Elaine who loves all the groups on the 4AD label but has never heard of the one N fronted. This ob-scurity seems to become a pattern: each time a cult label he's been on pushes through to wider acceptance, N is guaranteed to have left it months before. Which is rather like me, Stevie, leaving this world just when I did. Death is the only god who comes when you call, and sometimes before, but death is not the end of everything. In the salty seadog bookshop on Minories I am also a presence: Jenny lets N slip through the odd order for a free book of his own choosing, and the first thing he asks for is the big new Penguin compendium of my poems. Heigh-ho.

George Melly: In 1985 N is renting a big overheated room in a semi-detached villa—a carpeted cocoon of slightly urine-scented mediocrity—in the southern suburbs of London. "Ah, deepest Streatham," sympathises Merlin Unwin, who publishes his father's fishing books—one of which I review for *The Times Literary Sup-plement*, calling it "a kind of pornography." N attends Merlin's ca-sual pep talk wearing a double-breasted Jaeger suit his mother has bought him in the hope that it will nurture the sensibility the media are beginning to call "yuppie." The much-signalled aspiration is quite misguided, for the young urban professionals of the mid-1980s are politically spineless and aesthetically clueless: only snobbish fools pay for water they could get free from a tap. N carefully distances himself by mixing his mother's suit with strange sandals and sweaters. He paints his room on Wavertree Road olive green and lemon yellow. The place is actually not so bad—the bay window overlooks a cypress tree, Renaissance reproductions decorate the walls, and the Picador bookstand looms in a corner. N has a bed, his red Baldwin twelve-string guitar with its spidery, unamplified sound, and a typewriter to tap out lyrics on. You can borrow June Tabor records from the Streatham library, or join Ruskin in admiring the Lombardic polychromy of the bell tower of nearby Christ Church. Better still, you can take the 159 bus up to Trafalgar Square and see the National Gallery or the ancient Roman rooms of the British Museum for free. You can linger in Soho or finger literary fragments in the Loeb Classical Library at Foyles. It takes an hour to get to central London on the bus, so there's lots of time to sit upstairs in the front seat gazing at passing parks and buildings, or admiring posters for the new Pogues album, which is called *Rum, Sodomy & the Lash* in tribute to my memoir of navy life, *Rum, Bum and Concertina*. Postmodernism has, rather excitingly, collapsed high and low, past and present: historical forms can be the very latest thing, and you're free to collide the refinement of the opera house with the vulgarity of the music hall. With John Chilton's Feetwarmers I'm reviving raucous big band jazz, while the Pogues are reheating rambunctious Irish folk music. Tom Waits has fused a junk shop with Harry Partch. Along the route of the 159 bus—stop-starting between the nowhere and the somewhere—N has lots of spare time to daydream about the records one might make, reviving and channelling rebellious, rum-soused, rain-soaked things. One might make an EP about threesome sex, or one about death. One might melt down Brecht, Juvenal, Kierkegaard, and Matthew Arnold and turn them into whispery cabaret songs about television and pop music, the new "bread and circuses." One might, indeed, take as one's subject the kind of wide-screen historical violence on view in the National Gallery: those big, graphic paintings of Saint Sebastian, Holofernes, John the Baptist, and the rape of the Sabines. So much blood, so much sexy atrocity! If Derek Jarman and Peter Greenaway can get away with it, anyone can.

H. G. Wells: While I may be best known, latter-day, for my early science fiction—*The Time Machine, The Invisible Man, The War of the Worlds*—I would humbly suggest that I put my best foot forward, as it were, with my whimsical trilogy of middle-class manners: *Kipps, The History of Mr. Polly,* and *Alway.* Of the three it is *Alway*—the comical misadventures of an artists & repertoire man in a 1980s world of independent record labels—that spans genres and squares the circle, placing a Pollyish or Kippsian fellow seven decades into the future. Michael Alway is a silver-tongued Englishman, originally from the West Country, who inhabits the Barnes and Richmond area of London. He is alert and birdlike, with delicate lips, a long hooked nose, and warm hazel eyes that dart about as he extrapolates seductive visions of worlds which can never be: "I'd like you to think about a record about pastry chefs and England winning the Ashes, Nick. With a silly-ass Ian Carmichael character narrating in the style of a teacher in some Michael Powell version of *St. Trinian's.* When it comes to the sleeve I've got an idea featuring lime-green ecclesiastical lampshades." When N first meets the charming Mr. Alway—in 1982, in a pub across the road from 4AD's office—the Englishman is in the employ of a company called Cherry Red, which occupies an elegant suite of offices in Westbourne Grove. Boyish, with a shaggy haircut and short trousers (this is before he starts dressing like a bowler-hatted Edith Sitwell), Alway has been close to groups like the Soft Boys, the Monochrome Set, the Subway Sect, and Everything but the Girl. But he explains—"and this is all highly secret, Nick, but I'd like you involved"—that he is forming a new label called Blanco e Negro, distributed by the major label Warner Bros. Well, two years go by, and when N moves to London Alway has already been ejected from Blanco e Negro after spending a king's ransom on the artwork for a series of "neuro-activity modules" by a clever but commercially hopeless Peterborough group called Sudden Sway. A man called James Nice has in the meantime released a cassette of Happy Family demos—accompanied by a booklet of dark musings extracted from N's diary—on his label Les Temps Modernes, and it has been reviewed favourably in the *New Musical Express*, so N's stock is in the ascendant. Alway and N meet in the kitchen of Mike's house in Barnes and decide they must find a way to make records together. Over cups of steaming black coffee Mike outlines his vision of a new label, to be called él Records after a 1953 film about sexual paranoia by the Spanish surrealist Luis Buñuel. An affable press officer called Dave Harper will assist. N opens his notebook and plumps for the artist name Momus, which he has scribbled down while reading *Aesop's Fables*. Momus is a god both obscure and unjustly exiled: he's been banished from Mount Olympus for simply doing his job, which is to mock. The money for the first Momus record will come from Brussels, where Alway has forged links with Michel Duval's elegant label Les Disques du Crépuscule and a distribution company called Himalaya. And so, carrying only his guitar and a light overnight bag, N is packed off on ferries and trains to the Belgian capital, where he records—in the jazz studio on the Rue aux Fleurs where the young Jacques Brel first recorded—the "three songs about threesomes" released, in 1985, as *The Beast with 3 Backs*.

Ernst Ludwig Kirchner: As an expressionist artist of the Berlin school Die Brücke, I am particularly interested in the look of things. The record released under the title *The Beast with 3 Backs* has a cloudy green sleeve designed by Mike Alway. The number 3 in the title is rendered as a snake, lending the sleeve an edenic resonance. "The beast with two backs" is a Shakespearean description of sexual intercourse, of course, but what would a beast with three backs be? Would the third back belong to a tempting snake or an observing outsider, an adulterating interloper, one of the voyeuristic spectres that hover—as Freud observed—over every act of sexual congress? As in a garden, everything on this sleeve is green except for the small black-and-white photograph of me watching dancing peasants in Frauenkirch in 1920. I am in the great chalet I rented, the Haus der Lärchen, wearing a leather jacket, a cigarette dangling from sharp lips, my paintings stacked behind me. As delicate as a Pierrot, I have come to Davos in order to recover from an addiction to Veronal and morphine. N finds that I resemble David Bowie, who is a drug addict recovering in Switzerland himself at this point, and indeed a collector of my work, although he tends to talk more about my friend Erich Heckel. N has carefully cut this image from a book he has borrowed from the art library of the University of Westminster. Here I stand at the edge of the picture, a melancholic Pierrot, a singleton observing couples, an artist among farmers, and it is an image of what Momus will always be: the third party, the adulterer, the voyeur, the critic, the oedipal son impotent to intervene in the parental bond that made him, the pale observer doomed to record a form of life he can neither enter nor alter. The recording sessions on the Rue aux Fleurs have been spooky, with N supplementing his whispery vocals and shivery twelve-string guitar with ghostly choirs created by an ancient modular synthesiser, the muted gong tones of a prepared piano, and the medieval throb of a tenor recorder. The session engineer, perhaps affected by the strange atmosphere, falls ill—literally green at the gills. As for me, I eventually commit suicide in the Alps, condemned as "degenerate" by the Nazis and unable to escape my demons.

Peter Porter: What could be more exciting than your first interview appearance in a publication you've been reading for years? It's your first validation as a professional, your chance to blow your own trumpet into fresh ears! And yet when freelancer Jim Shelley arrives to quiz N for a half-page feature in the *New Musical Express*, the young Scot spends most of the interview "quoting proudly, fidgeting constantly," and discussing a lubricious Australian poet living in London: myself. I suppose it's neatly reciprocal that a poet who places music far above his own art should be lauded in this way by a musician who apparently feels that someone else's poetry ranks far above his own music. Playing to the gallery, no doubt (but *what* gallery? The Oxford University Press's moribund poetry imprint, the squeaky Picador bookstand?), N cites my definition of good writing as "essential gaudiness" and laments the fact that only a handful of people have turned up to a reading of mine he's attended at a Kensington wine bar. Perhaps that's because, as Clive James once put it, my poems are "so freighted with learned references that I can't even tell if I don't know what they mean." N's first releases as Momus are greeted in the British music press with similar bafflement. Jack Barron's review of *Circus Maximus* in *Sounds*, for instance, calls N "an intellectual exhibitionist who has swallowed The Bible, Plato, *The Encyclopaedia Britannica*, *The Rise and Fall of the Roman Empire* and *Roget's Thesaurus* and ended up with indigestion of the cranium." And do you know what? I don't think the book you're reading shows a single sliver of evidence that this man has learned anything from his mistakes. Bless him.

Nicolas Roeg: By the time N moves to London his Greek and French friends Babis and Zoe have separated. Zoe has tried living in Brixton with Babis and a flatmate called Robert, but it hasn't worked out. Zoe finds her own room in a ground-floor flat at Draycott Place, a short walk from Sloane Square. Chelsea isn't what it was: Thomas Carlyle's house is now a museum, and Granny Takes a Trip, the Chelsea Drugstore, and Syd Barrett left long ago. The flat is like something out of my film *Performance*: a hippie bootlegger called Mick is renting it from an elderly gay man who lives upstairs, so the place is full of boxed-up rock records that don't exist in any shop: Pink Floyd's *The Massed Gadgets of Hercules*, David Bowie's *Neo-Expressionism*. In the basement bathroom there's a huge demonic goat's head—a prop made for one of the Rolling Stones' tours. Soon after visiting her new room N becomes Zoe's lover, and not long after that he takes over the room itself—Zoe moves up to Tufnell Park for greener scenery and fresher air. N spends the next five years living, singing, and playing guitar in this "canary cage," as one visitor calls it. The room is tiny, but doesn't lack charm; one would shoot it in wide angle, I suppose. There's a bed with a bright red duvet, some theatrical claret-coloured velvet curtains, a bookshelf from which a page of Chinese newsprint hangs over a fluorescent tube, N's red Baldwin guitar and his Picador bookstand. There's also a ghetto blaster with a tiny television screen in its fascia, the kind of gadget Thomas Jerome Newton might have marketed through World Enterprises. To pee, N squats over the basin and aims between his legs at the flow of fresh water. You could add some cutaway shots of record sleeves (Brel, Gainsbourg, Jake Thackray), perhaps a view of the long mirror that stretches between the two barred windows. They overlook posh Bray Place—in the mid-eighties it's just where you park your BMW to do some shopping at Next, but back in the 1960s this was where Antonioni filmed bits of *Blow-Up*. Two American girls are living in the flat: N meets them in the shabby living room or the basement kitchen, which is lit with a blue fluorescent tube. Cindy is a sort of Sally Bowles who sings in an unremarkable band called Hearts on Fire, Sharon is from Hawaii. At some point Cindy is replaced by a junky called Barbara who tries to sell the television set for a fix. Because he's on the dole N gets his rent paid by Kensington and Chelsea council. Dinner mostly comes from the Chelsea Kitchen on the King's Road, where a takeaway chicken Kiev, bulging with hot garlic sauce, costs three quid.

Muriel Spark: I am in Tuscany with my amanuensis Penelope Jardine, but N is spending the summer of 1985 in France. In July he's on a fruit farm in Normandy with Philippe Auclair, who records on él Records as Louis Philippe and sounds like a one-man Beach Boys. Along with one and a half billion other people they watch the dreadful Live Aid concert on television: when it falls to art to save the world, both art and the world are probably doomed. Afterwards N makes his way south, joining his mother and brother in the Cévennes. Mark has just graduated from the Aberdeen English department with his own first, but Jo picks this moment to tell her sons that she has changed her mind about the value of education: "I now see that it is just as valuable to have a practical skill like knowing how to raise chickens or repair galvanised wire mesh fences." Miss Jean Brodie herself could not have pulled off a more provocative volte-face! (Like the filmic Miss Brodie, Jo is not just in her prime but also spotted often in the company of Gordon Jackson, who happens to be married to her husband Graham's sister.) In a holiday villa halfway between Saint-Jean-du-Gard and Lasalle, N is reading Nabokov's *The Real Life of Sebastian Knight*—a novel in which the narrator is writing a biography of his own brother but, it transpires, may actually *be* his own brother. Well, one afternoon Jo and the two brothers are walking down the Avenue du Pasteur Rollin in Anduze, a pleasant village in the shadow of the limestone Languedoc scrublands, when N spots the lonely, gnome-like figure of Lawrence Durrell approaching, carrying a cloth shopping bag. Since the Durrells and the Curries have both lived in Greece and worked for the British Council, Jo greets the writer like an old friend. He seems pleased to be recognised, but isn't terribly impressed by the British Council connection. He's come on the bus from Sommières and is trying to find a café where a journalist is meant to be interviewing him. Perhaps he's early, or just thirsty—anyway, Durrell agrees to stop in a bar for a pastis. He's been awarded some sort of tedious *medaille*, and tells the literary tourists what a pain it is to have to travel up to Paris to receive it. "But you can't turn these things down, of course . . ." He's working on a travel book about Provence, which will eventually appear as *Caesar's Vast Ghost*. N chips in with the observation that Provence is of course the backdrop to Durrell's Avignon Quintet. Someone has given him *Monsieur, or the Prince of Darkness* as a birthday present, and N has chucked it aside after six pages, but he doesn't tell Durrell this. "Yes, yes," Durrell replies, darting of eye and bulbous of snout, "but of course that was fiction, the approach was quite different." Jo chooses this moment to embarrass N hideously: "Nicholas is a writer too," she announces. It's not in the least bit true. Blushing intensely, N considers changing the subject by asking how Durrell feels about the Larry character in Gerald's books. But no—for God's sake, don't mention the brother!

Tom Hibbert: It's early 1986 and Nick "Brainy Professor Spook Bloke" Momus has released his first *meisterwerk* (that's an album to you, matey). It's called *Circus Maximus* and is "jolly good," but why does the steamy Scot insist on appearing naked across the gatefold sleeve, shot full of more arrows than, er, a hedgehog or a pincushion? Suffer for your art if you must, old bean, but do put some trews on! Ver Mome (as nobody calls him) lays down these v. knowing songs (and yes, we do mean that in the biblical sense) in a cheap and chilly studio called Alaska, right under Waterloo Station's eastbound tracks. N quite literally has to stop strumming his guitar every time a train goes by, which is . . . well, quite often, actually. One song is ruined by the sound of a *Smash Hits* ex-editor—yes, cuddly Pet Shop Boy Neil Tennant—clopping through Waterloo Station in kinky boots and a tragi-disco overcoat, filming the video for "West End Girls." Indeed, *Smash Hits* soon becomes a new family for Sir Nicholas of Bogus, for he happens to have taken up with a droll writer-designer on our staff, a lass called Vici McD with "interesting teeth." N starts popping up (mostly wearing clothes, thank goodness) at our Carnaby Street office, where he gets friendly (but not familiar) with Lola, soaraway Sylvia from Inverness, Ian "Jocky" Cranna (who used to manage Orange Juice) and editor Steve Bush. At about this time the pallid perv starts bumping into Lord Neil of Tennantshire in pet shops, post offices, Polish restaurants, the ICA (snoot!), and out at Pinewood Studios, where he's invited to magical mystery tour–type parties with silly names like "Bingo Bongo Bango" thanks to a certain string-pulling "press officer" called Murray Chalmers—and ends up larking on bouncy castles with members of Depeche Mode (as you do). Irony ahoy: this ligging lark is almost like being a pop star oneself, murmurs Baron Momers de Mome (in medieval French, probably). For life with Vici is a dizzying round of VIP passes, slap-up feeds, hobnobbery, and whooshing white-knuckle Addy Lee cab rides ("on account, please") as the pair shuttle between Soho and her very "Festival of Britain" flat in one of Brixton's dodgiest council estates. Thanks to the Vix—an "avid scribbler" and graduate of the Royal College of Art—Momus features pop up in the unlikeliest of places: *Smash Hits, The Face, Morpeth & Pegswood Used Car Gazette*, and the *New Pervecy-clopedia* (okay, we made up the last two). So an artist who would normally be down the dumper before he'd even been up it (steady, steady) begins to look—to the Man on the Clapham Omnibus, an omnivorous reader of "ye style press," probably—as if he's going right to the very toppermost of the poppermost.

Jean-Marie Straub: No, no, and again no! Ambition in the 1980s will only open a politically progressive artist to accusations of selling out from his allies and active sidelining from his enemies the moment they begin to see the outlines of the wooden horse. Outright resistance—that banal negation which lets the enemy set the agenda and choose the field of battle—is liable to turn into a gesture as superficial as the sans serif imperative printed on a Katharine Hamnett T-shirt. CHOOSE LIFE, says Hamnett! DANCE DON'T RIOT, says the *New Musical Express*! As politics in Britain becomes increasingly ruthless under Margaret Thatcher—a radical conservative figurehead intent on bringing back Victorian values, ending the welfare state, privatising public assets, and fighting her own country's miners as well as foreign navies—a sludgy undertow of guilt-driven tokenism, aided by the remorseless creep of identity politics, sees the left hand completing the work the right has begun. If the bien-pensant and nominally progressive bourgeois class is not actually camped out at Greenham Common protesting the arrival of American cruise missiles, it's attending WOMAD, Peter Gabriel's world music festival. Various isms become new sins modelled on anti-Semitism but leading only to schism. Marxism is the ism the eighties most needs, but is most liable to forget amid the growing clamour of calls for "respect" and frantic identitarian efforts to massage stigma with euphemism. There's anti-racism, of course, exemplified by progressive organisations like Rock Against Racism (some clever-clogs in the music press transmutes this into a "race against rockism"—an apparently righteous struggle to mock all claims to authenticity). There's anti-sexism, manifested more by Athena posters of muscled male models cradling babies than calls for actual pay parity between men and women. Anti-homophobia has to contend both with an explicit government policy aimed at the prevention of the promotion of homosexuality and the arrival of a deadly new epidemic called AIDS. Ageism, weightism, transphobia, and ableism add to the neoliberal victim litany, at least until the right takes over identity politics—a process that arguably begins with the unrepentant masculinism of the book *Iron John*, published in 1990. The progressivist clock is being set back, and the question arises: What should the artist do? Sandy Nairne's 1987 documentary *State of the Art* catches formerly radical artists backpedalling and recanting: Beuys signs autographs like a rock star, Cindy Sherman is guest-editing *Vogue*, while Victor Burgin talks about a new "complexity" somehow overlooked by his 1970s agitprop slogans ("What does possession mean to you? 7% of our population own 84% of our wealth"). My answer to this question is to make films with my partner Danièle Huillet which explore modes of being, modes of art, and modes of performance, production, and distribution that are explicitly—even frighteningly—non-capitalist. This can involve resuscitating the classicism of Corneille or Hölderlin or restoring the otherness of the music of Bach, all the while employing Brechtian and Bressonian alienation devices. I believe this is what N is also doing with a record like *Circus Maximus*. Of course, this strategy of summoning alternative worlds where different values prevail is not without tinctures and limitations of its own. The postmodernism of the 1980s is encouraging a playful historicism, an investigation of classicism's "return to order" that fits—as it appears in the work of a filmmaker like Peter Greenaway, for instance—all too well into

Thatcher's vision. And if one isn't neutralised by becoming fashionable, one is muted and marginalised in the usual ways: Straub-Huillet films never leave the art house circuit, and Momus records fail to break out of the independent charts. We both end up serving as a vindicating sign for the endless variety and luxurious waste built into the capitalist mode of production: the repressively tolerant version of Bataille's "accursed share." As Tocqueville has the masters say in *Democracy in America*: "You are free to think differently from me and to retain your life, your property, and all that you possess; but you are henceforth a stranger among your people. You may retain your civil rights, but they will be useless to you, for you will never be chosen by your fellow citizens if you solicit their votes; and they will affect to scorn you if you ask for their esteem. You will remain among men, but you will be deprived of the rights of mankind. Your fellow creatures will shun you like an impure being; and even those who believe in your innocence will abandon you, lest they should be shunned in their turn. Go in peace! I have given you your life, but it is an existence worse than death."

Ezra Pound: The little labels of the 1980s—upheld by a rabble of "zines" in which Nunkus, Punkus, and Swanky could have their say—were not unlike our small poetry magazines of the teens, beginning with Miss Monroe's *Poetry* and continuing through Mr. Lewis's *Blast*: while these ships of penny paper might escape the Scylla of lucre, they risked running aground on the rocks of that stern Charybdis, the cult of personality. 4AD, él, Creation, Mute, Rough Trade, Factory, each was a bully pulpit, an ambo built upon a creed, and that creed upon a man. Discovering his hendecasyllables to be out of step with the chryselephantine tastes of Ivo Watts-Russell, N found himself—somewhat unexpectedly—repeating the experience with Mike Alway, the *tyrannus minor* of él. At first all seemed well; N was drafted to ghostwrite the prospectus of this "most westerly of the indies," and was happy to contribute fantastical sleeve notes for records by concocted groups like Bad Dream, Fancy Dress ("One day, gentlemen, they will be old bags. But not yet, not yet!"). He was delighted to herald his own releases with pungent apothegms: "One man's martyrdom, another man's matinee" ran the pre-encapsulation of *Circus Maximus*, the disk in which he would "sing the Old Testament to the new instruments," and his EP of Brel covers was self-explanatory (which didn't stop N explaining it to all who would listen in the *NME*). But in escaping greed N fell prey to creed. Alway's favorite record was "Sugar, Sugar" by the Archies, and N increasingly felt that the English confectioner tended to treat musicians as regrettably meaty pretexts for his *visionem grandem*: wispy yet waspish cartoons in which swarthy bakers might pilot gondolas brandishing cricket bats and incanting *adeste fideles* in stentorian *pronunciamento*. In this wise was a fond parting foretold between N and his friend and mentor Alway: Atropos herself, cutter of threads, decreed that the second Momus album—indeed, the next seven—should appear on Creation Records, imprimatur of an intelligent imbecile, an erstwhile train driver called Alan McGee. "We don't sit around reading French novels here," was McGee's first declaration to Momus, before sealing a generous recording deal (50/50 profit splits) not in blood but generic ketchup from a Wimpy Bar on Chancery Lane. Upon hearing that the blond *Edimbourgeois* hoped to be bigger than David Bowie, the ginger Glaswegian spake with winged words: "That's good—most groups who come to me say they want to be bigger than the Mighty Lemon Drops."

Flann O'Brien: Friday emerges new-shorn from a mews house in Mayfair reeking of diaminobenzene. Improbable cuts and colourings are free at the Vidal Sassoon academy, where—in exchange for a few hours of scalp—the students tonsure as they please, talking around and above as if your presence were an afterthought. You can watch yourself in the mirror being transformed into an altogether new man: the great change the church has so often promised—but ever failed—to make. Sometimes you look like a rake and sometimes a fool, but what does it matter? You're being londoned, dining upon the crumbs that fall liberally from a great table. Afterwards—for you planned to buy *Die Harzreise* by Heine, do you remember?—you walk up to Grant & Cutler, the international bookshop on Great Marlborough Street, and fondle pale editions of Pierre Louÿs or Clarice Lispector. These are—as only you seem to know—the beautiful people. You would never steal a book from Grant & Cutler, but why not steal a character or two, with such a tempting empty pocket on your left buttock? Bilitis the goose girl! Macabéa the jilted Brazilian lass run over by a yellow Mercedes! You could use these little people in your own work, for aren't there too many characters in this world already? Make them sleep in a hotel, but don't fall asleep yourself, for then you may lose control of the rascals! Of course, they may rise up against you, these characters from the realms of magic, asserting their rights of assembly and association, defying your authorial will by insisting on lives of unaccountable dullness. In that case you may be justified in threatening the ungrateful sprites with some horrid accident or disease, just to keep them on their toes. Events, that's what we need! Why not invite these shoplifted characters to a party up at Zoe's house? You could bring Paul Quinn, the Scottish crooner with the generous grin, the one Edwyn Collins says can copy any singer's style, alive or dead. Zoe might like him. And Tammy and Shira, the Lampert sisters, will surely be there. Tammy and Shira are better than sunspots, milk, or lizards peeping from holes. The sisters are better than tubas played at the zoo by old men driven to theology by excesses of porter. Oh, God's teat, you forgot to buy the Heine! But London the great wet nurse will keep banjaxing you as you nestle towards her nipple, her cornucopia. Euclid, even the Jesuits, could become bigger men here—begin anew, and end askew. An ending one can see coming is a thing I never will agree with.

Ovid: "What's the book?" It's 1987 and the voice is warm and Glaswegian. The speaker is Yvonne McGee. N is visiting the Creation Records office at 83 Clerkenwell Road. He's keen for his alter ego Momus to release an album with the label, and has told Alan McGee—Yvonne's orange-haired husband—that it might be called *Vicious, Delicious, Ambitious.* The book is entitled *The Erotic Poems* and is by me, Ovid. It's a Penguin Classic from the black-backed Germano Facetti period (my favourite of the various Penguin designs, to be honest with you) and contains translations by Peter Green under the following headings: "The Amores," "The Art of Love," "Cures for Love," and finally "On Facial Treatment for Ladies." When N reads this out to Yvonne, she laughs. To be honest with you—an expression Alan drops into every third sentence— these could be alternative titles for the next few Momus albums on Creation, although N likes to joke that each record is provisionally entitled *Haggard Masturbator.* Alan—who has a power-pop group called Biff Bang Pow, a small son called Dan, and a subsidy from the Enterprise Allowance Scheme—keeps swallowing medications for his bad stomach. Creation is a sort of family business at this point, a motley rabble circulating between two offices overlooking— through a sort of fishbowl window—the jewellery district of Hatton Garden. There's Alan—visually a cross between Andy Warhol and the bubbly lad in Millais's ads for Pears soap—his wife Yvonne, and accountant Dick Green. Hangers-on—artists possible and actual—drop by often, sprawling on the floor in black leather trousers: the uniform is easy to buy, since Leather Lane is nearby. Alan often seems bored—he spends much of his time on the blower with obstreperous managers, pushy song publishers, anal lawyers, and major label A&R men. "One day, to be honest with you, Nick," he says, putting down the phone on a record executive, "I'm gonna turn into one of these people I hate!" At the same time he likes to boast that the London music business is run by a hundred influential people, and that he knows ninety of them. The networking is clearly paying off: Alan has put together a distribution deal for Creation with Warners. It results in an offshoot label called Elevation, and gives WEA the right to elevate the Creation acts they think have commercial potential. Momus, god of mockery, gaunt minstrel of modern angst, isn't one of them, although he has helped Alan confect a rap group called Baby Amphetamine, staffed by a couple of dreadlocked checkout girls from the Virgin Megastore. Alan writes a silly rap called "Chernobyl Baby," which—chanted by the girls over a backing track featuring a drum machine and a duck—gets decent press and does okay. For Elevation Warners have chosen the Weather Prophets, an anodyne but intelligent group fronted by the half-German Pete Astor, and Primal Scream, a floppy floral guitar group led by skinny hippy Bobby Gillespie, Alan's best friend from school. The Elevation deal will be short-lived, for reasons that become apparent when Momus tours Germany with Primal Scream that summer: his new album *The Poison Boyfriend*, on Creation, is being displayed in record shop windows everywhere because Rough Trade Deutschland is handling distribution and cares about each release. The Primal Scream album *Sonic Flower Groove*, on the other hand, is nowhere to be seen—WEA Germany have bigger fish to fry, and indie record stores aren't interested in major label releases. But let's get back to the more interesting tales in my black paperback of love poems! My cover depicts a *tablinum* fresco from Pompeii's famous House of Fatal Love. (The *tablinum* was essentially the home office of a Roman villa.) In the fresco Mars stands behind Venus with one hand down her blouse, while a baby Cupid hovers nearby. Venus is married to Vulcan, the dull but jealous god of fire. Vulcan walks with a limp and has hands hardened by the various volcanoes and thunderbolts he has to manage. (This is all in Book 2, Part 15 of my *Art of Love*, in a section entitled "Respect Her Freedom," by the way.) Venus and Vulcan have one child, Harmonia. The love of Venus's life is Mars, but Vulcan, alerted by the sun, gets wind of the affair and traps the couple naked in a net. All the gods of Olympus ridicule the couple, who

> *can't hide their faces, are even unable*
> *to cover their sexes with their hands.*

Momus, the god of mockery, is among them. Ridicule—and exposed genitalia—are very much his cup of tea, to be perfectly honest with you.

Jean Paulhan: As publisher of the *Nouvelle Revue Française*, I value good writing. *The Poison Boyfriend* is—like all pop records—a piece of writing spun out across chords, rhythms, and musical colours, and it rests on certain precepts. One is that "real writing"—which is to say the conscious and skillful assembly of language for the delight of strangers—is central; this is N's strength, the quality that separates him from the hacks, yodellers, and chancers all around. The album's first song, "The Gatecrasher," describes a shortsighted outsider at a party, frightening the girls and scorching his throat with stolen vodka. The guitars and flutes (sampled, appropriately enough, from a track on Leonard Cohen's *Death of a Ladies' Man*) provide an aquamarine churn capable of bearing a stream of free-associative lyrics documenting, apparently, the speculations of an observer about this outsider. Or is the gatecrasher merely observing himself in the mirror of his own heightened self-consciousness? There's something of Brecht's Baal about the stranger, and therefore something of Villon and Verlaine. His "flowers of evil" are mere ruminations, idle thoughts about terrorist explosions and the private life of the Führer. The pungency of his character is summed up in a Brechtian "quotable gesture": the man pushes a finger into his ear and, without thinking, brings the bitter wax into contact with his tongue. It is said that the modern tragic hero fights his destiny while his ancient counterpart "tastes it," and this is what the gatecrasher—a fresh "adulterer" to add to the lineage established on *The Beast with 3 Backs*—is doing, with a certain grim, articulate satisfaction: he is savouring his failure in advance, and relishing the taste. I will not make any messianic claims; if we consider the album to concern the evolutions of a single character, he is less a prophet or a devil than a Des Esseintes, a brittle dandy who allows disgust to eliminate most of the possibilities open to him. Across eight songs we see him progressing through landscapes in Islington and Ireland, envisioning his life as a series of battles *perdu d'avance*, seeking solace in the works of artists who know how to "flame into being," recoiling from political disillusionment in favour of the consolations of comedy, and, finally, finding peace in a diffuse and febrile eroticism. The album ends with the "little death of a ladies' man"—a sexualised take on Klee's epitaph: "Here lies the painter Paul Klee, somewhat closer to the heart of creation than usual, but far from close enough." Our gatecrasher, however, is lying not under the sod but between the legs of a woman, trying to get closer to Courbet's "origin of the world." His has been a trajectory from books to girls, from Marx to Freud, from Brel to Gainsbourg, from Kedourie to Badcock. To explain this last reference I must tell you that N is at this time—at the behest of his Greek friend Babis— a frequent gatecrasher himself. At the London School of Economics he attends lectures by Elie Kedourie on Hegel and Marx, but is disgusted when the conservative dismisses Marx as a philosophical fraud. Much more sympathetic is Christopher Badcock's class on the psychoanalysis of culture. Extending the Darwinian idea that "ontogeny recapitulates phylogeny," Badcock claims that since an individual, in the womb and afterwards, passes through the same stages as its species, cultures and individuals may be analysed using the same tools. He links Freud's stages of psychosexual development to cultural modes like animism (narcissism), totemism (the Oedipus complex), polytheism (the latency stage), the Christian era (adolescence), and psychoanalysis (sexual maturity), arriving at the conclusion that civilisation is a kind of collective neurosis. N finds this incredibly liberating: perhaps his sickness is not his own fault but something he can pinpoint in the culture around him? Perhaps one can—just by talking or singing it through—"shrink" this neurosis that passes itself off as a toxic form of normality? N returns to one of the criticisms Momus made of the Titans: man has a design flaw, for the gods have failed to place a window in his chest. By means, precisely, of his dirty records, N will now try to install this window and, in Kafka's words, "keep the peephole clean."

Christopher Isherwood: One's first visit to Berlin—that whirlpool of illicit excitements—is sure to create a lasting impression. N's initiation comes at the end of a Primal Scream tour that has been colourful, if checkered. The Glaswegians—so tightly packed into their van that guitarist Jim Beattie has to sit on a basketball—fart unrestrainedly and clamour for peep shows, booze, and pills at the approach of each new city. At Cologne N's backing tapes go missing, forcing him to play his set on a borrowed acoustic guitar. At Dortmund there is a sort of banquet in a basement, during which the members of the Scream compete to shock N with tales of their disadvantaged youth in various slums. At Bielefeld he joins them onstage to belt out a cover of "Loose" by Iggy and the Stooges, to the evident delight of a spotty audience of British soldiers. At Hamburg N tries to interest Bobby Gillespie in a pitched battle down at the docks between squatters and police, but the lank-haired vocalist and tambourine player would rather sleep. As the van approaches Berlin an oleaginous, moon-faced hanger-on called Halibut is reading to Bobby from a book about the occultic child murderer Gilles de Rais. They click a T. Rex tape into a cassette machine with half-flat batteries and the ghastly seasick dirge makes N turn round and snap: "For God's sake put that out of its misery!" The backseat Satanists glare like fourteen-year-olds caught bunking off chemistry class. It's a literal breath of fresh air when the van reaches the Kurfürstendamm and N discovers that a cinema next door to the hostel is showing Éric Rohmer's *Four Adventures of Reinette and Mirabelle*. Sitting in the air-conditioned Cinema Paris, the junkie lore of Johnny Thunders fading rapidly from his memory, N almost weeps for joy. Rohmer's philosophical heroines are fresh as a daisy, the perfect antidote to the queasy banality of rock nihilism. After the tour's final show at the Loft there's the usual backstage party, with a queue of girls offering themselves up to the bands. As usual Bobby gets the prettiest one and N the cleverest, a blond student called Daniela. The musicians proceed to various parties, bars, and clubs, with N nominally in charge of Bobby: "Make sure he doesn't pass out in a gutter somewhere," says Crusher, the tour manager. N discovers that Bobby is never quite as drunk as he pretends to be: the chance of sex brings him back to a canny state of alertness. The night goes by in no time. There's a visit to Monika's candlelit flat—the Loft's hippie mother, she tapes up N's gaping Doc Martens with silver gaffer tape. Next comes the Beehive, an impossibly fashionable gay club where Grace Jones records play and one dandy has a tiny record player strapped to his head. Berliners really do go the extra mile! The boys end up in a bar where model planes dangle from the ceiling and Blixa Bargeld serves them drinks. N gushes: "I feel as if I've come to Rome and met the pope!" He tells Blixa he's called Momus, but the Bad Seed mishears: "So, welcome to the Vatican, Mormons!" N spends the next four days in Berlin, sleeping in Daniela's bed. He obtains a day pass to cross into East Berlin and walks around Alexanderplatz sipping at a bottle of banana liqueur, little knowing that this will one day be a different country and his local neighbourhood. In the penultimate full year of East German socialism, blackened buildings cluster around the Soyuz-like Fernsehturm. There are black American soldiers with crates of vodka, looking like extras from a Fassbinder film, shoe shops with hardly any shoes, and bookshops outside which customers queue in the rain for new titles. Losing his way near the Brandenburg Gate, N asks a flower seller how to return to the West. "The West? That's not so easy. One requires a pass."

Peggy Guggenheim: I have always been frightfully enthusiastic about artists, despite—or even because of—their wild and headstrong egos. I've found them more than willing to share their extraordinary dreams and visions with me. What is crucial—in whichever city one finds oneself—is to create "salon conditions." Someone with a pleasant flat and the right connections must host a regular event to which all the great talents of the day should be invited. These conditions are fulfilled for N in London in the mid-1980s thanks to a new and lasting friendship with Thomi Wroblewski, a Polish Canadian ten years his senior. Thomi lives on the Gray's Inn Road with a Californian textile dealer called Junna. Although he makes his living as a graphic designer, Thomi is better known for his cooking. His suppers—given in a suite of rooms dominated by intelligently saucy books, African stools, and Moroccan lanterns—are attended by the writer Michael Bracewell, the minimalist composer Laurence Crane, the art dealer Andrew Renton, the fashion editor Hamish Bowles, the soprano Melanie Pappenheim, the sexologist Shere Hite, and many others. It's Mike Alway who makes the original connection, just before N leaves él Records. Thomi—rotund, warm, and garrulous yet also streetwise, with just the tiniest whiff of erotic cordite around his edges—shows N his portfolio in a patisserie on Old Compton Street. It contains record sleeves for Siouxsie and the Banshees and Talking Heads, but N is more impressed by Thomi's covers for John Calder and Peter Owen, bibliophiles publishing some of the most daring and cosmopolitan lists of the day. Thomi's designs—featuring murky nude figures and postmodern graphic motifs—have something dark and transgressive about them. His bookshelves heave with volumes by Bataille, Leiris, Mishima, Beckett, and Burroughs, and his conversation is peppered with casual gossip about Brion Gysin and James Grauerholz, or anecdotes about John Calder and Sam Beckett. N is soon drawn into this world, meeting the ebullient Calder himself—a short, stout, double-breasted Scot—in due course. He befriends Michael Bracewell, the promising author of a "London clubland" novel, *The Crypto-Amnesia Club*, and *Missing Margate*, a postmodern story about an architect who blows up his own buildings. Bracewell is the de facto leader of a reading group called the Quick End (also featuring Mark Edwards and Don Watson, with Kathy Acker clucking around the edges like a mother hen). The Quick End is named for a line in *More Pricks than Kicks*: "Well, thought Belacqua, it's a quick death, God help us all." The narrator delivers a flat riposte: "It is not." The group reads regularly in, for instance, the fin-de-siècle orientalist splendor of Leighton House. N's first visual project with Thomi is the sleeve for his first Creation release, a sensational record featuring three songs about death. The lead title is taken from an operetta by the painter Oskar Kokoshka: *Mörder, Hoffnung der Frauen*. N wants the cover to look like a bloodied record of ritualized murder, so Thomi shoots him naked, enacting a grotesque ballet with the flat-chested and kabuki-masked Zoe Pascale in the attic studio above Calder's offices. Alan McGee comes along to the shoot and is impressed enough with the results to invite Thomi to take N's press photo or "Walker print." And so we find the three men, as dusk falls across Soho one evening, almost involved in a scene of murder themselves: N—shaven-headed and performatively loutish in his big Chinese coat—is being photographed in a courtyard next to a sign saying MODEL when two black pimps approach. "This is a very foolish place to take photographs," they tell the trio, and demand Thomi's Nikon F2. The affable Canadian, unruffled, manages to talk the situation down, and the three return to the Calder offices all abuzz. The following spring Thomi shoots the cover for N's most iconic album, *Tender Pervert*, in Hyde Park in the middle of the night, using flash and a special medical film that renders the colors tungsten-cold. N, copying a horned devil pose he's seen in a photograph of Picasso—but also hoping to look something like his hero David Bowie—stands in front of a cherry tree laden with blindingly pale blossoms.

Egon Ronay: Just like me with my food guides, N is trying to find some interesting ambience as well as decent food. Well, not so much the food, to be honest. Like most British people he doesn't care much about eating. He prefers drinking. The London places he visits must have something else going on. Ambience, activities. There's the Man in the Moon pub at World's End, where he meets his musician friends Douglas and Kevin. Douglas has an electronic project called si-cut.db and Kevin is the mournful talent behind the él group Always. A block away there's the King's Road branch of the Dôme, which is a postmodern British take on a French café. You can sit there with a cappuccino and a copy of *The Face* magazine. If you want the real thing, go to South Kensington. There you can read today's *Libération* and the brainy magazine *Actuel* at the French Institute. The café above Habitat is quite a pleasant place to lurk with a book. At the Tate there's a "wild octagon of mirrors" in the basement that allows the young British lecher to peep sheepishly at tourist girls. The V&A also has an enormous refectory, a buffet like a Victorian barn. Then there are the evening places, the basement folk clubs still basking in their sixties glory: Bunjies, just off the Charing Cross Road, and the Troubadour at Earl's Court, where N's friend Tammy runs a poetry club called Terrible Beauty. The Bull's Head at Clapham hosts God's Little Joke, a weekly variety show featuring a parade of loser poets and failed balladeers punctuated by the odd unsung genius (Preacher Harry Powell, for instance, a verbose, comically embittered singer in the Brel mould). They're calling this the New Routes Acoustic Scene, but it's just people strumming in pubs. N typically orders a whiskey and ginger ale (Ken Tynan's tipple) and sits back to enjoy the show. Like British cuisine, much of this fare makes you queasy, but there may be ideas worth stealing here and there. So what? Good chefs steal. That's what they do.

Niccolò Machiavelli: Should the prospective potentate desire a smooth transition to princedom there are several precepts it would be wise for him to follow. First and foremost he should consort only with women, for it is women who hold the purse strings in the market, and women who control the levers of power in the music industry. Female journalists, a female press officer, a female radio plugger, a female manager—all control the paths to greatness via entrances that can be moist, warm, and welcoming. Our prince should motivate women by coming, from time to time, into their beds, but he should be wary of possessiveness and exclusivity, for these women must also flirt with the men who control the radio and the press—they must, in other words, seem constantly available to all, even if this is only an illusion. Should an attractive blonde with a gap between her front teeth (let us call her Jennie) happen to be proofing a Momus record sleeve there in the new Rough Trade distribution centre on Collier Street—awash with an influx of money from the Smiths—our prince should ask her out for a drink and become her lover, assisted no doubt in this mission by the great quantities of ecstasy she is consuming (our potential potentate should take care not to touch the stuff himself, for the world in which *everyone else* is on ecstasy is ripe for exploitation). If Jennie's friend Margie, an artist manager, should then become intrigued by descriptions of the potentate's great vitality—supposedly left-swinging and shaped like a whole bag of aubergines in a boxing glove—all the better. Our prince-in-waiting should hasten to depart on a tour of France and Switzerland with one of Margie's pop groups—let us call them the Loved Up—and make love with the manageress "performatively" (extemporizing in whispers, for example, between thrusts, a strange poem about waves crashing tempestuously upon rocks) in a hotel room in Montmartre. It should not be necessary to hide these amorous episodes from the view of others: the impish record company boss—let us call him, for instance, Alan McGee—might well be planting playful seeds of gossip throughout the Clerkenwell Road building that houses both his own Creation Records and Out Promotions, staffed by Nicki and Dave Harper (last seen assisting Mike Alway at él). The insinuations will prime the pump for Nicki's amorous interest, which will then become a song entitled—I say this speculatively, yet the title pleases me—"The Hairstyle of the Devil," which Nicki will not only promote to radio stations (successfully, we presume, since the record will be A-listed by BBC Radio 1), but also garnish with her beauty: the tall and lithe plugger, Greek American, will appear on the twelve-inch sleeve ministering to our prince in a barber's shop as he sits—a pretender awaiting his inevitable coronation upon a red plastic throne—having his hair primped and permed by an Italian barber. The press release, furthermore, will recount the whole story: how Nicki was dating the boss of a successful record label—let us call him Martin Heath at

Rhythm King—simultaneously with Momus, and how the two men, through her, grew fascinated with each other. And here—pay heed, for this is important!—we discover the secret dynamic of what has been called, in modern times, "the homosocial": that it is precisely through women that men express their feelings about each other, and that if you want to get on in the world of men—who are, alas, the true potentates of the music industry, and of all others—you must do it not with letters, not with cassette tapes, not with gossip about football teams, not even with your profound common interest in money, but via women.

Saul Bellow: In 1987 I publish *More Die of Heartbreak*, a novel in which narrator Kenneth Trachtenberg anatomizes his uncle, the lustful botanist Benn Crader. Flush that year with cash from a publishing advance, N buys his first word processor, an Amstrad PCW 8256. The green columns and flashing cursor create a luminous grid of bars through which the documents peer like startled beasts in zoo parkland. N immediately wants to type; he wants to hear that constant industrious tapping, and see slender documents fattening and swelling as they feed on his thoughts. Inspired by my novel *Herzog*, he begins to write letters he may or may not send. He writes to celebrities, to crushes, to his boss. He makes a diary of his Primal Scream jaunt and sends it to Alan McGee. The result is that on their subsequent tour together McGee keeps mouthing the phrase "More tea, vicar?" This, it turns out, is because N has complained in his document about the Glaswegians farting in the tour van. Other letters bring embarrassments of their own. N is a member of the ICA, the swanky yet minimal arts club on the Mall, and starts to notice an interestingly ambivalent, doe-like figure flitting around its bars and lobbies. This is Lois Keidan, who works for the Live Arts department. She resembles a female David Bowie (who, incidentally, has just paid to fix the ICA's leaky roof). Each glimpse of Lois—surrounded by a halo of effulgent glamour partly conferred by her job—is accompanied by a flutter of shame on N's part. He begins to keep a diary of his sightings, writing lines like: "Lois's face in profile looks like a Ford Anglia" or "Lois is a thin man you could fuck." At the same time, he's educating himself about the kind of artists Lois is dealing with in her job: Pina Bausch, Michael Clark, the dance company DV8. One day, impulsively, he does something that Herzog never did: he mails the diary to Lois. This is embarrassing on many levels. Lois is possibly queer. The impression N gives in the document is that he himself may be gay, and may be seeking a suitably ambiguous beast, some satyr of the genders. But caution is called for: Lois has had a stalker, and worries that N might be another. Eventually they arrange to go for dinner at a restaurant in Chinatown. Lois talks about Plato's idea that we are half men, destined to search fruitlessly for our missing selves. N describes his work, his aspirations. But nothing is resolved, and N subsequently bulges with self-consciousness whenever he sets foot in the ICA. A letter to Neil Tennant of the Pet Shop Boys fares no better. It spouts on for pages about how tempting it must be to blurt out the secrets of one's sexuality, despite the fact that this might be a career-ending event (the gayness of the Pet Shop Boys is at that time a matter of broad innuendo). The letter sounds like an old-fashioned attempt at blackmail, and Neil is not amused. Nevertheless, the Pet Shop Boys select "The Hairstyle of the Devil" as their favorite new single. Word filters back through mutual friends that Neil has suggested that Momus sign with their old manager, Tom Watkins, and perhaps record for the label the group is planning to launch, Spaghetti Records. Nothing comes of this; Spaghetti signs a Scottish disco sissy called Cicero instead. Gradually the Herzog thing is forgotten and the Amstrad is set to more useful tasks: compiling articles about French singers for the World Music pages of the *New Musical Express*, or composing Momus lyrics. Unlike the ill-judged letters—irrevocable once sent—files stocked between a word processor's green bars are soft and infinitely malleable, tolerant of endless reflection and refinement. The Amstrad documents, their desires and ambitions muffled, learn circumspection and the cork-heeled reticence of the British.

J. G. Ballard: It is the future and I am dead. You met me once at the October Gallery in London, do you remember? William Burroughs was showing his shotgun paintings. He'd exploded colours onto canvas, squeezing the trigger of a shotgun, unapologetic about that awkward William Tell game he'd once played with his wife. Bill stood jawing like a cheerful old ghost. Genesis P-Orridge was there too, you told him Serge Gainsbourg's address, I remember that. How is Genesis? Oh, I'm sorry to hear that! I can remember things quite clearly now: after death, one's memory inches towards perfection. Somehow the technology of the future is allowing you to write in my voice, using my thoughts and memories, even though you and I are different people. I'm not quite sure where I am, but I know that you are on the Place d'Aligre in Paris. You have just bought six books, mostly by old French poets. You've looked at some secondhand clothes in Guerrisol, but nothing has taken your fancy. On the terrace at Le Penty you've downed a *noisette*, which is what the French call an espresso with milk. You are writing your memoirs for a distinguished New York publisher. You always threatened to become this sort of elderly francophile littérateur, didn't you? A man of letters, a flâneur, and a dandy. You're in your element, N. Today you want to write about encounters with two women you loved, Jane and Beatrice. You will use me to do it, because I share your interest in twisted sexuality. Jane and Beatrice were friends at art school. Beatrice we already know about: your great first love.

Nothing happened in the seventies with Beatrice. One day in the mid-eighties she came down to London and asked to stay with you. It was Easter, and the Draycott Place flat was empty. You slept on the sofa in the sitting room, fully clothed, and gave Beatrice your "canary cage" room. Late in the morning she still wasn't up. Suddenly a powerful surge of lust sprang up in you. You took all your clothes off and just walked straight into the room where Beatrice was. It was one of those moments when the mask on the face of reality slips and you feel as if you're living a dream. You must have looked absurd, with that gigantic erection bobbing at your waist! Beatrice was lying in your bed. She calmly held back the duvet in welcome. You lay on top of her and came almost the instant your cock touched the warm flesh of her tummy. With Jane it was more complicated. She invited you to a house where she was doing an artist's residency. You had just written "A Complete History of Sexual Jealousy (Parts 17–24)" and I was working on a detective novel, *Running Wild*. Late one night Jane came into your bedroom and told you that sex was something she could scent like a spoor on the breeze. You held her hand and just said: "I like you very, very much, Jane." Later you came into her room and touched her ear gently. "You're very tender . . . but it just makes me wish my boyfriend were here." You cried. The boyfriend was in South America, his name was Michael. Jane went off to Igloolik and spent six months with Inuit people. They were alcoholic, and the men beat the women, Jane said. You made music for her exhibition. You were in love with Jane, but—as with Beatrice—believed the situation to be hopeless. She was religious, and naïve. You told her on a Scottish train once that there was a present you wanted to give her: cunnilingus. "Is that a kind of cake?" she asked sweetly. But one day Jane too came to the "canary cage" and you lay on the bloodred duvet and banqueted together on cake. I'm not sure if I would have put it quite so coyly, but this is your memoir. And I remember everything.

Derek Jarman: It's amazing what petty things we can take pride in. When I was diagnosed with HIV no one quite knew what this disease was or what it meant. It was still getting referred to in hushed tones as "the gay cancer." There were rumours that it was a death sentence. But at least I could congratulate myself on being an early adopter. In 1987 the British government took it upon itself to educate people about the risks. A leaflet headlined "AIDS: Don't die of ignorance!" was pushed through the letterboxes of twenty-one million households. The leaflet said that the high-risk categories were homosexuals, intravenous drug users, and "fast-track heterosexuals." This term fascinated N. Who were these "fast-track heterosexuals," and how could he become one? A campaign designed to urge caution might have had the opposite effect, you see, and made some people want to live dangerously. I got a bit of stick—in, for instance, that *Face to Face* interview I did with Jeremy Isaacs on Channel 4—for remaining sexually active after my diagnosis. I would head up to Hampstead Heath. As I told Jeremy, everybody knew me up there, so they also knew my condition. At the time I was achieving a sort of queer canonisation. The young were seeking me out. N's Irish friend David Butler used to come and see me at my flat on the Charing Cross Road. People would make day trips to look at my clapboard cottage on the alien shingle at Dungeness, in the eerie shadow of the nuclear power station. I met N after he sang on the soundtrack of my film *Blue* in 1993. I wasn't well at all; my face had come up in unsightly welts, and I kept losing and regaining my sight. For the soundtrack Brian Eno kindly donated his home studio in Woodbridge, so N worked there with Simon Fisher Turner on a song called "Cock-Sucking Lesbian Man." Eno's mother was hovering around, but Brian himself was away somewhere. The lyrics were mine; N added melody and arrangement and sang. The refrain went: "I am a not-gay." N and Simon started cracking up during the sessions. They were doing this coming-out statement—a refusal to be categorised, really—as a kind of football chant, and in the middle of it they just got these fits of paroxysmal giggles, the kind you could almost choke on. Death hung over that film like an Yves Klein shroud. "Well, that'll go down in history!" I said, rather cheerfully, when we watched the sequence together in a preview cinema in Soho. When N shook my hand that evening—it was our first meeting—he said: "I'm very pleased to have met you!" The choice of verb was telling. We both noticed, and although it was dark I sensed a blush. It was as if he were saying: "I'm glad I had the opportunity to meet you before you croaked, Derek." I got a lot of that. There was obviously a near future in which I no longer featured, except for my features: my films and photographs of my face. It turns out that N's brother Mark is an academic who specialises in the literary implications of verb tense, and the presence of death in narrative. So he's particularly focused on the future perfect: that which will have been. The future perfect makes us aware of a perspective beyond the end of the story: it might be the narrator's perspective, or God's, or the way that history remembers us. It's essential to any kind of narrative: a future ordering of events, the now seen by a then that is—from the audience's perspective—still to come, yet unreachable: a flash-forward to a flashback. *Blue* is a film absolutely soaked in the "will-have-been," or what David Bowie much later called the "not-quite-yet." The suffusing, inescapable colour is the light of a pitiless future that stretches to all horizons: the permanent state that awaits us all. You'd half expect the audience to be turned to stone, petrified by that blue view which can only exist beyond the moment of our own destruction, somewhere in the terribly perfect, perfectly terrible future.

Robert Walser: Only much later did literary fanatics, as mad in their own way as me, decode my microscripts—the tiny stories I had been writing in a Gothic calligraphy of my own devising on postcards, calendar pages, envelopes, business cards, receipts. At a time when the ink pen and the foolscap page completely terrorised me, these provisional and private scribblings in pencil were a clear way forward. On a scrap of toilet paper I sketched out a miniature cosmology in which a voyeuristic god masturbates in order to create new worlds with his seedy explosions. On the back of a beer mat I placed a cautionary tale about some homosexual ice skaters whose honesty becomes their downfall. In the margins of a communist pamphlet I inscribed with careful illegibility the self-epitaph of a Maoist who wishes he had been a double agent, and on a handbill for a dubious club in Zürich I imagined an effeminate man who uses his presumed homosexuality as a cover for adulterous adventures with the wives of the men who disdain him. One day I found a strip of Japanese paper, and on it composed a rambling picaresque about a beautiful young man destined to die young, who shames himself and his mentor by living to a ripe old age. An unfilled prescription picked up from a clinic floor became a pretext for a story about an invalid whose heart is on the wrong side of his body. Another scrap—the backside of a billet-doux—anatomised exhaustively all the jealousies that exist in this world. And then I scratched, with a pin on an ice cube, the tale of a man who pretends to be cold when his heart is actually warm. Unfortunately, that manuscript melted. A tale about sanatoria was inevitable, since I was by this time living in one, so I wrote a microscopic *Moritat*—on the back of a ticket authorising a bus route through the mountains—about a man who deliberately keeps his lover feeble. My final *Mikrogramme* was about a man who remains innocent no matter how many sins he commits; it may have owed something to Wilde's Dorian Gray. But the thing I am most proud of is to have hidden these tales in a place where no one will ever find them: on a long-playing gramophone record by Momus called *Tender Pervert*.

Joe Orton: The normies had found a new way to kill the queens—with some sort of swamp malaria, apparently. A monkey fever shipped in from the great grey-green greasy Limpopo. Of course, they could simply have pushed us under electric milk floats, or left us to smash each other's skulls in with hammers. That was highly effective in my case. But killing us wasn't enough—they also had to make it clear that our way of life wasn't a thing they endorsed at all. And so in the spring of 1988 the Conservatives enacted Section 28, a piece of legislation designed to make schools and libraries in Britain stop "promoting homosexuality." Isn't that a scream? Presumably homosexuality might otherwise have advanced through the ranks, eventually reaching the position of major or even general. The Edna Welthorpes of the world were up in arms again. N—who was "queer" without actually being, you know, omi-polone—was furious. If the government was planning to gag the nancies, camp must fall to others. There had to be a quantum of mincing, you see, for Blighty to remain even half amusing. And so the 1988 album from Momus was code-named *The Homosexual.* N was going to hoist all that stifled difference onto his own back. He was going to die for our sins, up there on Camp Calvary. There was a quote on the sleeve from Yours Truly: "Give me the ability to rage correctly." Along with a nice piece of advice from Deuteronomy: "Circumcise the foreskin of your heart." And lashings of Mishima, Gide, and Bataille—the usual suspects. There was just one snag: according to Creation Records, the Canadian licensee Polygram wouldn't touch an album called *The Homosexual* with a barge pole. It reminds me of the palaver I had with my script for the Beatles, and how their boring, closeted manager Brian Epstein thought *Up Against It* would bring the lads into disrepute. What a hoot! All Momus had to change was the title: his record became *Tender Pervert.* And all the Beatles would have had to do was act; a film should be masquerade, a splash of carnival, a chance to dress up! McCartney later said the reason they rejected my script was that they weren't gay, but what would have been the harm in pretending? The fans would have loved it, and it might have provided more interest than an actually gay group being actually gay. The Section 28 legislation was very vehement about homosexuality not being allowed to pass itself off as any kind of "pretended family relationship"—there was a moral panic about adoption at the time—but what it condemned gay people to was passing. The masquerade was to be ours, and it was to be in the direction of a pretended, supposedly aspirational, dullness and normality. Fuck off, seriously. In those conditions, why shouldn't straights rise up and pass themselves off as gay? What is a scapegoat, really, but a sheep in a cape?

Alexander Graham Bell: When I invented the telephone in the 1870s the last thing I had in mind was that it should be used for sexual purposes. And yet this is precisely what occurred to N, an Edinburgh lad like myself, brought up just across Charlotte Square. A sort of pervasive sexual paranoia led him to explore the erotic possibilities of being connected telephonically to a person of the opposite gender. Actually, the idea was first put into his head by his mother. In the late 1970s she was having an affair with an accountant, and after one protracted conversation asked her teenaged sons: "Do you think a man could get excited just by listening to a woman's voice on the phone?" At the time the boys just shrugged—the idea of *anyone* getting sexually excited by their mother was somewhat grotesque—but the exchange must have lodged itself in N's mind. A decade or so later he had an unsuccessful date with a Scottish lass called Allison—pale skin, dark hair, Islington red lipstick, bolshy round glasses—who worked for a Japanese newspaper in London. I say "unsuccessful" because although N was invited into her bedroom, he never got beyond kissing. There was no follow-up date, but one day N had the filthy idea to call Allison's number at the newspaper and say nothing at all. He orgasmed on the second "*Asahi Shimbun*?" and hung up feeling intensely guilty. This event must have rattled N like a motorcar (that monstrous creation of Benz), because he was soon telling the *Record Mirror* that his songs were "like dirty phone calls to God" and singing about "the first obscene phone call" in his phonographic recordings (a system spawned by that fiend Edison). Calvinist guilt ensured that his career as a telephonic pervert was not very extensive—though I do recall overhearing, with horrible embarrassment, one conversation in which, exaggerating his Scottish accent, he promised to ejaculate over an art student's freckled nose—but it left deep scars in his psyche. For a while, any casual mention of the words "phone" or "telephone" would make him flinch visibly. The funny thing is that this was the era of hot chat lines, rap tracks about booty calls, and Nicholson Baker's *Vox*, a time when the association of sex and telephones had become utterly banal and even American presidents dialed with sticky fingers. But N, terrified by what he saw as a dangerous and omnipresent temptation, went the other way, avoiding and eventually abjuring phones entirely. Oddly enough, I entirely sympathize: I invented the telephone by accident while working on a cure for deafness, but refused to have one of the damn things on my desk.

Giacomo Casanova: Amorous confidence came to our protagonist but belatedly; it was the critical success of his light operettas that made him feel worthy of the attentions of women, but the good reviews came sometimes with cautionary advice: "How does this soft and tender poet lead his life guided by what dangles between his legs?" demanded one *Melody Maker* chronicler, as if the dangling beast did not, quite rightly, serve as a plump-headed Virgil to all men of vitality. The scribe continued with a description of how he had witnessed the "randy bedsit poet and chat-up merchant" in action at a party near Kew Gardens: "He was bloody good, apart from when one girl told him to fuck off." The early London years had in fact seen N rejected often as he rose through a dating purgatory of tired Irish nurses, activist Brixton teachers, and hearty Sloane Rangers before finding his niche as the "randy sod" *Melody Maker*'s readers were now being warned against. But something heartening began to occur. In response to records laying bare a pronounced interest in the erotic, letters from women began to arrive saying, *en substance*: "O thou giant corrupter, do not neglect me!" These communications came from girls of all classes and positions in life. There was the coal miner's daughter, who invited N to Nottingham. Shy N hid in the guest bedroom, but the slim, pale girl arrived in her slip and by morning the fireplace was full of crumpled tissues. With her big eyes and a tiny frame, she could be carted around London on the carrier of N's sturdy black bicycle. Another, a corvine and curvy Frankfurt disk jockey, arrived for a sex holiday and consented to be recorded during the demonstrative transports of her ecstasy; N used the guttural love cries as percussion in his recording of "The Homosexual." In 1989 he dated a Japanese woman for the first time and was impressed by her intimate knowledge of the work of Jean Cocteau. "Nicholas, you are torturing me!" she whispered as he bared her breasts in the shrubbery at Battersea Park. One ran a poetry club and liked to gasp "Slow down! Slow down!" during N's private performances. Another, meanwhile—halfway to becoming a gay man called Joe—had her breasts bandaged flat and was hurt one day when N accidentally used the wrong personal pronoun. Particularly rich was the era in which N was described as "the third Pet Shop Boy": two girls beat a path to his door in the belief—not entirely misguided—that he was a heterosexual Neil Tennant. While N had been swayed by Cesare Pavese's sad axiom that "intellect, like a great glittering machine, leaves most women utterly cold," he was beginning to discover that fame—even just a light smattering of the stuff, shading into infamy—can be a powerful aphrodisiac.

Angela Carter: "Be careful what you wish for." It might be a moral from Hans Christian Andersen or the Grimms. It might even be one of Sade's "misfortunes of virtue." Sometimes the saying is attributed to Goethe, sometimes to a Chinese sage. But there is evidence that it's right. Success—the fulfilment of wishes—kills its little winners with extraordinary efficiency. Studies have shown that musicians who have a Top 10 album die at the age of fifty-seven, on average. They croak wracked with the delights of drink and drugs, forked bloody by the demons of untrammelled self-indulgence. They are prescribed fatal painkillers by trusted personal doctors, they smash their expensive sports cars into the concrete walls of parking garages, they fall screaming from helicopters or prang their hoverboards in alligator swamps. Theirs are rich lives, fast and chaotic, profligate and prodigal, stuffed with peak experiences and fuzzy, drooling deliria. Theirs are the lives the Bible warns us against, and Satan advertises. Success stinks of goat, or perhaps resembles Morrissey, whom N sometimes glimpses slinking down the King's Road in a broad-brimmed hat, desperately trying not to be recognised. In 1989—incidentally, the year my body starts concocting the lung cancer that will kill me—N faces a dilemma: to be a pop star or not. To jump onto that golden bus or let it pass him by. He's already making enough money, thanks to his 50/50 profit split deal with Creation Records, to sign off the dole. He's at last having enough sexual intercourse. His acoustic guitar noodlings have turned into electronic throbbings. In the autumn of 1988

there's been a significant tour of France with Alan McGee's band
Biff Bang Pow. The venues have seemed to get smaller at each stop:
from a shopping mall via a country disco to an anarchist café. In
Toulouse, McGee throws a drink in the promoter's face and quits.
Momus continues, joining tours headlined by the Shamen and the
Beloved—dance groups influenced by the acid house sounds now
coming out of Detroit and Chicago. When he returns to London,
N records "The Hairstyle of the Devil" in a studio above a Beth-
nal Green lumberyard. It's Charles Aznavour recording with Kevin
Saunderson, the Pet Shop Boys wrestling a Colette story down
to four verses. BBC Radio 1 is playing the record daily to millions
when N enters the studio to make the follow-up: a bhangra-powered
piece of disco Buddhism called "Lord of the Dance":

> *In man is no abiding entity*
> *In things no abiding reality*
> *Fantastic illusion is everywhere*

The engineer's wife tells N: "I haven't heard your music, but Nigel
tells me that you're becoming successful, and I admire success."
This is what winning would bring: the blurry, blurring admiration
of the ignorant and the indifferent. Another track from the sessions,
"Lifestyles of the Rich and Famous," is a pastiche of the Stock, Aitken, and Waterman sound then conquering the charts. The narrator has lost his girl to a flashier competitor. He's not even on his own
side: "It didn't seem important . . . I was wrong." The values of the
mainstream are toxic, but what if one could become successful by
parodying them? What if a pastiche could pass itself off as the very
thing it was mocking? Smart people would understand the song as
a critique of opportunistic Thatcherism, the stupid would hear a
celebration of their own flashy aspirations. But that is clearly a path

to hell. The experiment is never tried: "The Hairstyle of the Devil" does well as an indie single, but stiffs in the mainstream. Neither Creation nor Momus sees any virtue in releasing a follow-up single. As Socrates said: "Life contains but two tragedies. One is not to get your heart's desire, the other is to get it."

1990–2000

I am a lie which is constantly telling the truth.

—Jean Cocteau

John Braine: Five years after graduating and moving to London, N has the sort of life he's always wanted. He's thirty and living in London in a room just off Sloane Square. He's signed off the dole thanks to publishing advances and the money he's made on European concert tours. The music press is ranking his albums on the Creation label among the year's best, and they're selling more than enough to make back their costs. American and Japanese women are beating a path to his door; for a while he courts a succession of graduates from Sarah Lawrence, the famous liberal arts college. In early 1990 he moves to Cleveland Street, renting a ground-floor flat in the shadow of the Telecom Tower, a suitably thrusting symbol of ambition. He invites an erstwhile Creation secretary—an elegant Felt fan from New Zealand who looks like a shorter, bustier Audrey Hepburn—to live with him and she moves in, papering her room with Andy Warhol cow wallpaper she's stolen from an exhibition at the Hayward Gallery. Dark-eyed, dimpled Vicky now works at the Design Council Bookshop and is dating Lawrence, formerly Felt's front man, who now has a neo-glam postmodern rock project called Denim. Lawrence arrives daily to eat spaghetti and watch the soaps, then retreats to Vicky's room to have sex. It seems to N that Vicky submits because Lawrence is her idol, rather than for the inherent pleasures of sex: she proclaims that she's never had an orgasm, and indeed finds it hard to believe that such things exist. Her passion is for other things: French girl-pop and *Twin Peaks*, mostly. Each new episode of David Lynch's cult series becomes a party in the darkened kitchen of the Cleveland Street flat, with a rotating cast of friends—Tammy, Douglas, Kevin, Vici, Iain, Malcolm, Phil—arriving bearing slices of cherry pie and "damn fine coffee." N buys a Sony Handicam and documents this newfound sociability on Video 8. There are tapes of folk gigs in clubs, tapes of recording sessions out at the Spike studio in Fulham, and tapes of his sex life, which is becoming increasingly demanding. On a particularly busy day in which N—like an overstretched gynaecologist—consults with three different girls in the privacy of his bedroom, Vicky explodes with indignation: "I hope you die of AIDS!" It's a rare moment of conflict: the flatmates stay the best of friends, and when Vicky has to go into hospital, it's N who comes to visit her.

Serge Gainsbourg: I never actually meet N, but I do hear from him. My attention is first drawn to a hagiographic article he's written about me for the *New Musical Express*. What's amusing is that it appears in the World Music section, as though France were Indonesia or Brazil. Then a mutual friend, a British singer in Paris called Bill Pritchard, gives me a CD of *Tender Pervert* with a handwritten letter from N confessing that his song "In the Sanatorium" is my song "Pull Marine"—a hit for Isabelle Adjani in 1983—"*détourné au clef mineur.*" This is a play on words: the song has been adapted into a minor key, but there's also a reference to the sleeve of my last album, *You're Under Arrest*, which shows me bruised and unrepentant in a series of police mug shots. My crime, listed prominently at the top right-hand side of the sleeve, is *détournement de mineurs*: the corruption of youth. Which is of course what old Socrates had to glug the hemlock for. The final request—one which I accept—is to meet N in Paris on camera: he is to interview me for a new music show on British TV called *World Café*. N's idea is that he will ask me some questions, then kneel at my feet and receive some kind of humorous symbolic imprimatur, some gesture nominating Momus as my authorised Anglo-Saxon licensee and successor. Gainsbourgism is not a franchise like McDonald's, but it's an amusing idea; British pop has always been important to me, but I've had little impact in the country where I recorded so many of my hits. Unfortunately, Channel 4 demands a two-thousand-pound subsidy from Creation to cover the cost of getting a film crew to Paris, and the interview is called off. The next thing you know Momus is recording his most Gainsbourgian record, entitled *Hippopotamomus*. And—pop!—just as it's about to come out I die of a heart attack, aged sixty-two. It's a personal tragedy for me and my family, of course, and a sad refutation of my theory that longevity is my destiny because "smoke preserves meat, and alcohol fruit." But I do live on, in Momus and in many other successors. I thrive—spores in agar—in the petri dish of culture.

Josephine Baker: I loved the fact that I got a mention in the song "Michelin Man" on *Hippopotamomus*. But Michelin U.K. didn't love their motif, their mastiff—damn, what's the word?—their mascot, thank you, getting compared to a sex toy. The song goes:

> *The Michelin man, made of rubber*
> *The Michelin man, Josephine Baker*
> *Make him Zeppelin big on your bicycle pump*
> *And he'll bump you 'til your bed's just junk*

Well, apparently those lyrics were read out at a board meeting, and it was agreed that legal action would have to be taken. I'm sorry, but it just makes me shriek with laughter to imagine that scene. "Now we turn to item three, a popular song which mocks our glorious leader, Bib." They must've had about twenty feet of white picket rail up their asses. The thing is, their mascot, Mr. Bibendum, is based on a character who's a bon vivant, a gourmet with a bulgy gullet. His image originated in a beer hall in Munich. *"Nunc est bibendum"* means, basically, what the hell, let's get drunk! Now's the time, baby! Sure, Michelin made tires, and nobody should drink and drive. But back in the twenties tires on cars existed so you could go from one fabulous restaurant to the next, and hang some big tires of flab on your belly. And as a big-spending high-lifer Mr. Bibendum would've loved to bump me and junk my damn bed, I know it. Especially if he saw me doing the *Danse Sauvage* in my banana skirt! So why he had to come off that album sleeve I just don't know. After poor Paul White had put so much effort into drawing him! Only his hippo head is left now, and how in the hell are you supposed to eat or dance or fuck with just a head? Hmm? Humans have no guts anymore. It's all been downhill since 1929.

Christian Enzensberger: The *Hippopotamomus* album is dirt. It is nothing. Zero out of ten is the mark the *New Musical Express* awards it, because marks out of ten have suddenly become a thing. This nothing will not—like previous Momus albums—make the critics' year-end lists. It will be consigned to the slurry huts, the charnel pits. This nothing is the moment when Momus and the surrounding critical community break apart: they no longer share common terms of reference, common understandings of the good. In the previous decade N has been able to publish articles about Brel and Gainsbourg in the music press in order to create a little context for his way of making records. (There was to have been a third article, an interview with Jake Thackray, a satirical British singer influenced by Georges Brassens, but Thackray designated a pub on the M4 which N, carless, was unable to reach.) With the arrival of the new decade a page has been turned. The music press no longer references Bataille, Baudrillard, and Nietzsche, as it might have done in 1981. Now football is the preferred metaphor. There are clear signs of the "lad culture" to come: in 1994 an ex-NME editor will launch *Loaded*, a monthly magazine known as "the lad's Bible," larded with moronic hedonism and ironic sexism. The so-called Hip-Hop Wars of the mid-eighties have been lost by the black artists, who are effectively banished from the covers of the three U.K. weekly music papers despite making the most original music of the time. The white indie guitar band now reigns supreme, although the "indie" will often turn out to be a major label in disguise. This state of affairs—this sad new something—is called "Britpop," and its symbol is the Union Jack. *Hippopotamomus* has been influenced by De La Soul and Little Richard, by Georges Bataille and Serge Gainsbourg and the Italian Futurists, but its most important manifesto is to be found in a book-length essay of mine called *Smut: An Anatomy of Dirt*. Published by Calder & Boyars in 1972, *Smut* looks into the transgressive and redeeming qualities not just of dirt itself, but of everything denoted as "dirty" by culture. The hippopotamus is an animal that delights in wallowing in mud. Transgression and the paradoxical sublimity of filth determines the content of the songs. "I Ate a Girl Right Up" features a narrator who wants to "cross the line dividing clean from dirty." The idea comes straight out of *Smut*, but reviews compare it to the big Hollywood film of the day, *Silence of the Lambs*. Where there are no common terms of reference there can really only be confusion, anger, conflict, and separation. The press release for *Hippopotamomus* proposes itself as an imaginary documentary—a tapestry of interwoven voices prefiguring the fake "oral history" format of this book—but it's really a scathing broadside against the values beginning to take hold in the Britain of 1991. This is no longer a culture willing to be educated about other ways of thinking and feeling. The breakdown in communications will lead, within three years, to N leaving Britain and taking up residence in Paris, where he will enjoy his greatest commercial success writing songs about sex for the Japanese.

Leonard Cohen: The first chapter of my novel *The Favourite Game* is about scars and how they mark the bodies of my characters. The second is about wrinkles and Russia. The rest is mostly about sex. But I am summoned here to speak of N, and his final farcical conquest of his teenage sweetheart. It happens at his sister's wedding. Emma is marrying Steve, who works in theatre. The reception happens at the Edinburgh Language Foundation on Great Stuart Street. No expense is spared. There are highland reels with fiddlers, and aunts and uncles unseen for years, and awkward cousins, and speeches to make you wince, and champagne. That's crucial. Lots of the very best champagne. Beatrice arrives without her sister, who is in Alicante with the rest of the family. N has come up from London. He's no longer the drooping plant of 1979 who sat in Beatrice's living room in Marchmont and twitched as she played *Songs from a Room*. (Beatrice came to my concert at the Usher Hall in 1976, and I became her favourite singer.) Now N glows with confidence. Now he is something of a ladies' man—firm, forward, frisky, building quickly to the pathetic climax which goes, always, in essence:

Won't you let me see your naked body

There's a certain effervescence at the collegiate stairwell. Heads are lightened. The whole scene is dizzy and fizzing. Beatrice is giggling, stuffing balloons down her blouse. N, the ladies' man, doesn't hesitate for a moment. He leads her upstairs to an empty classroom. The didactic strip lights blaze down on the whiteboard and there are no curtains, but champagne will keep the couple safe from shame. N sits Beatrice down and kisses her dry lips until they open and become wet. Soon they've slid from the hard chair to the floor. An expression of surprise but also respect comes over Beatrice's face. N should have acted like this years ago! She suggests they continue at her family house; it's empty this week. They leave the party without goodbyes—the dancers are far gone—and take a taxi to Marchmont. At the flat N is deeply excited. The front door cannot close too quickly, the kettle creeps with agonizing slowness toward the boil. He strips off his clothes until he's only wearing a pink shirt, from which his prong, alert and vengeful, protrudes. Beatrice is taking her time. She will drink coffee, she will shower, she will chat as if nothing unusual were occurring. But at last the moment of truth arrives. The lovers are on the bed preparing the favourite game. It is time for the old ceremony in various positions. Forgive me, I am not usually so self-referential. What's the line I came up with, once?

Hungry as an archway through which the troops have passed

Well, that is not how it is. Not at all. Impenetrability. The troops, in a heightened state of readiness for battle, must hang back. Willing at last, the beloved cannot be possessed. "This door was meant for you alone, and now I am going to close it," as the flea-ridden gatekeeper puts it in Kafka's parable "Before the Law." Or, if I can paraphrase what Marx said in *The Eighteenth Brumaire of Louis Napoleon*, himself paraphrasing Hegel: "History plays the first time as tragedy, the second as farce." That's a good line. N should put that in a song one day.

Ray Bradbury: It is the summer of 1992, and five musicians are setting off for a concert tour of Mars. N, the singer, is nervous about the approaching rocket flight—the longest he will ever have embarked upon. He goes to a general practitioner on Fitzroy Square to ask for Valium, but the whiskery old man chuckles: "If I prescribe Valium now, and the voyage is fine, you will always believe you need the same drug. But if you make this great journey undrugged, and all goes well, you will realize that your own resources are all you require." The doctor is right: once the rocket leaves the Earth's atmosphere the voyage is smooth and seems to pass in hours. Soon the five friends—Tammy, Douglas, Damian, Neill, and N—are being met by the Martian tour agency, which is called Creative Man. The air on Mars is humid and sticky, and at the arrival pad there are vending machines selling strange drinks called Pocari Sweat and Positonic Sports Water. The alien musicians slake their thirst, then the Creative Man operatives bring them in a people-carrier to Oykot, the great Martian capital, which spills and fizzes like a pacific surf of low white buildings toward the majestic volcano called Ijuf. The city is punctuated by soaring chimneys and crisscrossed by concrete canals. The musicians have been booked into a hotel atop a hill in the lively western district of Ayubihs. Zebra crossings zigzag across hot tree-lined streets at crazy angles, bisecting vertiginous glass-walled department stores that seem to have been styled after mistaken memories of Italy and France, or cinemas in the shape of ziggurats draped with curtains of concrete. N is interviewed by a group of fat girls—shy yet bold, with buck teeth, dressed in black—who produce a fanzine dedicated to him. It's called *Guitar Lessons*. Neill buys a briefcase marked, for no apparent reason, "Scottish Sheep Dog." Mars is a looking-glass world resonant with decontextualized echoes, phrases containing warped dreams of life on Earth, even misinterpreted visions of oneself: a record shop near the hotel features a display for a record by an artist called the Poison Girlfriend. For dinner N—unable to decipher the Martian script on the menu—orders randomly and receives "Congealed Egg of Trpong," which is vile and sulfuric, the ancient spawn of some crater-creature. On the hotel TV, porn plays constantly behind a blur of cubic pixels that make every act seem both vague and lubricious. Sex on Mars happens differently than sex back home: pubic hair seems to be taboo, and yet the most obscene acts are apparently perfectly acceptable. During breakfast—a nonsensical meal featuring hundreds of microscopic dishes—N observes crowds of demure Victorian-Martian schoolgirls making their way to school in impeccable pleated skirts and spotless jackets. On the radio they're playing his Glasgow cousin, Justin, but perhaps it's some new invention and everyone on Mars hears the music that means most to them? There's time for a visit to the invisible palace of the planetary emperor before the sound check at Club Orttauq, which is located beyond the top escalator of a closed, and yet still-open, department store. The ticket price would feed a family back on Earth for a week, yet the show sells out, and N is greeted backstage by Martian celebrities like Suilenroc, the monkey singer. N performs wearing a T-shirt he has bought in the nightlife district of Ukujnihs—it features a druggy pill-shaped design, yet real drugs are quite unknown on Mars; like the whiskery London doctor, the Martians seem to know that their own inner resources can match any intoxicant. And indeed the combination of rocket-lag and the skewed, surreal nature of everything one experiences in the Martian environment produces a more powerfully hallucinogenic effect than any mushroom or acid tab. On the hyperloop journey back from the concerts in Mars's second and third cities, Akaso and Ayogan, Douglas finds whale bacon sandwiches on the train menu. Identical ticky-tacky houses flicker by, punctuated by tiny mountains and plastic simulacra of Christian churches. The hyperloop reaches and leaves stations with an almost fascist exactitude, and the English announcements are made by a synthetic Joanna Lumley with a sympathetic head cold. Back in Oykot the friends dine beneath a gigantic golden turd designed by Philippe

Starck. The city seems to present itself to each band member as a personal utopia: percussionist Damian admires the massive bridges and hunts for men at dusk near the temple (the Martians follow a powerfully sexual cultic religion organized around the regenerating power of nature) while synth player Neill flirts with the elevator ladies in the Panasonic Museum only to find they're actually robots. Casio operative Douglas buys Gamemen and Walkboys in Arabahika, the "electric town." As the days pass, an unexpectedly warm and folksy side begins to replace the first brash impressions of Mars's cold futurity. The Earthlings visit the straw-floored bungalow of a fan—whether male or female it's difficult to say—called Urahihc, who shows N books by an artist called Okenak. A cross between the unsettling surrealist sex diagrams of André Masson and Tenniel's illustrations for *Alice in Wonderland*, the drawings make a strong impression. N returns from his first trip to Mars filled with a kind of nostalgia for the future. Back on Earth, he finds himself deeply unsatisfied with London, a city that now looks stubbornly prosaic, putty brown. This trip "through the looking glass" has been the first taste of a drug that will claim years of his life.

Yukio Mishima: Summer comes fleetingly to Edinburgh, bringing festival days that seem to hold sunset back until the last possible moment. The season cannot fail to remind a sensitive youth of the infinite fragility of life and the noble splendour of a death freely embraced. Each return to his homeland gives N—already, in his early thirties, too old for a beautiful martyrdom—a clear view of the slow encroachments of annihilation. In her New Town flat his mother's face is etched with new lines, visible when she stands by the living room window and gazes across Moray Place Gardens to the silhouette of the castle, illuminated at dusk by the exploding colours of martial fireworks. At the Lyceum they're showing my

Five Modern Noh Plays, and N is impressed by my reworking of Kan'ami's *Sotoba Komachi*. On the Lyceum stage a ninety-nine-year-old woman meets a poet in a park and tells him that anyone who compliments her beauty must die. It doesn't seem like a risk until, by some supernatural magic, the pair are transported back to a ballroom many decades before. Suddenly the old lady is young and beautiful, and the poet cannot prevent himself from falling in love with her. He announces that he loves her, regardless of the price he must pay. Death comes swiftly, but the poet is just able to hear the lady whispering the news that they will meet again in a century. This combination of ghostliness, morbidity, time travel, aestheticism, sexuality, and melancholy impresses N deeply, and inspires the style that will dominate his next two albums, *Voyager* and *Timelord*. It evokes wistful distances and epic journeys across regions of endless emptiness—the spaces one might see from a jet crossing Siberia, for instance. N calls the style "Science Fiction Melodrama." The first fruit appears in the form of a song called "Summer Holiday 1999," recorded for a Japanese compilation called *Fab Gear*. The song recounts the plot of Shusuke Kaneko's 1988 film *Summer Vacation 1999*. Four boys stay in a futuristic boarding school during the summer break. One commits suicide after declaring feelings of love for another. Suddenly a new pupil appears who is the dead boy's double. In the film the boys are played by teenage girls, adding a new layer of ambivalence and homoeroticism. After the crude provocations of *Hippopotamomus*, the new style represents a return to sensibility and refinement. There are traces of an "electronic inwardness" N has discovered in Japan, but also a foreboding: we are in a world in which love is new but "the weather's wrong." This landscape becomes blindingly bleak as we advance into it, weeping over a young couple who—surrounded by herons and cranes—have opted to die together in the snow, or an astronaut who has returned from a space voyage so long in Earth years that he has outlived everyone he ever knew. These are themes familiar to me: to die young is a tragedy, but to live on might be worse.

Jacques Derrida: I never met N, but I did meet his brother, Mark, whom I personally found to be a much more interesting character, outstripping his elder sibling as the neglected Epimetheus outstrips Prometheus. This was not clear to me the first time we interacted, for I was being hounded by Marxists and was in such a furious mood that I whirled away from Mark with a flourish and a conspicuous plume of silence. (Not having, at that point, listened to any Momus records, I also would have been ill-prepared at that moment to make comparisons.) But, yes, on the second occasion—which is of course the first I can actually remember, since the original meeting, the blanking, has been itself blanked out and sublimated in my memory—we engaged for a few minutes in casual conversation at a literary conference. N never met *his* hero, David Bowie, but I suspect that that would have been a similar moment for him: an apex, a zenith, a fulcrum. I found Mark a very thoughtful academic, a man whose silences, combined with his Brad Pitt–like good looks, spoke volumes. These lacunae were the very inverse of N's seemingly endless mediated self-dramatisations, with which I did eventually familiarise myself, in idle moments, as a footnote to my reluctant study of the music of Scritti Politti (who had named a song after me, for reasons not immediately obvious). I particularly admired Mark's complete abstention from the charades of social media—which, had I lived, I would have abjured rigorously and also written an interesting book about. I wonder if it is a coincidence that this family is full of experts in unreliable self-narration? I think not. Mark has an interesting lecture about self-narrators who use the third person in which he describes their father referring to himself as "Currie" while he re-creates, leaning enthusiastically across the family dinner table, the many conversational victories that have made up his working day. One of the axioms Mark lives by is Nicholson Baker's insight that the explanation of self-consciousness must ultimately turn outwards. This later guided his interest in Knausgaard (whom, had I lived, I would have ignored and also written an interesting book about). To Mark it seems clear that the main similarity between N and his father is the homology between Bill's self-narrations in the third person and N's technological self-archiving. (Of course, Mark has actually read my books *Archive Fever* and *The Post Card*—N's copies of these stand unopened on his shelves.) There is also common ground between Jo's assertion that she dresses to please herself and N's belief that he has, as a creative person, an "internal locus of evaluation" that makes him impervious to criticism. One need simply point out, with Freud, that this *Innerlichkeit* is more crowded than one might at first suspect: a hall of mirrors, an aporia, a *mise-en-abyme*. I agree with Eno: enough about genius, let us hear more of scenius! I am speaking of course of Brian Eno, not his brother, Roger.

Wyndham Lewis: It was all a great nonsense: the record labels with their fiercely independent ethos were as greedy as the gallerists and dealers had been back in my day. High ideals were not preventing Rough Trade from sinking, despite the money still pouring in from the Smiths' back catalogue. Daniel Miller—now dating Nicki, N's ex—had to step in to save Geoff Travis and the whole circus from bankruptcy. Major labels all had fake indies on their roster, and Creation was in negotiations with Sony, currently being castigated by George Michael for treating artists as "software." N didn't think that was such a bad thing to be—he even thought *Software* might make a funny album title—but he didn't believe Dick Green at Creation when he said that Sony part-ownership "would be good for Momus too." Meanwhile Nicki tantalised N, telling him that Daniel at Mute had been "intrigued" by the triangular situation sketched out in "The Hairstyle of the Devil" (the *disque-à-clef* detailed a love waltz between Nicki, N, and Martin Heath, the handsome ex-soldier running Rhythm King Records) and that in consequence he might want to sign Momus to Mute. We call this kind of intrigue "homosocial": ambitious men are fascinated with money and power, and therefore with each other. So they use women as proxies, go-betweens, sources of pillow talk, basal ganglia. But the message Nicki brought from Daniel was that Momus could only sign to Mute as a mainstream proposition like Erasure or Depeche Mode. There could be no solecisms, no self-indulgence, in short none of the things that make art really worth doing. A demo session was arranged at the Mute studio on the Harrow Road, but when N turned up there was no engineer to help him, and he couldn't even find the power switch on the desk. His manager did her best, but all she could achieve was an extension of his already-existing Creation contract: three more albums. N had little choice but to keep "optimising his marginality." Standing still in capitalism is a nigh-impossible task: in the early nineties if little labels weren't being bought up they were going under. Meanwhile the era was seething with new hordes of the veriest tyros: ruddy-faced, elemental, listless, and grinning types, these trivial fellows began arriving, seemingly, from nowhere, but mostly from an asylum called, apparently, Mad-chester. The press embraced their puppet swagger all too eagerly, and so dawned the era of the New Lad—a gammony bourgeois scion passing himself off as the very thing he most feared: a prole-tarian. Scurrying away from all this, N made two records in 1992: a melancholy pop album of "chill-out house," *Voyager* (influenced by Massive Attack, PM Dawn, the Jazz Warriors, Definition of Sound, Deee-Lite) and a Vorticist cabaret record, *The Ultraconformist*, in-fluenced by Brecht and by myself. The latter claimed to have been recorded live at Frida Strindberg's cabaret on Heddon Street, the Cave of the Golden Calf, "on or about December 1910," but this was a contractual convenience on behalf of Richmond Records. Actually N made it with Doug Martin, his regular engineer, at the Spike in Fulham. Creation, high as kites, barely seemed to notice the flagrant violation of N's exclusive contract. Six months after *Voyager* came out Alan McGee invited N to his "presidential suite" at what was now to be known as the "label of love" and played him the Creation Momus release from start to finish, his ruddy face fixed in a rictus that was at least 80 percent pharmaceutical. "Spacewalk" was belatedly launched as a single. Somewhere in the farthest reaches of glittering galaxies it hastens still, the loneliest man-made object in the universe, its critical transmissions unheeded.

Corinne Day: It's shit to be dead. I hate it. Do you know what happens? You just loop back through the life that you lived, repeating everything. So here I am back in the nineties, being accused yet again of encouraging "heroin chic" and asked how I discovered Kate Moss (I didn't). The best photographers of the time were me and Wolfgang. We were the ones that got it: we did the drugs and went to the parties and knew the people. Before me there'd been Nan Goldin. And after me there was still Nan Goldin. Bloody brain tumour! I had so much more to do. Wolfgang went on to win the Turner Prize, and headed off more in an art direction. But when he was still a student he photographed N for a German magazine called *Tempo*. For an article by Christian Kracht, who became a famous novelist later, Wolfgang shot the first pictures by a houseboat on the Thames, but didn't like them. So he photographed the second set in N's flat on Cleveland Street. N squatted on a pile of phone books, looking like a goblin with a bowl haircut. At around the same time Brad Branson shot him for *Vogue*. He was styled by Isabella Blow. She put him in a Comme des Garçons shirt with transparent plastic sleeves. "*Love* the eyebrows!" is all she said. When it came time to pose for the sleeve of *Timelord*, N went to Paris. Benedikt

Taschen had asked him to write some stories for a book he was doing about Pierre et Gilles, and N did these charming little fables. So he asked Pierre et Gilles to take one of their kitschy, glossy studio shots of him. They'd already done Marc Almond and Erasure and Mikado. They wanted three thousand pounds for the shot, which N thought was reasonable. He arrived at this big open studio in Le Pré-Saint-Gervais. Birds were flying around, very Francis of Assisi. There was a cute Vietnamese boy assisting. A fax came in from Bronski Beat, and Pierre and Gilles chortled. "We don't work with pigs," said the Vietnamese boy. The porn star Jeff Stryker had been their last model. Downstairs they'd built this amazing set from silver-sprayed Jell-O moulds. It was very Jules Verne, like a time machine for a crusading knight. N had a shaven head. He wriggled into a rubber suit of armour. There was a knife and some fruit. Later, when P&G were working on the retouching, N asked them to add a tear: the Bangladeshi girl he'd fallen in love with had been sent off to Sylhet for an arranged marriage.

Ernst Kretschmer: I am the man who first outlined the complex of personality traits we call schizoid, building on Eugen Bleuler's clinical work with patients exhibiting avoidant personality disorder. In my 1925 book *Physique and Character* I describe how the schizoid seeks to deaden all stimulation from the outside, like a house with the blinds permanently drawn. It's a line that, seventy years after I wrote it, finds its way into a song written by a Scottish man for a Japanese woman to sing. *Shyness* is an album negotiated between London and Tokyo by fax. While in Tokyo in 1992, N has purchased a mini-album called *Melting Moment* by an artist called the Poison Girlfriend. It's a gorgeous confection of melancholy ballads and lush strings, somewhat reminiscent of Massive Attack's "Unfinished Sympathy." N, knowing that singer Noriko Sekiguchi must be a fan of his own work, contacts her label to ask whether she would like him to co-write and produce her next album. A reply comes from Nippon Columbia in the affirmative, and soon Noriko is in London. She's a tall, slender, reserved woman fond of straw hats and red wine. The recordings are made with session musicians— Simon Fisher Turner, the bass player from the Tiger Lilies, Louis Philippe—in a basement on Berwick Street in Soho. The songs combine sadomasochistic themes—there's a take on Mishima's Madame de Sade, for instance—with a strong influence from the hippy-baba records of Brigitte Fontaine and Areski, all delivered with the lush string pads and ambient squiggles then in vogue. N gives Noriko some of the songs he's written for his own next album, *Timelord*, which is now focused more narrowly on the tragedy of Shazna's banishment to Bangladesh. In December of 1993 he flies back to Tokyo to promote the album and tour with Noriko. He's astonished to discover her hiding, at their press events, behind dark glasses, and further perplexed when the manager of Wave Shibuya refuses to let him sign copies of *Shyness* in the store, setting up a table outside on the street instead. It turns out that Noriko has had feelings for N, but—like a house with drawn blinds—has succeeded in hiding them. N, preoccupied with Shazna, has failed to notice anything. Noriko's boyfriend—who happens to be the manager of Wave Shibuya—is filled with paranoid rage: banishing the puzzled N to the street is his attempt at revenge. How sensitive schizoid artists—the hyperaesthetic rather than anaesthetic type of schizoid—can be to their own feelings, and yet how insensitive to the feelings of those around them! I once speculated about the type in language which I still find rather beautiful: "What is there in the deep under all these masks? Perhaps there is a nothing, a dark, hollow-eyed nothing—affective anaemia. Behind an ever-silent façade, which twitches uncertainly with every expiring whim— nothing but broken pieces, black rubbish heaps, yawning emotional emptiness, or the cold breath of an arctic soullessness." And this, indeed, is the impression created by the Momus album *Timelord* when it comes out. "Momus has changed," says Taylor Parkes in the *Melody Maker* review of the record. "The man sounds exhausted, embittered, the songs have lost the perilous wit that smoothed their sides and deepened their darkness; what is left is a cold, crumbling skeleton with one huge teardrop hanging out of its eye."

Raymond Radiguet: They called me Mr. Baby. I was the sensation of Paris when my novel *The Devil in the Flesh* came out. It was the frank tale of an affair I'd had at sixteen with a married woman whose husband was away at the front. Jean Cocteau adored it and persuaded his friend Grasset to publish it. The company poured a fortune into promoting the book, which, aided by scandal, became an immediate bestseller. Well, like Cocteau, N had a teenage protegée, the daughter of a Bangladeshi restaurateur. Shazna wrote to the singer and the pair began to meet in clandestinity. N—ostensibly a tutor—came several times to Shazna's family house in South Woodford, or to watch her receive prizes at school. When rumours of this reached Shazna's parents they engaged her to the son of a wealthy Dhaka businessman, and moved him into the family home. Shazna ran away, joining N in Manchester, where they visited the Dry Bar and the Haçienda club. In response, Shazna's brothers and fiancé made a frightening scene at Creation—which was at the time upstairs from a Bangladeshi sweatshop in Hackney—demanding N's address. This happened, as fate would have it, the very afternoon a new group called Oasis were making their first visit to Creation's offices. Telephone negotiations with Shazna's family led the couple to believe that they would be allowed to marry, but the goalposts kept moving. At first it would merely suffice for N to become a Muslim. This was quickly achieved: he began to attend talks at the Central London mosque by Yusuf Islam, a convert who dressed with elegant sobriety and made devotional music. N told the musician—formerly known as Cat Stevens—that he too was on a spiritual path, made an oath, and left clutching a certificate. Shazna's father (head of the Bangladeshi Welfare Association in Spitalfields, and therefore a man with a lot of face to lose) then declared that N would have to visit Mecca on a hajj, a pilgrimage. The next of these "trials of Hercules" was that N would have to bring his father to meet Shazna's father. This he did, ushering the perplexed Bill (in London to address a committee at the House of Lords about the effects of acid rain on fishing) into an angry room containing Shazna's family, an imam, and several relatives of the prospective fiancé. It was the kind of incendiary situation Bill occasionally had to deal with in his language college, and he handled it with dignified aplomb. He was taken upstairs to meet Shazna's father, who was in bed with a heart complaint. Meanwhile, in the downstairs room, the most hotheaded of Shazna's brothers danced about in a way designed to suggest that he might have a revolver or knife under his leather jacket. N escalated the situation by saying that Shazna had been abused by her fiancé. The boy's uncles jumped up enraged, and the imam tried to calm everyone down. Father and son could only extricate themselves by playing out a theatrical capitulation in which N burst into tears and Bill laid a hand on his head, crooning soothingly: "My son, my son." As they headed towards the Central Line Bill said: "Well, that's probably the most dramatic scene we'll ever be in." Shortly after this, on the pretext that her grandfather was dying, Shazna was whisked off to Bangladesh, where she was held as a sort of captive and shown a succession of new potential husbands. N managed to get a single phone call through to her. "Listen," said Shazna, "stay strong. Don't disintegrate." As the weeks went by, N worked on things from his mews house in a tiny alley just off St. Martin's Lane, faxing, phoning, and sending letters. He engaged a feminist lawyer to glean information on his behalf in Sylhet. Word came back that a marriage had taken place, but no one quite knew whose it was. In fact, Shazna was still unmarried but had fallen quite seriously ill. N bought an open-ended Singapore Airlines ticket from Dhaka to London. He wrote to the British High Commission, who were very sympathetic and surprisingly cooperative. In Dhaka they asked Shazna's father to bring his daughter in to renew her passport. Whisked into a private room at the embassy, Shazna was told that the air ticket was available should she wish to escape back to Britain. She hailed a baby taxi on a dusty Dhaka street, went to the airport, and boarded the next flight to Singapore. From there she contacted N with the news. At Heathrow police ferried her to a different terminal, just in case the family had managed to find out her route. The lovers were reunited at the arrival gate. In June of 1994 Shazna and N married at a registry office in Glasgow—with the Momus track "Rhetoric" playing on repeat and a small group of close friends in attendance—then left to begin a new life in Paris. Someone had tipped off the Scottish tabloid newspaper the *Daily Record*, which flew a journalist and a photographer to Paris to interview the couple. Photos were shot in front of the Arc de Triomphe and at Sacré-Coeur. The tabloid's fee was generous enough for N to place a deposit on a duplex apartment, a *garçonnière* on the Rue Caulaincourt in Montmartre. The story, spread over two days, ran on the cover of the Scottish paper under the headline "RUNAWAYS WED IN FEAR." My own tale ended much less happily: I died at twenty of a heart attack, of tuberculosis, of typhus, of poisoning by oysters, or of the sheer intensity of my precocious fame, depending on whom you believe. Cocteau, inconsolable, turned to opium.

J. D. Salinger: So right after Shazna and N ran away to Paris, following the stink they'd kicked up with her family and all, they were staying at this dive hotel in Montmartre. It was a crummy cheap joint but the sun shone in through the window and the times were good.

Shazna wore an edible candy necklace and slid around on roller
skates. The hotel maid stole her wedding ring one day when they
were out. But it was a phony gold ring and N replaced it. So anyway,
some Japanese record company called Cru-el had asked N to write
songs for Kahimi Karie. She was this cute mousy Jap girl who hid
behind her hair and was the girlfriend of Cornelius, some big singer
named after a monkey. N had been to dinner with them in Tokyo
the year before. They'd eaten at an Indian restaurant in Roppongi.
Then Keigo and Mari (their real names) brought him back to their
flat and he played with their cat and all. This is on video somewhere
because at that time N was taping everything. And what he noticed
was that the camera loved Mari. You just couldn't keep your eyes off
her. She had this way of sort of crossing her eyes like, you know, a
butterfly had just landed on her nose. Well, in the Montmartre hotel
N wrote this cutesy song called "I Am a Kitten." He stole that idea
from some fancy book, a novel all done from the point of view of
a cat. Soseki wrote it, but N of course spiced it up with some extra
nooky—the cat is horny as hell and wants to make time with his
lady owner after seeing her naked and all. The funny thing is that N
was back to making songs in the style of good ol' él Records. "The
Camera Loves Me" and all that bull. To write a song like that N just
had to think: "What would él do, for Chrissake?" And he knew the
Japanese would lap it all up and he would make a hatful of dough. So
he found a bassist, this jerk called Bertrand Burgalat who thought
he was Serge Gainsbourg. Jeez. And a drummer called Czerkinsky
who used to be in a band called Mikado and also thought he was
Serge Gainsbourg. Christ. Then Mari arrived with her manager to
record the four songs they'd picked and they banged them out fast.
Burgalat turned out to be a pretty good bassist. He could play a
mean piano too. Trouble is, he wanted to be the producer. I swear
he just took over that swivel chair and ran the desk his way. And it
did sound good, retro and authentic and all. It even had that 1969

stereo effect where there's totally different stuff going on in each speaker. N secretly hoped people would hear Mari's naked voice in the left cabinet and just hump it like dogs. He once did that with a Ludus record. So, when the Japanese put the record out they still had N down as producer. *Kahimi Karie sings Momus in Paris*, produced by Momus. Bertie Burglar (that's what N and Shaz called him) got mad as a nest of hornets. He pitched his own goddam Kahimi Karie record to a different label, and this time N wasn't invited. Shazna got ornery too. Perhaps there was a visit from the green-eyed monster, perhaps she just didn't want to stay home alone while the others were having fun in the studio. She got in touch with this big-shot film director jerk called Leos Carax. He'd put out a call for subcontinental chicks, so Shaz went for a screen test. The film was probably phony all along, but Carax liked Shazna and they became friends. And that was all fine because, you know, he was dating Carla Bruni. But there was something goddam fishy about it too, because when N asked one day if he could come along—he was a big fan and all—the word came back that Carax would only talk to girls.

Salvador Dalí: All the British people are homosexual, so it is natural that N has taken a catamite. Of course, Shazna is a female, but that is a mere detail. Very affectionately, I shall call her the Catamite, and imagine them as two homosexuals. It is undeniable that she makes a charming impression. With a little moustache she would be as nice as Charlie Chaplin. The Catamite's quick brown eyes and absurd sense of humour make her a most engaging consort for N, who is himself a miniature genius. I say that not because he is small, but because only Dalí can be considered a great genius. Dalí however is impotent, a royalist, a Catholic, and a masturbator. N, the miniature genius, is still very potent. As a matter of fact he has a most impressive prick. I would like to paint this organ disguised as a sceptre—perhaps I can work it into my next commission from a pope? That is the nice thing about being here in heaven: not only does it resemble the landscape of my own paintings, but it is full of rich patrons. And Dalí, even dead, loves money. But we were speaking of the Catamite and her impulsive charm. One day she throws open the iron shutters that connect their duplex *garçonnière* to the Rue Lamarck and shouts: "Armageddon is here! Armageddon is here!" Like that, do you see? Just to scandalise the people at the bus stop. It is her humour. She is a great Surrealist, like Dalí. The Catamite is naughty, and so she amuses the circle of friends that this homosexual couple begins to accumulate in Paris. From the Catamite's cramming school there is one classmate, Claudia Squitieri, who is the sixteen-year-old daughter of Claudia Cardinale. Very beautiful, like her mother. She visits for pyjama parties, and the homosexual couple are invited to the apartment of Claudia senior, whom I myself encountered many times in the Café de la Paix. And of course there is Ariel Wizman, who presents—together with the actor Édouard Baer—a programme on Radio Nova called *La Grosse Bulle.* They play the kind of easy listening music that is at this time coming back into fashion. Ariel has a naughty grin and a taste for practical jokes. One evening he and Édouard are petting a lady's poodle in a restaurant when suddenly they seize the animal and start high-stepping toward the kitchen yelling gaily: *"Au micro-onde!* To the microwave!" The lady almost dies of fright. Ariel loves Perrey & Kingsley and that funny American group, the one with the Hitler look-alike, what are they called? Oh yes, Sparks. N and the Catamite meet Sparks at a party at the Montmartre studio of Kuntzel+Deygas, and N asks the brothers if they are really rivals. What a magnificently stupid thing to say! Dalí is a great admirer of stupid remarks, for they often conceal an extreme intelligence. Also in their circle is Toog, the poet, and his wife, the paranoid-critical artist Flo Manlik. Philippe Katerine is an ironical songwriter who has recently moved to Paris from Nantes and says he still feels like a tourist. He is writing for Kahimi Karie too: one song is called "J'apprends le français" and is about the kind of French poor Mari is learning from Parisian lotharios. Another amusing visitor is Jeremy Scott, the fashion designer. With his hooflike shoes, skeletal frame, and dyed red hair, Scott is a flamboyant ungulate like the one in my painting *The Burning Giraffe*. Speaking of my paintings, you must know *The Persistence of Memory*, with its melting clocks? Well, it is the persistence of memory that begins to undermine the charming homosexual marriage of N and his catamite. Arranged neatly on his bookshelves, you see, N keeps his diary, which might be entitled *The Journal of a Magnificent Prick*. Here are detailed all his sexual exploits from years before. And although these stories are all in the past—for N is as faithful to Shazna as I am to Gala— a voracious curiosity compels the Catamite to take down and read these terrible pages whenever N is out. When he returns, they fight like weasels in a sack. There is a proverb of the Catalan fishermen, you know, *Tenen els plaers de la vida, bona entrada i mala eixida*: the pleasures of life have a good entrance and a bad exit.

Mikhail Bulgakov: Jesus, the devil, hell; these ancient things are undoubtedly real, though modern secular relativists may try to squirm and deny them. In my novel *The Master and Margarita* I depict the devil visiting Soviet Russia as an urbane foreign gentle-man called Woland. A fellow who looks like a suave magician, with a sinister talking cat called Behemoth, capable of ripping a man's head off—it should be clear who that is, no? But the vain poets Woland encounters are unable to read the signs; such things are not in their cosmology. N is the same. Long ago he wrote,

> *Hell's a manner of speaking, hell's a gleam in our eye*
> *It's the way we get on in this world, not where we go when*
> *   we die*

Like all atheists, N cannot credit Mephistopheles as anything other than a metaphor. And yet Satan has a distinct smell: of sulphur, certainly, but also of rose petals, motor oil, tincture of benzoin, camphor, cardamom, and the scum that forms on warm apricot juice. It is this odour—the sickly-sweet smell of success—that begins to hang in the air during N's second year in Paris. He and Shazna have moved up to a gorgeous new flat on the Place du Tertre. Through the window is a leafy square populated by café terraces and painters, surmounted by the breast-like swellings of the domes of Sacré-Cœur; if you lean out you can see pale Paris spreading out far below. The couple now have a kitten—a *"super-mini chaton"*—called Little Meowy, which is often terrorised by an enormous black cat set loose by the bar next door—the first omen that Satan is ranging the roof tiles. One day, returning with a new printer under his arm, N meets Iggy Pop on the street, being sketched by three artists. "Iggy! What are you doing here?" The American singer drawls: "I come here. I have friends here." Shazna now has a job as a cyber-hostess at Cyberia, the internet café in the Pompidou Centre. The internet itself is becoming a temptation: N has just one regular email correspondent, a New York advertising executive called Regina who hopes to lure him to New York, and a career in that dreadful profession. Online there are now things called "newsgroups" which offer "binaries": algebraic incantations that, if stitched together in the right order, become images of Japanese women. And yet why bother, when the real thing is close to hand? Mari Hiki, a huge star in Japan thanks to the hits N is writing for her alter ego Kahimi Karie, arrives with her manager Fumiko wearing a David Hamilton T-shirt. The women sit cross-legged in N's sunny living room—furnished with bookshelves and chairs made from ingeniously folded cardboard—responding to fan mail and recording programmes for Japanese radio. Mari has a new boyfriend, a preening male model called Jerome she met making the video for another Momus-penned single, "Le Roi

Soleil." The song casts her as a revolutionary who, intent on poisoning Louis XIV, decides to sleep with him instead. It is a scenario
that might stand for the 1990s as a whole: the indie counterculture
which once aspired to overthrow the dominant order has joined it
in bed, giggling behind a spreading fan of banal irony. Jerome turns
out to be a bastard: he tries to involve Mari in threesomes, attempts
to make himself her principal songwriter, and smashes N's equipment after a concert, offering to carry a suitcase full of electronics
then deliberately dropping it down a staircase.

Francis Lai: Cast as Satan in "The Hairstyle of the Devil,"
Martin Heath has now become N's song publisher. Not content to
reap the considerable rewards of Kahimi Karie's success in Japan,
Heath—who's now the head of Arista Records in London—comes
to Paris to encourage N to sign a "cocktail singer" who can duplicate Kahimi's success in Europe. N places an ad in *Nova* magazine
for a girl to sing songs inspired by my soundtrack for the soft porn
film *Bilitis*. The successful candidate is a half-Thai art student called
Laila France—pretty, playful, and flirtatious. Unfortunately—as
she herself admits—she has a "voice like a duck." Arista turns her
down, but Laila keeps coming faithfully to N's flat on the Place
du Tertre every Wednesday afternoon to co-write. The similarity doesn't stop at Laila's name, which sounds like an anagram of
mine—the songs themselves sound like recombined versions of
my tracks, which is interesting because I used to meet the singer
Bernard Dimey in the Taverne d'Attilio on the same square thirty
years before, when I was working with Piaf. In the spring of 1996,
Vicky Spook, N's old New Zealand flatmate from London, comes
to stay for a couple of weeks in the apartment. She, Shazna, and N
all sleep on the same futon. Vicky, convinced by certain looks and
smiles that Laila and N are in the throes of an affair, confides her
suspicions to Shazna. In fact, the only sexy thing the songwriters

have done is make a humorous Macromedia Director animation in which sperm trickles from Laila's mouth while her eyes roll heavenwards like a Saint Theresa depicted by Pierre et Gilles. In case of doubt, Laila takes the file away and adds her own ending: a caption which declares chastely: "I love my boyfriend Luc." Nevertheless, the suspicion Vicky has unleashed—and the flirtatious lifestyle the three friends embark upon as they try to hook the New Zealander up with Parisian men—shakes the marriage to its core. Before long Shazna takes up with one of her customers at Cyberia, a graphic designer. N, meanwhile, meets temptation in the form of a tiny Japanese girl. He's walking one day at Les Halles when a stranger approaches and throws her arms around him: "You're Momus!" N invites Yoko to the empty Place du Tertre flat and, after coffee, casually slides her miniskirt up her thighs. "Oh, thank you!" Yoko breathes. When the new Kahimi Karie and Laila France albums appear there's a floaty song on each containing a suitably demonic moral:

> *If this lazy suffering*
> *Can bring erection to the lap*
> *Of just one man*
> *It hasn't been in vain*

Even that's a pastiche: "If one life has been saved by this photography session," runs a line of *Sprechgesang* on Howard Devoto's collaboration with Bernard Szajner, "it has been worth it."

Marcel Proust: The suit was of a rough blue hemp, and, with its rounded collars and almost Maoist aspect, it recalled the clothes that N had worn in his twelfth year, when he had first dressed up in what his father called "your togs." Emerging from marriage, and from fidelity, perhaps reminded N of that first emergence into autonomy, that transition into informality and colour that had succeeded, during those precious school holidays of the early 1970s, weeks of enforced uniformity. In late 1996 there came but one scene of rage and grief with Shazna: during one terrible night she tugged ferociously at N's wedding ring, demanding that he take it off, weeping and shouting that he no longer had any right to wear it. The ring, however, was wedged beneath a swollen knuckle, and eventually the thunderstorm passed and the couple settled back into an uneasy slumber. A trip to New York was quickly approaching, and N was nervous. One morning, stirred by a tender anxiety, N made a final amorous approach to his wife's recumbent form. It was in the moments preceding dawn, before the cafés on the square were open, before the pale light of coherence had encroached upon the red futon. Shazna, like a proud captive in an Ottoman seraglio, feigned sleep. Years later she would declare that the marriage had collapsed because N had wanted "a Third World wife," and that she had rebelled at the idea of walking in his shadow. In those last days of cohabitation she defiantly brandished a book by Jonas Mekas, a selection of his diaries entitled *I Had Nowhere to Go*. Shazna did find a refuge, however, on the Rue de Buci, in the apartment of the man who would soon become her second husband. N, meanwhile, was spending a great deal of time at the residence of Georges Condominas, an anthropologist with a pretty mews house in the Butte-aux-Cailles quarter. Condominas himself was always on a voyage of cultural discovery somewhere, but his taste was indicated by the straw ritual artefacts, Mnong masks, and Vietnamese musical instruments that decorated his walls. Ocora albums of proto-Indo-Chinese ethnomusicology lay, neatly stacked, by the record player. More significantly, this was where Yoko had her little room, and where N could meet her friends as they passed through Paris: Young Kim, the Korean American who was soon to become the partner of Malcolm McLaren, or the talented Japanese composer Hirono Nishiyama. Yoko—like Mari Hiki, and like me, Marcel Proust—was one of those advanced souls who knows the people and the culture most worth knowing. In the Vietnamese restaurants of the Thirteenth Arrondissement, where fish darted through great limpid tanks, N was now free to sit in the refreshing company of this new circle, dressed in his round-collared TGV suit, writing notes for songs designed to thrill the Japanese. "One Thousand 20th Century Chairs," "Le Roi Soleil," "Cat from the Future" . . . These new works, recorded with Kahimi Karie in a pleasant studio on the Rue de Seine, would surely resonate like anthems on the other side of the world, spread successfully through the western districts of Tokyo, and bring their progenitor all the wealth and position he could desire.

Kathy Acker: There's a man, we're calling him N. He's also known as Momus, Nicky, Bluebeard, and Plumphead. I know this man, we talked at the wedding of my ex Don Watson. We talked mostly about property prices in Brighton. I think Plumphead was surprised that I wasn't wearing a headband and brandishing a machete. I wasn't Rimbaud inside a woman's body. He went home that day with my friend, a filmmaker called Vera. They lay there in her flat in Ladbroke Grove, drunk on Don's champagne, fucking. Then Vera got pregnant and had a daughter. DNA tests showed that the baby wasn't from Plumphead but another man she'd had that same weekend. I've always thought it's funny how Aeschylus portrays Clytemnestra in the *Oresteia* as a sexual deviant. Women have needs. Anyway, in early 1997 N has fled from a marriage that has broken down in Paris. He's back in London. Things have changed since 1994. The East End is exciting now. In Hoxton Square you can peep at cookery right down the extractor stacks. Tracey Emin has a studio there, and an artist called Greg is living like a hermit in a signal box in Dalston. Georgina Starr has made a comic book showing a world based on love lyrics from Momus songs. Tracey gives a lecture about how Billy Childish pissed on her once when they were living together. Only people who really love each other piss on each other. There's a good chance that Labour might get back in after the next election. N takes a penthouse flat near the Barbican. He buys an office table and Arne Jacobsen chairs and props copies of *Studio Voice* and *CUTiE* and various Game Boys on the bookshelves. The seventies revival is in full swing and everything's safari suits and lava lamps and Stylophones. David Bowie has gone drum'n'bass, but sensible people prefer Squarepusher. N goes straight into the studio to make *Orgonon*, his album with Laila France. It's all about fucking, and Wilhelm Reich, and not fucking because it's your period. Then in the same studio he makes a record called *How to Make Love (Volume I)* with a Welshman called Anthony Reynolds. That goes out under the artist name Jacques and is also all about fucking. London by now is full of either people who've done better at being Momus than Momus ever did—Pulp, the Divine Comedy, White Town—or people who were brought up on Momus records and want to be his friend, like Dickon Edwards the queer diarist or Ant the louche Welshman. Everybody seems to be fucking members of Kenickie or the riot grrrl bands. N is now touring America regularly thanks to a magician called Matthew Jacobson who starts a label called Le Grand Magistery. N has this sense of how you ought to present yourself to Americans as a European. And of course the Japanese are paying for his lifestyle, and happy to fuck him if he needs that. So his 1997 album *Ping Pong*—which is also about fucking, of course, and about being sponsored by Lufthansa to fuck Japanese girls and being censored for fucking and being the only animal that fucks in a world where fucking is a criminal act—is a sort of self-pastiche. Oh, did I mention that the other three important things about 1997 were table tennis and *buk-kake* and playing the theremin? Also, N briefly gets back together with an old girlfriend, an *i-D* journalist who introduces him to her friend Bidisha. Bid is a precocious teenager who went to Oxford and has written a novel called *Seahorses* and has her own column in *The Independent*. It's a big mistake on the ex's part, because Bidisha and N are soon fucking, mainly because Bid loves N's flat near the Barbican. It gives her somewhere to go. Otherwise she would just be living with her mum. N takes Bid to the Edinburgh Festival and they buy retro-seventies nylon shirts to look like each other. One day Bid decides that it might be a good idea to try heroin because it's fashionable. N says that if she does he'll split up with her, because junkies are always bad news. But Bid goes ahead. When Diana dies in a car crash, Bid basically doesn't give a fuck because she's stoned out of her mind. One day she phones N to irritate him with a real-time description: "I'm heating it on the spoon. Now I'm taking a hit from the glass pipe." She sends all his love letters back with a note in her backward-slanting murderer's handwriting saying that she'd only be interested in "a purely physical arrangement." Then she shaves her head and gets tattoos all over her body, which she later regrets. Bid also stops writing novels and becomes the kind of critic who writes about the many crimes of Israel or says that heroin is great and that all men are dogs. But underneath that she's a twee, tiny, and nice person who believes secretly in chivalric romance. Oh, did I mention that 1997 was also a really shitty year for me, Kathy Acker, and for literature? Because I died in Mexico that November of breast cancer. I was only fifty.

Pete Shelley: N's first words to his Mancunian songwriting hero Howard Devoto were: "Do you know who I am?" They met at a Snub TV party in 1990, around the time that Howard was working with a guitarist called Noko and N was sounding suspiciously like a certain group from Salford. "You're M-M-M-M . . ." stammered Howard, possibly for comic effect or possibly because he genuinely couldn't remember N's artist name. But he must've been impressed by N's fannish devotion, because he requested that the Scot conduct a Luxuria interview for Super Channel. During the interview, N asked Howard whether he wrote juicy phrases in a notebook, and if so, whether he would read something out from it. "I do," Howard replied, "but my bag is over there and *I can't be seen to move.*" He said "*I can't be seen to move*" in audible italics, with a flash of widened eyes, a comedy version of that punk face that was shorthand for affront, aggression, and boredom when Lydon pulled it. On Howard, though, the stare evoked a deer in headlights or a spoof Bond henchman. "The bus is better than the train," he added. In 1992 Simon Pettifar from Black Spring Press—the man who midwifed Nick Cave's first novel—published lyrics collections by Howard and Momus simultaneously. The Momus collection was called *Lusts of a Moron* and Howard's was titled *It Only Looks as If It Hurts*, which is the kind of thing a protective parent might say to a child exposed to a violent film. In 1997 N was trying to get Howard to duet with him on a comic tribute called "The Most Important Man Alive." Howard had a job at a photographic agency in Clerkenwell, not far from where N was living. The Mancunian seemed lonely and horny, and was clearly keen to meet Kahimi Karie. He expressed this by borrowing a copy of a book called *How to Make Out in Japanese* from N's bookshelves. Unfortunately Kahimi had never heard of him. Howard eventually decided not to add his voice to "The Most Important Man Alive," but he and N did go for dinner a few times. One evening N took Howard to the Japanese Canteen on St. John Street. Between the salmon teriyaki and the dessert he started giving his hero a hard time about the sexual sadism in the song "Permafrost." Howard disappeared off to the bathroom, and when he came back N saw suffering and reproach in his eyes. He felt suddenly sad for guilt-tripping his hero. A decade later, when Howard reformed Magazine, he changed the song—which is about drug rape in the Arctic—to make it more consensual: "*You want me* to drug you and fuck you on the permafrost." It was not improved. Another time N had to send Howard a DAT tape. Curious about his house, he decided, stalkerishly, to deliver it by hand. The place was a modest brick terrace house in the Hasidic area of Stoke Newington. N pushed the stampless package through the letterbox, listening for any sign of Howard inside. Perhaps he could be heard narrating a chapter of the audio autobiography he plans to leave to the National Sound Archive? No signs of life emerged. The next time they met Howard said: "Oh, you should have rung the bell." At the close of one of their dinners, Howard rose from the table and said: "Let us go, then, you and I . . ." Recognising the reference to Eliot's *Prufrock*, N recited:

> *When the evening is spread out against the sky*
> *Like a patient etherized upon a table*

The last time they dined Howard seemed happier. N was on steroids for his sick eye, and quoted the master to excuse his jumpiness: "Blame my deadening intensity." But Howard was relaxed and happy. He had a new girlfriend—his inamorata, he called her. She wrote plays for Radio 4 and seemed nice. "Do you know who Howard is?" N asked her. "I *think* so," said the inamorata.

Kamo no Chomei: There is water under rock. Time carries on like a stream that flows on the bottom of the ocean, and no two moments are ever the same. Disasters befall us, the people we love leave us or die, and the structures we build are like bubbles on the surface of a swiftly flowing torrent that sweeps everything away. I was writing *An Account of My Hut* in thirteenth-century

Japan, but in the late twentieth century human life hasn't changed much. People still need dwellings, no matter how much their lives are filled with motion. And they still fall ill and suffer. N drives to Greece with Toog in 1997, and the friends take the ferry between Bari and Piraeus. N washes the case of his contact lens case in the tap water of his cabin bathroom. That turns out to be a mistake, because his right eye is soon looking sick and red. By the time they get back to Paris it seems to be a case of conjunctivitis, but Moorfields Eye Hospital in London confirms the infection as something called *Acanthamoeba keratitis.* It's a rare but potentially blinding condition, according to the specialist, a small dapper Irishman called Mr. Larkin. And so begins a two-year ordeal of inconvenience and pain. Moorfields is a short cycle from N's flat on Long Lane. At the eye hospital this interesting case is greeted with apparent delight, much probing with ophthalmic torches and much dazzling with slit lamps. N becomes familiar with the refracting phoropter, the dwindling letter chart, the hushed crowds of medical students, the trips to the hospital pharmacy. He even appears—a worst-case scenario—in a BBC documentary about parasites. The amoebas are living on the surface of his eye; like humans, they have dug in and made little cities on the white and blue globe. This is painful, but the treatment is worse: biopsies are often conducted without anaesthetic. "We just need a small sample of the cornea, there won't be much discomfort," reassures Mr. Larkin before pushing a sharp scalpel into N's eye, screwed open with a vise. It hurts like hell. There is no known treatment for this condition, so an experimental variety of drops is prescribed, along with powerful painkillers, immune suppressants, and steroids. When N goes on tour—which he does at least once a year, breaking America, or at least the college circuit—he carries a cooled flask of chemical cocktails and is more drugged than any rock star. Light hurts him, so he has to wear heavy sunglasses. In Chicago super-groupie Cynthia Plaster Caster wants to cast his penis, but N is too ill to summon a respectable erection, lying there on Cynthia's kitchen floor with his dick in a thermos of dental molding paste and his tongue on the clitoris of the "plater," a Chinese American architecture student called Janet. It just feels like the eye hospital. He'll look pathetic next to Jimi Hendrix, but at least he'll create a compelling image of rock's decline and fall. There's no question of cancelling these American tours, because career comes first and losing the eye entirely seems like a very remote possibility. And yet that is exactly what happens; apparently an eye can evaporate like dew on the stem of a daisy. N wakes up in Atlanta on the morning of his thirty-eighth birthday to discover that he is effectively blind on the right side. Only a vague smudge of light is visible, as if filtered through frosted glass. Back in London an operation is performed and a donor cornea—apparently from the victim of a traffic accident in Plymouth—is attached. N's body is now partly female and partly dead. For a while this operation restores some sight, but the eye is beginning to swivel out of line and the result is double vision, which is worse than none at all. N begins to wear a black eye patch he's bought in a New York drugstore. He likes the dramatic effect: walking down the street, he has the impression of being famous, or at least remarkable. When it becomes clear that the treatments are failing, Mr. Larkin signs him into a room at Moorfields—the same hospital where his hero David Bowie was operated on three decades before—and a stern regime of chemical drops is attempted, with alarms going off every two hours throughout the night. N soon feels as if he's back at boarding school. He's sick of the treatment and sick of the drugs, which have made him tense, snappy, and hairy, bringing out an inner brute, a Hyde. Nothing is working, and little veins are now growing across the optic nerve, making blindness inevitable. At last Mr. Larkin agrees that treatment can cease, and N is tapered off the hated steroids. Jekyll returns. He's lost the use of one eye, but still has the other. At no point in the process has he wept or sunk low in spirit: it has been a technical malfunction, nothing more. And in the meantime technology has provided new ways of seeing: digital tools and the internet are like new eyes. Making the best of a bad deal, N portrays himself on the cover of his 1998 album *The Little Red Songbook* as a cyber-baroque dandy, the right side of his face covered with an optical head-mounted display. All this happened twenty years ago. It is now the end of the fourth moon of 2019, during the last month of the Heisei era, and N is writing this in his hut in the twelfth district of Paris.

Agatha Christie: A most puzzling affair has summoned me, Hercule Poirot, back from retirement, and indeed, as it may seem, from death. And yet a fictional character such as myself can never die, never having truly lived except in the pages of detective stories. What has surely died is my profession itself, or at least its traditional fictional representation, for any credible depiction of detection in the twenty-first century would have to involve hour upon tedious hour of that abomination known as "googling." *Chapitre un*, the detective googles, *Chapitre deux*, he googles some more. What has happened to the little grey cells? Who would read such a monstrously boring narrative? Since—in the name of my profession, and indeed of my existence itself—I refuse this humiliation, my investigations are of necessity quite limited. Take the affair of *Stars Forever*. The facts are, on the face of it, quite simple: in early 1999 a Scottish songwriter called Momus announced that he would make thirty song portraits for a thousand dollars each. These pictures in sound would apparently make their sitters famous. The scheme was successful, for within three weeks all thirty portraits had been reserved by affluent fans keen to take their place in the pantheon of apparent immortality, or perhaps some Valhalla of notoriety. The patrons included the artist Jeff Koons, a multiplicity of Japanese girls, several English homosexuals, and two record shops. Three months later the finished record was released—there is ample proof of this!—and yet it seems no longer to exist. In order to clear up this mystery I attempted to contact representatives of those digital services now tasked with archiving and delivering music on demand only to discover that—unlike the Belgian railway—they are apparitions of an unfathomable abstraction, automatic lighthouses blinking on a sea of complete silence. I decided that this line of enquiry was a red herring, and turned my attention to the previous release of this Momus, a record called *The Little Red Songbook*. It seemed clear to me that some crime had been committed on this record, and that the *Stars Forever* album had been made partly as self-vindication, partly as a clever ruse to repay a debt run up, in all probability, by legal fees and a modest out-of-court settlement. I began to scent, at the centre of this affair, a regrettable episode of lèse-majesté against a concealed king or queen. And so I, Poirot, dressed impeccably in a gown of Chinese silk, my moustache waxing in its trainer, sat down in the Art Deco apartment at Florin Court, Charterhouse Square, to which the BBC has consigned the television version of myself—an apartment visible, incidentally, from the northern window of the penthouse in which Momus wrote and recorded *Stars Forever*—and listened to *The Little Red Songbook*. The experience was one of great deception, *mes amis.* To the accompaniment of the mocking, quacking sound of the *mirliton* or kazoo, and a very cheap harpsichord, almost every song on this disk offers some insult to an eminent personage, some affront against public decency. There are foul and lubricious attacks upon Lucrezia Borgia, M. C. Escher, and Beethoven, and songs describing sexual practices so vulgar that Poirot must shudder to name them. At first I wondered if the actionable insult had been against the Method actor referred to as "Harry K-Tel," but reasoned that the song's continued presence on the record proved that this could not indeed be the offending squib. What I must discover is the trace of a *missing* song, removed in the wake of the threat, perhaps, of a multimillion-dollar lawsuit. And then a great revelation came to me, and I slapped my own forehead, momentarily dislodging my *garde-moustache*. But of course, Poirot has been a greater imbecile even than Chief Inspector Japp! He must only consult the principal witness, Momus himself! On the singer's website I discovered a mail link, and wrote a short missive explaining my interest and asking for an explanation. N replied with commendable alacrity, but seemed to speak in riddles: "Appropriate personal pronouns she / her . . . The high analogue baroque . . . Synthesis as artifice, therefore inauthenticity . . . To remake oneself, and then marry oneself . . . Forcing others to accept one's presentation of self . . . Time travel is to time as reassignment is to gender . . ." While these were no doubt excellent topics for a master's dissertation, I needed something more precise. I sent a further letter expressing thanks, but demanding specifics. Where were you? What happened? The reply that came was only marginally less frustrating. "We both had records out and shared a promotion company. I sent my *Songbook* and thought she would be flattered, but she was waiting as I emerged from the Fez club under Time Cafe with a little thug in a baseball cap. 'Great show, Nick! This is for you.' And when we opened the fat envelope there was this absurd packet of papers about slander and plagiarism and God knows what else. The court threw out the injunction immediately, but she came back with more papers, again to the Fez club, right when I was sound-checking. I freaked out: she was like a vengeful robot, something out of Stanley Kubrick." This, *hélas*, was the last communication I received from the Scottish singer. There is perhaps an important clue in "Stanley Kubrick," but I must confess myself unable, on this occasion, to say more. Since it is so much out of character for Hercule Poirot to fail to bring a case to a satisfactory conclusion, I can only entertain a strong suspicion that I too am being portrayed, ventriloquised, misrepresented. Perhaps lawyers forbid further elucidation; lawyers are great enemies of clarity. As for the curious, they need only google, and in so doing watch me—and all my brothers, the great detectives—disappear in a cloud of smoke, like steam from the chimney of an ancient locomotive puffing its way implacably toward the Orient.

Umberto Eco: The nineties of the nineteenth century were a decade of flamboyance, dandyism, cosmopolitanism, decadence, and orientalism, and the nineties of the twentieth century to some extent reiterated those tropes. Throughout the decade N was caught in the monstrous shadow of Morrissey, the second coming of Oscar Wilde. At first—in letters to the press and interviews—he defended the singer against accusations of racism, but little by little began to agree with them. He also had dealings with the closest thing the 1990s had to Aubrey Beardsley: Jarvis Cocker. The Pulp singer had written a letter asking Momus to produce *Separations*, but received no reply. He was still, however, willing to appear in the 1993 documentary *Man of Letters*, which followed Momus from Helsinki to London. Apparently, Jarvis and N had shared a girlfriend at some point, or so the unreliable narrator suggested (the character was modelled on the elder of the two devils in *The Screwtape Letters* of C. S. Lewis). Derek Jarman, the Dante Gabriel Rossetti of the age, was too ill to appear in the film, and died before the decade was even midway through. (Rossetti himself never lived to see the 1890s he had helped prepare.) Two interwoven developments determined N's experience of the twentieth century's closing decade: globalisation and digitalisation. N was quick to see the implications of the latter, predicting in a 1991 essay for the Swedish magazine *Grimsby Fishmarket* that "in the future, everyone will be famous for fifteen people." Globalisation—the escape from the national straitjacket—was equally liberating. Not only could a British citizen live, after the signing of the Treaty of Maastricht in 1992, visa-free anywhere

in the European Union, but one could escape the strictures, preju-
dices, and limitations of one's national cultural arbiters. Neglected
by the gatekeepers of the British music industry, N found much
greater success in Japan and the United States. He never appeared
on the British music programme *Top of the Pops*, for instance, but
in 1998 was flown out to Japan by Kahimi Karie's management to
appear on *Music Station*, whose ten million viewers far outstripped
the British equivalent. The song he was performing, "One Thousand 20th Century Chairs," drew its title from a book published by
the German publisher Taschen, and was set in Les Olympiades, the
towers that dominate the Vietnamese area of Paris. Globalisation
provided a broader and more cosmopolitan canvas. Between 1996
and the century's end N spent most of his time on American stages
incarnating a certain idea of the European dandy yet promoting—
in magazines like *Raygun*, famously illegible thanks to the grunge
typography of David Carson—the Shibuya-kei scene he knew from
Tokyo. In *The New York Times* Eric Weisbard noted: "When those
on the rock fringe do reach out now, it's to people like themselves,
who just happen to live in other countries. Nouveau cabaret acts like
Momus in London, Kahimi Karie in Tokyo, and the French-singing
April March in Los Angeles use their sophistication to make common cause across national boundaries . . . Yet the worldliness these
performers manifest inevitably promotes an ideal of affluent cosmopolitanism." You can already sense, in that caveat, the backlash
against internationalism, multiculturalism, and cosmopolitanism
that would begin in the early decades of the twenty-first century.
And yet, back then, visas were still easy to come by: for a two-week
tour of the U.S. it wasn't unusual to be given a working visa valid for
a whole year, and N soon graduated to the O-1—the American "genius visa." Much better received critically, financially, and sexually
in New York, Berlin, and Tokyo than he'd ever been in London, N
decided to leave Britain for good. He bade farewell to the 1990s,

and to London, in a wild New Year's party at the studio of Gilbert and George. Dressed in a kilt and leather eye patch, N danced the millennium into oblivion in a scrumlike huddle with the gay performance artists, a couple of Japanese girls, and his Greek friend Babis. In the early hours of the new millennium Sophia—the St. Martin's student who inspired Pulp's song "Common People"—attacked N with kisses behind a pillar as her amused husband looked on. The new century seemed to be starting well.

part
five 2000–2010

I am a man, and therefore have all devils in

my heart.

—G. K. Chesterton

Gore Vidal: In March of the year 2000, having recently turned forty and recently gone half blind, N moves to New York. He has resolved, with his remaining eye and the remaining half of his life, to see twice as much and live twice as fast. How did Martial put it?

"Tomorrow will I live," the fool doth say;
Even today's too late; the wise lived yesterday.

Certain developments have made the move possible from a purely pragmatic standpoint: N has made the soundtrack for a perfectly dreadful Film Four movie called *The Low-Down*—some wit at the channel suggests it would be better titled *The Let-Down*—and has a tidy sum stashed away in the bank; enough to send his earthly goods on ahead to New York, where they will mostly sit in boxes in a Manhattan Mini Storage unit in Tribeca, gathering a light scattering of dust when the towers of the World Trade Center collapse nearby. The other propitious circumstances are a yearlong U.S. visa and an invitation from the Knitting Factory to mount a regular cabaret of some kind, to be webcast from a new online facility called Knit-Active. N pitches *Electronics in the 18th Century*, a regular hour of retro-futurist flimflam enacted by two synthetic aristocrats, the Duke of Atari and the Earl of Amiga, played by himself and

Torquil Campbell, who—in addition to being the lead singer of a group called Stars—is the nephew of Andrew Wylie, the infamous literary agent. A small audience of about twenty-five people assembles, scenes from *Chitty Chitty Bang Bang* are projected, and N and Torq spar their merry way through an improvised stream of quirks, foibles, jabs, and squibs. For some reason my name comes up a lot: "As Gore Vidal says, there is nothing worse than a poodle when one is trying to concentrate." Of course, I never said any such thing. On those occasions when Torq is indisposed (when, for instance, the police fling him into the cells overnight for smoking dope in Central Park), the Amiga role is played by various members of Fischerspooner, a narcissistic collective of performance artists whose minimalistic electronic songs are being championed by impresario Larry Tee as the spearhead of a new movement called Electroclash. To N it just looks like warmed-up Sigue Sigue Sputnik, but there's no denying Casey Spooner's ambition: high on a catwalk at Gavin Brown's Enterprise, spotlit and singing Wire's song "The 15th" into the cinematic gale unleashed by a huge fan, he suddenly has his entire costume snatched away by an assistant. When N interviews him for an audio documentary called Fakeways: Manhattan Folk, Spooner says he's trying to make an American version of Bollywood. Of course downtown art mogul Jeffrey Deitch is all over Fischerspooner. Deitch is the closest Manhattan has to a Warhol at this point, although strong competition comes from the painter Peter Halley, who, with Bob Nickas, is running a magazine called *Index* from his painting studio on West Twenty-seventh Street. N gets a feature, and Kahimi Karie a cover. Photography is by Wolfgang Tillmans and a young man called Ryan McGinley, who is flown to Berlin for the Momus feature—his first international assignment. Editor-at-Large Steve Lafreniere becomes the Virgil to N's Dante during his two years in New York, affectionately dubbing him "the Heliogabalus of Orchard Street." This bucolic address—

where Orchard meets Hester, and the old Jewish Lower East Side dissolves into Chinatown—becomes the hub of N's American Empire, a tiny nation both too homosexual and too Asian ever to be representatively Yankee. The cabaret soon falls by the wayside. N's hope has been to ape the success of the drag artist Justin Bond's rival act Kiki and Herb, but *Electronics in the 18th Century* fizzles. The Scot returns to his minuscule apartment and Shizu, his Japanese girlfriend, who is given to wearing sweaters embroidered with the words "I LOVE MOMUS." The couple—too hetero for this gay new world—spends the spring of 2000 exploring Manhattan and adjoining Williamsburg on matching Razor kick-scooters.

David Foster Wallace: Rika appeared in N's life shortly after he arrived in New York. He was giving a concert one evening at the New York University gym on Washington Square. Dusk had fallen, and between sound check and stage time N was lingering in the lobby when he noticed a small, pretty Japanese girl with a straight fringe, wearing a hooded yellow coat that made her look exactly like a fluffy chick. The girl drifted out onto the square and N followed. She walked down MacDougal Street, past the great spreading plane trees and the old men playing chess, and entered a record shop. N, too shy to make any kind of approach, went back to the gym. When the show was over the girl came up and introduced herself as Rika, and her taller friend as Mie. Email addresses were exchanged; N needed help finding an apartment, and Rika said she had some good leads. They met the next day at the Lotus Cafe on Clinton Street. N learned that Rika was studying painting at Hunter College and that she'd not only been aware of his attention the evening before, but had been deliberately willing him to follow her. They shared a taxi back to Brooklyn, and began kissing passionately on the Williamsburg Bridge. Rika had a sparse studio apartment upstairs from a woman who played excruciatingly loud music;

it was apparently some kind of feud. She took a strangely long time in the bath before arriving in bed. The sex was somehow stilted, and afterward N explained that he would soon be joined by his "real" girlfriend, Shizu. This set a limit of a few short weeks to their affair, and Rika began to develop feelings for Ryan, a fellow art student. She would get these huge crushes on people, and drink heavily, and self-harm to get attention. But she was fine as a friend; true to her word, Rika helped N find his apartment at 38 Orchard Street. ("I haven't come all the way to New York just to live in Brooklyn," he quipped, hoping to justify spending a thousand dollars a month on a single room bisected by a loft bed.) Then Shizu arrived from Japan—the deal was that they'd live together for the length of a tourist visa, then Shizu would return to Japan to make money, then N would stay with her in Tokyo for three months, subletting the Orchard Street room, and so on. Shizu was very permissive—she'd encourage N to seduce the girls they met in New York. But Rika was different—although she'd still sometimes stay over at Orchard Street (she was working as an assistant to Rainer Ganahl, who had a studio nearby), the relationship resolved into pure affection: she and N would hold each other close on the high bed deck, and N would whisper in her ear "I love you, Rika," as they fell asleep. Rika always seemed vigorously happy in N's presence, so it took him a long time to realize that she had a bipolar and manic side, and that love and drinking brought out disturbing and self-destructive behavior in her. Ryan was appalled one day when Rika started hacking at her wrist in front of him with a broken beer bottle, and the pair split up. Rika soon met an Austrian, Walter, who was part of Rainer Ganahl's set. She graduated from Hunter and they got married. For a while she seemed radiantly happy, but then suspicions began. Rika claimed that an outsized pair of knickers had been found in their bed, and she believed that Walter was having an affair with some enormous woman. When 9/11 happened Rika declared that the collapse of the towers had been one of the most beautiful things she'd ever seen. N couldn't accept this. He also had trouble understanding Rika's art, and one day Rika phoned up and screamed for about half an hour, accusing N—who was embarking on an art career of his own—of knowing nothing about painting, nothing about art, and nothing about beauty. It turned out that a portrait she'd been making of N had appeared in a photo a Dutch magazine had published of his apartment, and Rika felt that her work was merely providing N with an arty backdrop. The force of her rage was unsettling, but they were soon sitting together again at Vanessa's tiny dumpling shop on Eldridge Street, smiling at each other, forgiving everything. Whenever he was with Rika N just wanted to smile. With Walter she would also blow hot and cold; once on Houston Street a baby bird had fallen out of its nest, and Rika called Walter to rescue it, as if only he could do that. Rainer Ganahl told this story at her funeral. Yes, Rika died, in August 2002, days before her twenty-fifth birthday. The crisis struck while N was touring the States. Mie kept sending mails: Rika was in a mental hospital, Rika was threatening to kill herself. N hurried back to New York and came to visit the ward. Rika was mute and pale, but willing to communicate by passing scraps of paper on which she wrote things like "WALTER IS LIER" and "I AM NOT SELECTIVE MUTE" and "I FEEL LIKE MY LIFE IS BORD GAME I LOST." She looked beautiful, like a frail capuchin monkey with a mushroom haircut. The consultant seemed terrified to discuss her, and reluctant to get people involved who weren't family. Mie and N ended up bringing Rika's mother over from Japan to take her home. Thinking all would be well, N went to Paris and then Scotland, where he was joined by Mie, who was exhausted by the situation and needed to get out of New York. But when Rika's mother came, Rika persuaded her that everything was fine and that she should return to Japan. And then, the day after she was released from the hospital, Rika made this big wall-scribbling installation in Walter's loft on Kent Avenue—he was away at his sister's place—and then downed a bottle of whiskey and took pills and settled a razor blade on the edge of the bath. N's last communication with her had been from a phone booth in Le Marais. Rika claimed that she'd been pregnant in the hospital, and had an abortion during a thunderstorm. She said that her marriage was over. She didn't want to come and live with N and Shizu in Tokyo. Now she was going on a journey to "a paradise-like place." She told N "thank you" before hanging up. N was alarmed, and alerted mutual friends in New York. They went straight to Kent Avenue and rang the bell, but Rika didn't answer. Her last phone call was to Thuy Pham, a friend who owned the fashion label United Bamboo. She agreed to see him the following day, but said she couldn't meet that evening because "I have to do something with my body." Walter sent N an email the next day; he had visited the loft with his sister. "She was in the bath tube." Reading this in Edinburgh, with Mie by his side, N let out a deep howl of grief.

John Cage: The title of this memoir, *Niche*, puts me in mind of the Zen Buddhist proverb I learned from D. T. Suzuki while sitting in on his classes at Columbia: "*Nichi nichi kore kōnichi*: every day is a good day." In pre-9/11 New York, every day really is a good day. N might wake up with a Japanese friend, then breakfast on green tea and a plastic mug full of garlicky eggplant congee. He might dress in his quirky rags from Domsey's, the huge thrift warehouse over in the Hasidic part of Williamsburg, and head across Allen Street to Vanessa Weng's hole in the wall, where they play Cantonese opera in the kitchen and give you five juicy hot dumplings for a dollar. Soho still has reasonable enough rents that a place like Printed Matter can offer acres of artists' books behind a wrought-iron façade on Mercer Street. There are relics of downtown's former status as the center of New York's art world in the form of lofts like the Thread Waxing Space, the Drawing Center, or Space Untitled, a factory-like gallery with a café attached. N might visit his storage unit in Tribeca to pluck out a book or kick-scoot his way across the NYU campus to Sixth Avenue, where he keeps a mailbox not far from my loft, where Merce Cunningham still, at this point, lives. In this New York you can still see Gerard Malanga limping along Broome Street. There are still physical record shops like Other Music to look into, and you can borrow clunky old VHS videotapes from Kim's on Avenue A. Depending on the weather, one might want to see the show at the New Museum, which is still on Broadway, or head across to Pierogi in Williamsburg, PS1 in Queens, or the Noguchi Museum down at the waterfront. In some ways this is still the age of the long boom, the dot-com bubble, and "irrational exuberance." The art world is very much setting the agenda, hmm? A necessary port of call is Aaron Rose's new space Alleged in the Meatpacking District. Here you might be served tea by Susan Cianciolo in a sort of conceptual restaurant, alongside Michael Stipe and Björk and the Italian twins from Blonde Redhead. After dark N heads with Shizu and the artist Hiroshi Sunairi to Passerby, a tiny bar on West Fifteenth Street run by British gallerist Gavin Brown. There's a flashing disco floor installation by Piotr Uklanski, and Elizabeth Peyton is probably playing Oasis records from a turntable in the corner—we do wish she wouldn't, hmm, ha ha ha! The sign behind the bar states: EUROTRASH NOT SERVED, which is funny because almost no one else goes in there. Closer to home N's map includes a murky basement bar on Mott Street called Double Happiness, a multimedia lounge in Soho called Void, and a place called Sway where you can't dance but you can sway. N might sprawl on a broken chair in Pink Pony on Ludlow drinking sweet chai, or there could be a feeding frenzy of gallery openings in Chelsea, and interesting people to meet: baleful crooner Stephin Merritt, fashion design trio threeASFOUR, eccentric inventor Brian Dewan, or

Harmony Korine, the enfant terrible of independent film. One evening Harmony invites N to his Gramercy Park apartment for a sort of heroin-fueled drum circle and they write a song together, which is stillborn because Korine is mostly smooching—so to speak—in the other room with Kahimi Karie. The song begins:

> *Before I wrote the book I wrote*
> *Before these roses pushed up in my throat*

I am tempted to make a mesostic:

> *roses pusHed up*
> *in my throAt*
> *the book i wRote*
> *pushed up in My throat*
> *i wrOte the book i wrote*
> *pushed up iN*
> *mY throat*

Alan Lomax: Black men working the chain gang under the whip and the gun made some of the best music I'd ever heard, like "Go Down Old Hannah," which is a song addressed to the sun:

> *Go down, Old Hannah, well, don't you rise no more*
> *Don't you rise no more*
> *If you rise in the morning you'll set the world on fire*

I recorded these songs with my father down at the Texas penitentiary. Later I traveled the world as a folk collector—to explore, but also to escape the McCarthyite witch hunts of the 1950s. I came to believe that the working songs of weavers and woodcutters were some of the finest music known to man, as great an achievement of the human spirit as any piece of chamber music or symphony. Yet this culture was hidden, downplayed; in the age of automobiles, television, and atomic explosions we'd somehow become deaf to the sound of our own voices. Sometimes the Library of Congress helped me find these work songs, sometimes it didn't. Old people sang them, mostly. You just had to capture them on tape recorders that were more or less portable—rather less than more, in fact! I had assistants in the field, official and unofficial. And amateurs everywhere took up the cause. N was one of them. At first it was a somewhat whimsical interest for him: he liked the proximity of the words "fake" and "folk"—one pointing to the synthetic, to creativity and innovation, the other to tradition and authenticity. Well, but, see, collectors like my father and myself, we were never selling you the idea of purity. We weren't interested in what was "unspoiled" or "untouched by human hand." We knew things were hybrid, that songs moved and changed as they got passed from place to place and from race to race. People now talk about "cultural appropriation," but that's how culture works. Nobody owns it: it moves around, changes hands, breeds, gets dirty. I don't mind at all that N took the title of my TV series *American Patchwork* as the name of his record label, nor that he started an organization in his New York apartment called the Fakeways Institute and treated Manhattan bands as if they were Native Americans, Appalachian fiddlers, or Negroes in the cotton fields. Of course he was playing around with some kind of provocative fusion of postmodernism and ethnomusicology, but he was still entirely within the tradition of folk music as I would see it. The horizon of authenticity is a receding one: for every untrained outsider there's an even more "real," even more intuitive singer who could point a finger and accuse that fellow of faking it and selling out. It's a fruitless dispute, of course. Everyone could be fake, and everyone could be real. Purity is not the point. The point is that we sing our lives, and sing them boldly and joyfully. When N made his *Folktronic* album in his Orchard Street apartment in 2000, I believe he was thinking about what folk music might mean, but also making actual folk music, just like Lead Belly or the fiddlers Hamish Henderson and I recorded in the Inner Hebrides. It was hot that summer in his apartment, so N recorded naked. He got so excited by songs like "Robocowboys" that he wrecked his ears playing them back far too loudly in the headphones. I guess the style started with the EP he'd recorded in London in 1999 with Kahimi Karie, *Journey to the Centre of Me*. N was buying a lot of second-hand folk records in Spitalfields Market, and listening to medieval music he would borrow from the Barbican Library as well as the artists who drew inspiration from that music in the seventies, people like Gryphon and Caravan and Nico on her *Desertshore* album. Well, Polydor offered a good budget for a new Kahimi EP, so N recruited the Dufay Collective. They were musicians who played at Shakespeare's Globe theater, and they had these wonderful medieval instruments: crumhorns, sackbuts, shawms, regals, cornetts, and viols. The raw edges and unstable tunings of these ancient instruments reminded N of early analog synthesisers, so he mixed in the sounds of Moogs and Prophets and Korgs. That record didn't do well in the market, and became his last project with Kahimi. But the new direction really excited N, and he continued it with *Folktronic*. In fact a whole genre sprang up that came to be known as Folktronica, and included people like Four Tet, Broadcast, and Múm. After the record came out N continued the project in his first solo art show, which was called *Folktronia*. He set up two tepees in an art gallery in Chelsea. LFL on West Twenty-seventh Street was transformed into a forest with digital projections of trees, aromatic hay bales, and the sound of birdsong. In one tepee you could hear extracts from *Folktronic*, like "Finnegan the Folk Hero," which is a song about an exploited web designer, or "Tape Recorder Man," which is a song about me. In the other tepee you could record your own misheard, misremembered versions. So there was this Chinese Whispers thing going on, a sort of laboratory version of how the oral folk tradition actually works. For two hundred dollars Momus would even make a folk tale about you, writing you into the history of this digital territory called Folktronia. It wasn't so different from what the boys in Silicon Valley were offering at the time—selling lots in spaces that weren't quite real, vending their bubbles with a mess of P. T. Barnum hoo-ha. It really was an American patchwork, and very much of its time.

Yves Saint Laurent: I appear in the narrative at this point for several reasons. First of all, I was invoked by a member of the public the other day when N was strolling along the Coulée Verte, a green high walk in the Twelfth Arrondissement of Paris. The dipping sun was gilding the fresh leaves of spring with an orange light when someone sitting on a bench, seeing the elegant and epicene figure of N approaching, shouted out: "Yves Saint Laurent!" The thin Scot was delighted because—frail and feline, reeking of perfume, talent, and heightened sensitivity—I have always incarnated one of his ideals of subversive male beauty. But please understand that when you invoke the dead you not only perpetuate our memory—for if we exist at all it is only in the thoughts of the living—but also summon our spirits. I suspect, from my position in this book, that I have been recruited to describe how N dressed in Tokyo in the early years of the twenty-first century. There's a kind of bathos here: think of all the things you could ask me instead! How well—if at all—do people dress in the afterlife? What did I really get up to with the boys in Marrakech? And why am I not ghostwriting a book by Jarvis Cocker or David Sylvian instead? It reminds me of those Japanese porn films in which Japanese men, given the ability to stop time and thus potentially to rule the world, use this super-power merely to have sex with Japanese women. Anyway, since I am here to describe clothes, let me speak of a photograph of N taken in April 2001. He is standing astride an orange folding bicycle by the Meguro River, and blossoms still hang on the branches of the cherry trees. It is April, and he has just arrived in Tokyo from New York. He will spend six months of the year here, sleeping between Shizu and Rie on a futon in a small apartment near the Meguro River, recording with Emi Necozawa and Kahimi Karie and feeling, if truth be told, deliriously happy. His clothes are mostly from New York: his patent plastic shoes and 1970s herringbone trousers are from Center for the Dull, the spunky vintage shop on Lafayette Street previously called Smylonylon and run by an eccentric Welshman called Chris Brick. A daring touch is the fur waistcoat from Domsey's warehouse in Williamsburg; this garment actually lured Robert Rauschenberg to approach N at an exhibition opening in Washington at which everyone else was wearing suits. (Perhaps the pop artist believed that N was dressed as the goat in his famous *Monogram* combine?) Slung over N's shoulder is a tomato-red rubberised bag from Berlin. It contains apartment keys, a wallet, a small white flip phone, and a Fujifilm FinePix digital camera. The look is topped off with a pirate eye patch and a widow's-peak crew cut. *Et voilà!* It's not haute couture, of course, but in a sense couture is for the lazy rich, those content to outsource their elegance to experts. The rich have money, but N has the time, the design sense, and the motivation to search for interesting garments in secondhand clothes shops all over the world. Nakameguro is an excellent place in which to continue the hunt; APC has a surplus outlet here, and there's a shop near the station called Per Gramme in which you pay for clothes by weight. The place to show off the resulting outfits—spliced as in one of those die-cut costume flip-books in which a pirate can be combined with a Scotsman and a peasant—is the Organic Cafe, where the area's population of musicians, magazine writers, fashion designers, and photographers congregate. Obey posters designate this a recognised site of international subcultural importance and a Groovisions mannequin guards the door like the fierce *Niō* at the entrance to a Buddhist temple. Inside there are stacks of *Relax* magazine, each featuring the elegant street photography of Masafumi Sanai, who shoots beautiful girls using a 6x7 format camera, natural light, and hand printing. Fantastic Plastic Machine's album *Luxury* hangs on the wall—the orange and purple sleeve is a reappropriated Verner Panton design. N lounges on a white vinyl sofa with Kahimi Karie and Emi Necozawa, who flatter him rotten. They scrawl ideas on napkins, admire a frizzy-haired Pre-Raphaelite photo shoot Mari has recently posed for, and plan records. Mari tells N that Cornelius, recording his new album at the 3D studio nearby, is expecting him to drop by at some point. And *Point* turns out to be the record's title. Its motto—"from Nakameguro to everywhere"—describes very much what this particular moment feels like, poised precariously on the edge of the golden age of globalism. It's what N's outfits are struggling to express: Nakameguro is a point of presence, a cluster of local particularities that—chopped up and regrouped as they might be by a world-famous fashion designer—express a sort of universality, a sort of sublimity. Tokyo in 2001 is the perfect playground for our spoiled world-child, an apex and zenith. There are still traces of the feel of the 1960s and '70s, soft echoes of a jet-set childhood. The world will not always feel so comforting.

Ernest Hemingway: The day the planes hit the towers the sky was very clear. It was a new fall day and everything felt fine. N was lying on the Orchard Street loft bed with a lithe Japanese fashion student. Fierce and elegant, she had the body of a pearl diver, brown from diving in the sun with a knife between her teeth. She'd flown in from London, and they were awake now and celebrating each other. After the scorch of pleasure N took pictures and then put on the winter lieder of Schubert. For the moment there was only beauty. A crash rang out in the city beyond, loud enough that N paused the CD and turned on NY1. They began reporting that a plane had hit the World Trade Center. "Let's go up onto the roof and see!" N pulled on shorts and a pink T-shirt and they ran up to force open the roof door. You weren't supposed to go up there. About a mile away the north tower of the World Trade Center had a hole punched right through it. The hole was black and smoking. But the city still looked clear and calm under a fine blue sky. A second plane flashed between buildings and it seemed to N that it must be an official vehicle sent to investigate. The south tower was hidden behind a big brick building in Chinatown, but instead of the plane what emerged was the sound of an explosion and a new puff of smoke above Confucius Plaza. This wasn't an accident, it was an operation of some kind. Before they went back down N asked the girl to take a photograph of him with the building burning behind. He was careful to look dismayed, but felt several different things. Excitement, amazement, distress, anxiety, confusion. Perhaps nobody had been in the building. Perhaps the fire would soon be extinguished. The couple walked to Division Street and N shot some digital video. The Chinese were watching in silence. What were those things falling out of the building? There was a lot of paper fluttering out, but also heavier, darker things. You could smell the smoke and dust. N felt no desire to get closer. They went back home. The television started reporting that one of the towers had fallen. Then the second one also. *Jesucristo!* There was a sort of mushroom cloud on the horizon now. The smoke was blowing endlessly toward Red Hook. That night the wind changed and N's apartment suddenly began filling up with smoke and dust and debris. N shut the windows quickly and flipped the bolts. But it was impossible to avoid the smell. It spread across the whole of New York City—the smell of fire and death and catastrophe that comes from the sky. To get away from it, the next day N and the girl went up to Central Park and looked at the statue of Alice at the Mad Hatter's tea party. They watched children launch boats on the boating pond. They returned videos to Kim's on Avenue A. In the East Village people were sitting outside cafés with their quivering little dogs as usual. But everybody looked shell-shocked. Life was continuing like a series of empty mechanical actions. To be normal was to be out of touch. Photographs of missing people started appearing on walls and lampposts. The ghost faces in those images were manic and desperate, as if clinging to the idea that they were still alive somewhere. American flags appeared everywhere from nowhere. The president said that he was going to smite the evildoers, whoever they were. "An eye for an eye leaves the whole world blind," read the graffiti on the sidewalk. When airspace reopened the girl took an Emirates flight back to Europe. It was only then that N got rattled. There were rumors that the water had been poisoned or that botulism or bubonic plague would break out. Someone was sending anthrax through the mail. The papers printed a crude note: "THIS IS NEXT. TAKE PENACILIN NOW. DEATH TO AMERICA. DEATH TO ISRAEL. ALLAH IS GREAT." A Vietnamese employee at N's eye hospital died of anthrax poisoning. Everything was potentially toxic. Muslims were advised by terrorist organizations to avoid planes and high buildings. Should one take a taxi? Should one buy bananas from a street vendor? N bought a bunch on Houston but threw them away before he reached Grand. America was squaring up to an invisible enemy. Who was it? A man in a cave? A cabal of covert operatives? You were either "with us or against us." N didn't like this new talk or this new feeling. America's problems were not his, and America's solutions were going to be worse.

Michel Butor: In 1962 I published *Mobile*, a "study for a representation of the United States," which documents my 1959 road trip across that nation using a jubilant and jazzy flow of facts and observations inspired by the painting style of Jackson Pollock. *Mobile* is like Tocqueville's *Democracy in America* randomised and rewritten by the young Allen Ginsberg; it's a textual collage juxtaposing the names of cities, flavours from the Howard Johnson's menu, products for sale in the Sears Roebuck and Montgomery Ward catalogs, Native American treaties, the history of the Freedomland theme park, dates, days of the week, the history of the 1893 Chicago World's Fair, accounts of the Salem witch trials, excerpts from the writings of Thomas Jefferson and Benjamin Franklin, road signs, and so on. What's remarkable is that a technique so mechanical and apparently random can be so exact, evocative, and expressive. Scrapbooks—like the marvellous series collated by the Japanese artist Shinro Ohtake—can tell us a huge amount about our lives in culture, and the ephemera they preserve only gains in value as time makes it rare. Of course, zoom out and you can see an artist's list of works as another sort of collage: the succession of projects is an attempt—continually corrected and refreshed, ripped up and recomposed—to set in aspic the flux of a sensibility rushing through a particular series of places and times. Looking back at his discography, N is able to evoke his own state of mind in any given year between 1982 and the present by remembering the album he was making then. Since his lodestar is the equally prolific David Bowie, and since the two have made approximately the same number of long-players, N can impose a second grid on the same time period and declare, for instance, that 1987 was the year of both *Never Let Me Down* and *The Poison Boyfriend*—one made in Lausanne, one in London—or that 2003 saw the release of both *Reality* and *Oskar Tennis Champion* (the former made in New York, the latter in Tokyo). N and Bowie are both artists inclined to pastiche the styles of others, so there are records on which they're colliding genres, coming up with "fake folk" or "plastic soul." They also have moments when they're bending gender and other moments when they're straightening up, moments when they're interested in America and moments when they're more European or Asian, and moments when they're trying to be mainstream and universal versus moments when they're happy to experiment in the margins. In the early years of the twenty-first century N is willfully embracing obscurity, influenced by the "glitch" laptop electronica then emerging from francophone countries (he's listening to Discom, o.lamm, DAT Politics, and two Belgian brothers who release records under the name of Scratch Pet Land). The manifesto for this work is provided by an essay by Kim Cascone entitled "The Aesthetics of Failure," published in *Computer Music Journal* in the year 2000. Failure is more interesting than success, and while the new world of shiny digital sound promises perfection, it also creates possibilities for exciting new kinds of failure, including the *wabi sabi* aesthetic of valuing technology that only half works (the fortuitously broken Waldorf Miniworks 4-pole filter with which Stefan Betke makes Pole records, for instance). I personally divide my own career into the era in which people were paying attention to me (the four novels I published in the 1950s) and the era in which they weren't (my experiments with painted and handmade books following the publication of my essay "The Book as Object"), but I can tell you that one state is no less amusing than the other. An artist may love to be read, interviewed, and discussed, but these things are secondary: what is delightful is to play and to persist. Success is merely failure you've found a way to sustain.

Viktor Shklovsky: A *yakiimo* vendor sells roasted sweet potatoes from a van. Like many other mobile Japanese tradespeople he has a melancholy, medieval-sounding street cry that issues in electronic form from the top of a compact white vehicle. There is one outside N's window at this moment—we are in the Meguro district of Tokyo in the year 2002—and he stops recording a song about Scottish vaudeville and turns to dangle a microphone out of his window to record the otherworldly melody. Since N loves *ostranenie* (my term for estrangement) and *verfremdungseffekt* (Brecht's word for the same thing), he ends up incorporating the sound into the song, forcing the listener into a strange world where the "Laird of Inversnecky"—a character invented by the Scottish comedian Harry Gordon—coexists with a Japanese seller of sweet potatoes. And now, by dragging me into it, he has added a dimension of Moscow in the 1920s, and formalist literary criticism. Is that an interesting world to drag people into? A world where Scottish music hall artists meet Japanese street vendors and avant-garde Russian formalists? It's quite possible that if one made a Venn diagram of these three areas of interest, only N would be standing in the tiny space where the circles overlap. Everybody else would be alienated (and not in an artistic way)! It's the kind of freakish, incomprehensible juxtaposition that expatriate artists tend to enjoy. I think of the American Paul Bowles, for instance. Living in Tangier, Bowles became fascinated by the privilege of being foreign and the incommensurable otherness of the host culture. In your modern dogma you would call this a kind of "orientalism" and warn Bowles to "check his privilege," but what you fail to see is that if an American foreigner is allowed to keep his host culture at arm's length in Tangier—by refusing to learn Arabic, for instance—there is an implied reciprocal politics which allows the Moroccan immigrant to do the same in America: to be in the place, but not of it. And this right of non-assimilation has obvious connections to the artistic virtue of estrangement. The *Fremder* stem found in *Verfremdungseffekt* means, in German, "stranger," and much of the moral dimension of politics revolves around the way one treats strangers: in order to contrast the liberal and tolerant Weimar Republic with Nazism, for instance, one only need write a song that begins:

Willkommen! Bienvenue! Welcome!
Fremder, étranger, stranger

There is a Jewish proverb: "When the housewife is lazy, the cat is industrious." In failing to integrate one still participates, but with different senses at work. When the left brain is blocked, stumped, or impaired, the right brain takes over. To the non-Japanese speaker, Japan becomes a succession of scents, textures, sounds, colours, lights, experiences, tastes, shapes, and emotions. N's Japan in 2002 is a rush of nonsensical impressions, a delicious regression to the primitive and the sensual, the lower cortex, the right brain; a reversion to the prelingual, to pseudo-babyhood. He becomes a homunculus, a cute and happy sensual monster in need of a mother, preferably with gigantic breasts filled with Calpis milk. As John Cage said: "As soon as I understand something I no longer have any need for it."

Philip Larkin: Whether in Belfast, Hull, or Tokyo, the same demons are always lying in wait: Lust, Sloth, Envy, the usual brood. N's first months in Tokyo are a sexual delight, as he lies sandwiched each night between two lovelies, Rie and Shizu. Rie kindly feigns sleep when business is afoot with Shizu, and has a tendency to grind her teeth when actually in the principality of nod. One morning N wakens to find Rie's hand gripping his knob—he doesn't take it personally: her teeth are still a-chomp. Alas, Rie is soon called away to marry a television comedian and bear his children. She is replaced by a flatmate who is more "dangerous" in Shizu's eyes, a bluestocking slim as a library slip. Keiko works in a famous art gallery and has already been intimate with N in a series of clandestine skirmishes. She has too much class to continue the flirtation at such close proximity, but Shizu takes the precaution of banishing N to the other room, where he kips in a kind of dog basket. This rankles, and N soon finds himself arranging an encounter at nearby Giggle Cafe with a disc jockey of ancient acquaintance. Natsuko is handsome and whippet-thin, justifiably narcissistic, and seems to live by modeling for a lesbian *mangaka* who has cast her in a sci-fi strip as some sort of Rocket Girl and is obviously deeply in love with her. The Giggle rendezvous goes well: Natsuko shows N a portfolio of studio portraits, in one of which she's casually spilling milk from her mouth across her pale, almost-flat bare breasts. Arrangements are made for N to take the Chuo Line regularly to her studio flat, a white room in Nishi-Ogikubo which quickly becomes a second home. Here—as well as annoying her cat Atom by tugging down Natsuko's expensive panties to marvel at her lovely coccyx—N learns a huge amount about Japanese pop music, coming to love, for example, Haruomi Hosono's wonderfully strange jingles compilation *Coincidental Music*, or Miharu Koshi's gorgeous 1984 album *Parallelisme*. "Life churns on like gorgonzola under a microscope" is how I once described the glum time I had in Hull, but there's a jazzy fizz to N's Tokyo life that might—should I have lucked into similar adventures—have made me quite a different poet.

Jacques Tati: I recognize the title of N's 2003 album *Oskar Tennis Champion*—his Tokyo LP, the follow-up to his New York LP—because it is also the title of my first film. In 1932 I wrote and starred in a comedy short directed by Jack Forrester entitled *Oscar, champion de tennis*. Alas, the film is now lost, but it's not hard to imagine its content: a series of slapstick gags set on a tennis court. My character was not yet Monsieur Hulot, but my central theme was already present: a Don Quixote is tilting—through a series of mute errors, clumsy accidents, and acts of subtle stubbornness— against the great windmills of order and geometry. Although I am a clown in the school of Keaton and Lloyd, I also share themes with the brilliant sociologist Michel de Certeau, who set the tactical—

in the form of furtive and cunning gestures of human defiance—against the strategic, by which he meant the oppressive overarching structures set in place by government and commerce. My masterpiece is *Playtime*, in which I build a graph-paper Paris—the kind Le Corbusier dreamed of making—and set Hulot loose in its plateglass labyrinths to squeak the chairs and crash the transparent doors. Since N has just seen the modernist towers of the World Trade Center slip, as it were, on a gigantic banana skin—religion, the irrational, resentment, the guerrilla resistance, self-appointed nemesis, call it what you will—he finds my worldview both topical and compelling. Embracing something he calls *vaudeville concrète*, N begins to make the kind of record that might have emerged if Georges Brassens had worked with Pierre Schaeffer, or Tom Lehrer had studied with Stockhausen. It's a powerful combination: On the one hand you have the conservative, folksy appeal of strong narrative lines and universal themes—all that is enduringly, bunglingly human. On the other is radical, innovative modernism, and with it a certain austere and progressive formalism. How to reconcile them? Well, one way is to do what I did: set a gangling clown loose amid skyscrapers. Another might be to perform the vaudeville in the lyrics and the *concrète* in the music by, for instance, bringing in a formalist collaborator—here, John Talaga, the "reproducer" with a license to fuck things up (excuse my French) musically. *Oskar* is a record that feeds on the clumsiness inherent in being a foreigner in Tokyo, of course, but also shows the first signs that N is becoming aware of himself as a disabled person, blind on one side—an affliction which makes it particularly trying to cross Shinjuku Station, for instance. The disability theme—which inevitably becomes a political correctness theme as well, since it is about a proclamation of victimhood—plays out in songs like "Beowulf (I Am Deformed)" or "Is It Because I'm a Pirate?" Here, Brechtian villains—Mack the Knives of various shades—hide behind their deformities, launching spurious requests that the world not rush to judgment: to call a pirate a pirate and invoke stereotypes that are actually accurate is portrayed by these rogues as an unforgivable act of prejudice. "Scottish Lips" continues the theme by suggesting a series of identities for which a labially well-endowed Scot might be celebrated: his cooking, his mind, his spirit—anything but his lips. Written by an "exotic" Westerner in Japan, these songs satirise anti-orientalism by inverting it, and mock the identitarian dogma that one can decide the attributes for which one ought to be prized by others. The themes converge: 9/11 has emphasised the frailty of modern progress, disability and the arrival of a new century have reminded our narrator of his own mortality, and I, Tati, have supplied the appropriate mode in which to address these topics: satirical slapstick. Uncle Oskar becomes a sort of King Kong in Le Corbusier's Radiant City, and the Bauhaus steps on a rake. Of course, the greatest banana skin of all—the spanner flying in slow motion towards the works—is death. Even our mightiest works will not last forever. There's something oddly comforting about that, I think. The aesthetics of glitch, failure, and slapstick—based on an embrace of deformation, hazard, error, and salvage—might contain a grim sort of salvation. It's the third law of thermodynamics: finally, the only way to be on the winning team is to side with the great falling apart.

Eva Figes: N had wanted to commence the next "chapter" of his life with a female voice, and first typed "Edith Wharton" on a fresh line. Then he was stumped, not having read any Edith Wharton (though he did remember bits of radio readings here and there). He went to his local Berlin supermarket and bought some box lunches—various world dishes precooked, untroublesome food to prepare while thinking of other things—and on the way thought of me, Eva Figes. He had once heard a programme on BBC Radio 3 in which experimental approaches to literary narrative were discussed, and I'd said something memorable about how it wasn't always necessary to describe the colour of the traffic lights. Standing, in fact, at the traffic lights on the way to Real (that's what his local supermarket is really called), N googled me to check that I was dead. Wikipedia said that, sure enough, I was born in Berlin in 1932 and had died in London in 2012, so I was certainly available as a narrator. (Writing this memoir, N has got into the bad habit of being rather pleased to discover that writers he likes are dead.) He also noted that I'd written a book in 1970 entitled *Patriarchal Attitudes*, and wondered if his desire for more female narrators was laudable or perhaps a pathetic kind of puppetry. Would I approve of the posthumous appropriation of my own voice? By a man? Probably not, but it was too late to know for sure. In a certain sense, even to be spoken about is to be given a little jolt, a little zap of life. N did like the fact that, as a Jewish refugee, I had fled from the Nazis. His sense of his own life in 2002 was that he was fleeing from a tepid yet insidious form of Nazism emerging in the United States. The world was once more mobilising for war of some sort. There was a "clash of civilisations," blah blah blah. One of N's standard lines about 2002 was that he had escaped terrorism and flag-waving in New York only to land in a far more dangerous city that could be destroyed by an earthquake at any moment. But as the year wore on it became clear that his Tokyo life was coming to an end along with his relationship with Shizu, who had taken up with an Irish American filmmaker called David (N actually introduced them). Unable to sustain a life in Tokyo, N at first returned to London and the arms of the Japanese fashion student with whom he had weathered the 9/11 attacks. Then he headed to Paris and took a room in an apartment at La Fourche, where the Seventeenth Arrondissement begins and Metro line 13 splits in two. The bifurcation is actually a nice visual sign for this moment of N's life, dominated by choices. Well, he stayed only a few months in Paris, attending headphone concerts by Japanophile laptop artists like Discom, Domotique, Kumisolo, o.lamm, and Shinsei, and paying five hundred euros for a single room in a flat belonging to an Irish translator. A trip to Berlin in early 2003 with some of these musicians convinced him that he was in the wrong city: for the price of a room in Paris he could have an entire flat in Berlin. N arranged to see a place on what used to be called the Stalinallee—now renamed the Karl-Marx-Allee but still redolent of Moscow with its "sugar baker" blocks and suprahuman scale. N liked the flat and took it, and so began a new chapter, a new prong to his fork. I, meanwhile, must be parked forever in a dark siding, because no narrator in this book gets more than a single paragraph. I find it deeply unjust. Please google me and read what I actually wrote while I was alive. Ha! That reminds me of a vignette, something that happened to N in his early months in Berlin. (N and I seem to be porous; my memories are his.) The Austrian composer Bernhard Gál invited N—which is to say me, for the mask slips—to a DAAD party and pointed out the concrete poet Emmett Williams, who was standing by a window. Impressed, N rushed over and said: "Hello, you were involved in Fluxus, weren't you?" What he didn't know was that Williams had suffered a series of strokes. "Read . . . my . . . fucking . . . books!" was all the old poet could muster. If you have to imagine us, the dead, spluttering out anything at all, it should be that. Read . . . our . . . fucking . . . books!

Rayner Heppenstall: I have been called upon to describe N's flat in Berlin in the year 2003, but since I am dead I have no eyes. I must therefore grope my way through it like Dunkel, the protagonist in my experimental novel *The Blaze of Noon*. The hallway is quiet, though I detect the distant rush of traffic on a wide avenue not far off. Closing the front door behind me I quickly bump into a button-back sofa, which I discover is curved. What's this doing in the hall? Just beyond it is something else anomalous: a magazine rack like the ones you might find in a newsagent's shop or on a railway station platform. There are thick magazines resting on its shelves, face out. I have no way of telling what kind they are, but the paper smells expensive. One has the impression that these publications must be trophies of some sort. Perhaps they are author's copies of journals N has written for? At the end of the hall a heavy television set sits on the floor, extinguished. There are rooms to my left and right—one faces the street and may have a broken window latch, for the traffic sounds louder here than it should and there's a draft. This is an enormous room that, on exploration, seems to be completely empty except for a most extraordinary object, a sort of inflatable vinyl igloo which stands at its centre. I enter the structure briefly and bounce cautiously on its padded floor. A strong, sweet smell of secondhand clothes is filling the room beyond—it takes me a minute or so to determine that various sheets and blankets have been tied together and suspended across the windows that cover the whole of one wall, above the radiators. Without exactly being Sherlock Holmes, I can deduce that nearby there must be some sort of secondhand clothes emporium. N has certainly bought these fabrics for their price, their colours, or their patterns rather than the way they smell. God's teeth, perfume turning to putrefaction! The room on the other side of the hall is a welcome refuge. Much smaller, this bedroom is filled with the pleasant sound of birdsong. There's a mattress on the floor, a pair of plimsolls, a desk, a clothes rail, some bookshelves, and several pieces of electronic equipment of indeterminate purpose. I mistakenly twang what must be an autoharp, and hurt my finger on its taut wires. Returning to the hall I discover another door, this time leading to a steamy bathroom. I begin to feel uneasy: Can someone be taking a bath in here? What will be the effect of an intrusion from a stray blind author who has mixed himself up with the narrator from his 1939 novel? One declared by Hélène Cixous, incidentally, to be the very first *nouveau roman*? Could this be any vindication for an act of impotent voyeur-ism? Cautiously, I move towards the source of the steam and extend a hand. I am touching the warm, wet flesh of a naked woman! "Is it you, Nick?" comes a female voice with a strong French accent. I can only assume that this woman is almost as blind as I am, or that the steam is indeed extraordinarily thick. And where is N, anyway? Could he be present in this scene only as the narrator of my nar-ration, the ghostwriter of my ghostwriting? Fumbling for the front door I find that I have missed the kitchen, which I now explore. It is pristine and spartan—clearly not much cooking is done here. At the end of the room there's a small pantry. Why do all pantries smell faintly of vanilla and cumin? Of course, were I filming this, you could see N's apartment, even if I could not. But the whole point of me being blind is that the novel needs to turn its gaze inwards now that cinema can handle the visual stuff so well. I want you to do a little more work and see, in your mind's eye, what I can only feel. In this way perhaps we shall invent, together, a new sort of novel. Wait, what am I saying? I mean autobiography.

Al Purdy:
Zombies were first hatched in Haiti, they say
to gibber through sugar plantations
sweetness is always suspicious to me
—it smacks of disintegration

What is this horrible certainty
swelling in me like a teal's egg?
snatched to tell somebody's tale
I myself am the walking dead

I cannot now speak of the A-frame house
that I built on the shores of Lake Roblin

but must relate the sickening life
of two skinnymalinkies in Berlin

One is called Anne, Anne Laplantine
the other the Niche of this memoir
they sit on a love seat in Prenzlauerberg
in the back room at Wohnzimmer

One evening, DJing on Schönhauser Allee,
Anne plays a file that is startlingly fresh:
N's voice, her guitar, all mingled and fucked
(much as they do in the flesh)

it brings him to tears—a music so sweet
(although sung in the voice of a goblin)
it can only compare to the A-frame house
I built on the shores of Lake Roblin

Raymond Queneau: In *Exercises in Style*, published in 1947, I tell the same trivial story ninety-nine times. A fellow is on the S bus moving through Paris when a quarrel breaks out between two passengers. Two hours later one of the men is spotted again at the Gare Saint-Lazare having a conversation about the buttons on his coat. The same events are retold with increasingly radical stylistic variations in sections headed Metaphorical, Hesitation, Anagrams, Futile, Gastronomical, Polyptotes . . . That last style, for instance, plays on the morphosyntactic variations permitted by grammatical variations on the same word. You can wax academic about conceptual literature, metafiction, and Oulipo's celebrated "Workshop for Potential Literature," but *Exercises in Style* is mostly a very funny book, liberated from banality by its own puckish invention. N's 2004 album *Otto Spooky* resembles it, as does David Bowie's 1979 LP *Lodger*, for both records apply styles in playfully arbitrary ways. *Otto Spooky* is the record David Bowie might have made if he'd worked on *Lodger* with ex-members of the Incredible String Band instead of an ex-member of Roxy Music. Berlin flea markets play a role, with their piles of scrap ripe for ironic recontextualisation; if we exclude the collaboration with Anne Laplantine, this is N's first Berlin album. But it's also a record dominated by the random discoveries of Google search, crowdfunded and cheered on by readers of N's new LiveJournal blog, *Click Opera*: the songs on *Otto Spooky* appear initially as mp3s there, next to a PayPal donate button. In the words of Henry Fuseli, N is now "the artist overwhelmed by the grandeur of ancient ruins," neglected by music publications but given a four-page spread in *Modern Painters* magazine. Financially the first year in Berlin is difficult: N and Aya the fashion student—who has joined him from London—are living by selling stuffed toys bought from Humana, the gigantic second-hand shop nearby, adapting them into "Momus dolls" and flogging them on the Momus website. It's a dung beetle strategy—you turn what's worthless into something salable, make muck into brass. What applies in the physical realm also applies digitally: *Otto Spooky* is neo-Elizabethan googlepop, an aleph-album proposing the search bar as the place from which everything in the world can be seen simultaneously, swooped down upon, pilfered. Needing a guitar solo, N would simply google "guitar solo" and edit the results until they fitted the song. He set about curating an obscure pantheon of search finds, setting figures down as statuettes in a miniature Japanese garden: Pauline Oliveros, Nold Egenter, Marc Bolan, John Barleycorn, Shimura Ken, Christine Rebet, Haruomi Hosono, Paul Klee, Shakespeare, Christoph Willibald Gluck . . . The result is like wandering in some sort of mad art biennial—a cavern of junk treasure where butterflies flutter upon paste jewels.

A rush of information becomes a spinning globe, a kaleidoscopic blur, an eclectic hoard. If he's lost, Spooky Otto, the "artist overwhelmed," is lost in wonder.

Karl Kraus: For thirty-seven years I published *Die Fackel*, my own magazine. Holding this paper torch aloft I proceeded to attack all that dismayed me in Vienna, assuming the persona of the ascetic satirist, the misanthropic pessimist, the intellectual flâneur, the irascible outsider, the mocking moralist—in short, the role of a Momus. A century later N attempted—with, let us be honest, a much lower wattage in his bulb—the same thing when he started *Click Opera*. At first it was simply a LiveJournal log of things he found interesting on the web, but soon *Click Opera* became a record of the artistic life of Berlin in the first decade of the twenty-first century, a love letter to Japan, a toolbox of the concepts and constructs N had acquired during his own intellectual formation, a cork slab pinned with pictures of his latest interests, and—thanks to a lively comments section thronging daily with intelligent people— a kind of seminar unfolding in a university without a campus. One could say, cruelly, that narcissism drove *Click Opera*—they said it of *Die Fackel* too—but a post-Calvinist didacticism also played a part; N after all came from a long line of Scottish teachers. The blog emerged from the technology of its time: most people were only now enjoying continuous DSL connections, and had not yet abandoned computers with QWERTY keyboards that encouraged long, thoughtful textual responses to data. How different from the lazy "finger food" approach encouraged by the iPhones and iPads that would soon arrive! "Today it is bad," sighed dear old Schopenhauer, "and day by day it will get worse—until at last the worst of all arrives." There is a saying in biology that "ontogeny repeats philogeny"—in other words that an individual developing in the womb mimics in mere months developments our species took millennia to work through: gills, dorsal fins, a tail. In the same way, N had spent the previous decade working through the digital equivalents of traditional media models, from the top-down monologues of websites to the hagiographies of fannish newsgroups—which is to say, from the godly to the saintly—and then from the squabbling, heckling rabble on bulletin boards to the calm symposium of pseudonymous students, broadly supportive, who would populate *Click Opera*: Cap Scaleman the eager young Swede, Pimmelkarl the surreal troll, Stanley Lieber the elegant fabulist, the kind and lucid Count Vronsky (who died tragically in Peru), and Marxy, the Harvard-educated Japanese fashion expert who served as *Click Opera*'s principal pantomime villain. The blog produced many thoughtful essays—"The Arrow and the Frame," "The Anxious Interval," and regular Lord Haw-Haw–ish accounts of how awful Britain had become—before it was killed off by the new modes and mores of social media. In its last days *Click Opera* was hounded by a satirical Twitter account called Twit Opera that offered reductio ad absurdum accounts of its entries. At its peak, though, the blog did its job: it was anthologised, it provided quarries full of material for the books N would begin to write, and it landed him columns in *Wired* and *The New York Times* (or, rather, their websites). Above all it gave N the sense that he mattered—here in the noughties, as a rather successful blog star—almost as much as he had back in the eighties, as a failed but interesting pop star. Two essays he wrote for *Wired* signaled the beginning of the end of the blogosphere on which *Click Opera* bobbed: in one N confessed that Steve Jobs's introduction of the iPhone had moved him to tears (he was immediately assailed in the comments section by American men telling him that men don't cry); in another he said that he was coming to the end of his interest in opinions, and hoped to replace them during the next decade with onions—with the pungent tang of those things of which the internet knows precisely zilch.

Frank Kermode: In November 2004 N compiled a list of his "objections to literature":

1. He disliked the sensory deprivation element of reading—the lack of colour, sound, texture, shape, and motion.
2. He disliked the sense that literature was something for an elite bourgeois class, usually university educated (like himself).
3. He thought that studying the literary canon had made him massively self-conscious about any act of reading, and he didn't like that.
4. He was usually living in some country where the bookshops stocked products he couldn't read.
5. He thought of literature as a moribund art form.
6. He had issues with language as an art medium. Prose, which appeared to be close to reality, was in fact merely close to conventions and assumptions about reality. Unlike poetry, it rarely had the power to startle.
7. The kind of writing that foregrounded the limits of language and explored the very autism N was describing— the "literature of exhaustion"—seemed to him tremendously depressing.
8. He thought that writers dressed badly.

N described this position as "post-literary," but perhaps it would be more accurate to call it a self-consciously anti-literary stance. He had studied literature, but his taste had come to contain a self-critique—a critique of himself as a literary person, and of the bourgeois class he had emerged from. Literature had been, at certain formative points in N's life, a kind of religion. Early Momus records had been seen by some as the work of a "singing author," a *cantautore*. But somewhere down the line N had decided that he was more interested in non-literary art forms—more intrigued by texture than text. And yet this stance turned out to be a mere hiatus, a sublimation. The repressed returned quickly, and with gathering force, thanks to four editor-mentors. First came the Swiss novelist Christian Kracht, who asked N to contribute a short story to his review *Der Freund*, and even wired a handsome advance from his hideaway in Kathmandu. A thousand euros for a tall tale entitled "7 Lies About Holger Hiller." N hadn't bashed out a short story since his student days, but this mythopoeic collision of the Brothers Grimm and the *Neue Deutsche Welle* seemed to write itself. Next he was approached by Xavier Belrose, a French publisher interested in a novel. Keen to concoct something pungent and libertine, N came up with the idea of an absurd bildungsroman about a family condemned to act out a series of obscene jokes (often featuring the punch line "this is the pig I've been fucking"). The English rights were picked up by the third figure in this story, Jeremy M. Davies, then of Dalkey Archive Press and now the editor in charge of the memoir you are holding. The fourth is Ingo Niermann, who commissioned two books about nations—Scotland and Japan—for his Solutions series, published in Berlin by Sternberg. A third "nations" book—a satirical fiction entitled *UnAmerica*—appeared later via Penny-Ante Press, and N wrote two more novels for Ingo, which appeared via a digital imprint in Berlin called Fiktion: *Herr F*—a picaresque take on the Faust legend—and *Popppapppp*, which posited the Fall's Mark E. Smith as the unwitting leader of a fundamentalist Middle Eastern cult. So, in the sixteen years following his declaration of himself as "post-literary" N published seven books. There were advances and translations and reprints and even royalties. The way N explained this to himself was sly: he was not making boring old bourgeois literature, he was lying for a living. Put that way, it sounded attractively scurrilous. And yet—as the original cover of *The Book of Scotlands* proclaims—every lie creates the parallel world in which it is true. That may not work as a defence in court or in bed with one's wife, but it's a good defence of poesy—and with that phrase we obviously tip a wink in the direction of Sir Philip Sidney, a man Elizabethan paintings show dressed to kill in a ruff collar and slash-proof gorget.

Chantal Akerman: I know exactly where to set up the camera: at the north end of the Laden Showroom on Brick Lane, opposite Oceanic Leatherware. We're re-creating a meeting that happened in 2003. N lives in Berlin, but he's back in London to play a concert at the ICA. He's been staying with elegant, lonely fashion student Aya. She has a new room in a Bangladeshi council flat and it's grotty and there's no Wi-Fi, so N grumbles and Aya explodes: "Well, go and stay with Suzy, then!" Suzy is his friend who writes for *i-D* magazine. N is probably supposed to back down, but instead he packs and leaves the flat, heading up Brick Lane in the direction of Clerkenwell. Hisae is a small boyish Japanese girl. She's hanging around waiting for her flatmate, who's peeing against a wall on Pedley Street. She walks straight up to N and says: "You're Momus, aren't you?" They chat until the flatmate returns, and N casually invites Hisae to the ICA show. He's settling in at Suzy and Ed's place when Aya starts yowling outside like a cat: "Nick! Nick!" He goes back to her, but can't stop thinking about Hisae. On the day of the concert he takes both Japanese students to the Pool Bar. They get on fine and exchange email addresses. Aya is at the London College of Fashion on Curtain Road, Hisae is doing graphic design at St Martin's. N soon "whisks" Hisae to Berlin ("whisking" is inviting a girl for a secret holiday and paying her plane fare) and feeds her strawberries on his bed, next to the eBoy poster of Berlin in cross section. But it's Aya who moves in, living with N until—halfway through

2004—a Swedish fashion designer invites her back to London to be her personal assistant. At that point Hisae takes Aya's place in the Karl-Marx-Allee flat. They buy an aggressive lionhead rabbit called Topo (renamed Baker and then Pok) and move house, mainly because Hisae doesn't want to live with the ghost of Aya lurking around. The rabbit is an absolute monster, but also a sort of small black son. The couple sublet a flat in downtown Friedrichshain, near the Boxhagener Platz market and a sweet little Japanese café called Smart Deli. Then Hisae has visa problems and has to stay in Osaka for a few months while N is doing art stuff in New York. In 2006 N takes a new flat near the Maybachufer market in Neukölln, and Hisae returns to live with him for four more years. She has visa problems again in 2010, and at that point N decides to move to Osaka to live with her there—which he does until late 2017. So he and Hisae live together for over twelve years! It's by far the longest cohabitation of N's life, a period of stable domesticity and happy productivity. But beneath the surface it's all much more complicated than that. We're going to need a lot of film stock.

Reyner Banham: Throughout the noughties each Momus album features a secret mascot on the inside cover. Open the Digipak gatefold on *Hypnoprism* and behind the hot pink disk you'll find Maria Callas. Prise out the orange *Ocky Milk* CD and there's Emperor Haile Selassie. Hiding under the acid lemon plastic in *Otto Spooky* it's me, Reyner Banham, in a big halftone blow-up. I'm a beardy fellow on a folding bike riding through London. I'm there partly because James Goggin, the designer, has the same oak-green Moulton in his studio. I'm one of his heroes, along with Ettore Sottsass and Enzo Mari. In the photo I look like one of the socialist cranks Orwell scorned in *The Road to Wigan Pier*—those fruit-juice drinkers, nudists, sandal-wearers, sex maniacs, Quakers, nature-cure quacks, pacifists, and feminists. But I'm really more like

Mr. Toad in *The Wind in the Willows*. When his canary-coloured caravan is nudged into a ditch by an automobile, Toad, rather than getting mad, becomes a dazed convert, frantic for a car of his own. I become a proponent, an enthusiast, an apologist for Los Angeles and its car culture. N starts visiting the city in the 1990s but never quite gets his head around it. There's the Roosevelt Hotel, the Museum of Jurassic Technology, Tower Records on Sunset, the Troubadour, Spaceland in Silverlake, the House of Blues, the Eames Office in Santa Monica, Venice Beach—attractions connected by tediously long car trips down boulevards where the only people walking seem to be crazies pushing shopping trollies. There are exiled friends who seem to be flourishing here, like Rafael Jimenez, the Spanish design student who laid out the lyrics collection *Lusts of a Moron*. But Los Angeles feels as alien to N as it had to Brecht and Bowie. In 2001 he performs at Modernbook and elects to be paid with accommodation rather than money. He spends a week where Pico meets Crenshaw, in the apartment of Amy Yao, whose sister, Wendy, turns up every day to chauffeur him around. N is reading my 1971 book *Los Angeles: The Architecture of Four Ecologies*, which parses the city via four ecological models: Surfurbia, Foothills, The Plains of Id, and Autopia. For me, the city is the realisation of the kind of postmodernity we were banging on about in the Independent Group in the fifties. We didn't call it that at the time, of course. Tom Wolfe and Robert Venturi describe it best: this is a new phase of the industrial age, a flipped version that replaces modernism's austere monuments of hieratic seriousness with all that's flimsy, temporary, cheerful, trivial, and demotic. This is Wolfe's "electrographic architecture": spectral, seductive, designed to be seen from the highway. It's air-conditioning, electricity, flashing signs, escalators, giant hamburgers, and Pepsi bottles. In L.A. I abandon my Moulton and learn to drive. I rave about the "sun-change" that defangs the puritanism of midwestern agrarian culture when it hits the coast. In

1972 I drive around in a "Baeda-Kar" filming the Neutra project houses for a BBC documentary called *Reyner Banham Loves Los Angeles*. Thirty years later N decides that his feeling about L.A. is best described as "lovehate." If he's good he'll come back, if he's bad he'll come back twice. The city is toxic, polluted, provincial, suburban, plastic, dangerous, sensual, bland. At its best it reminds him of Tokyo without the trains. So why do I preside benignly over *Otto Spooky* if we can't even agree on Utopia? I think it's because, whatever our judgments, we're both cultural journalists preoccupied with that Tolstoyan question: How then shall we live? We both tap into—and sometimes exaggerate—our enthusiasms to shake up preconceptions. Momus records become somewhat blurry and sparse in the noughties because *kulturkritik* takes up so much of his time, in so many forms: blogging, columns for *Wired* and *The New York Times*, music journalism for *The Wire*, lectures at the Architectural Association, reviews for the art and design press, books. It's his decade as a public intellectual. Later, when Cherry Red anthologises his records, they get a slightly different title: when it comes to music, the intellectual is not public but "pubic." Which—ha ha!— I guess means that N is finally owning up to being a dickhead.

Marcel Duchamp: Following certain amiable pronouncements of mine, anything could be designated as art: stories, strange objects, machines, wolf traps, chess games (played for the patterns rather than to win), smashed sheets of glass, scopophilic perversions, drawers full of documentation . . . It could all sit in galleries alongside the merely retinal pleasures of pigment on canvas. There need be no competition because there is no contradiction; there is no solution because there is no problem. Well, I'm here long after my bedtime to tell you about N's career in the art world, but to be honest it was all implied in certain statements I had made almost a century before. Alan Lomax has already told you about N's first exhibition, in which he created an imaginary land called Folktronia. In 2005 he returned to New York for a monthlong collaboration with Mai Ueda called *I'll Speak, You Sing*. Mai, dressed in high heels and a miniskirt, paced about the gallery chanting childish songs (*"Don't call me elephant, I'm gonna kill you!"*) while N— a shamanic red cloth draped over his head and a laptop droning at his side—improvised stories. "Speaking in a low, hypnotic voice," Roberta Smith wrote in *The New York Times*, "he made up oddly gripping tales that often centered on shocked disbelief and re-peated, almost choruslike questions. One tale, set in 1871, involved a mistakenly delivered letter through which one woman received another one's dead son as a prize." As a result of this N was invited, the following year, to appear as an "unreliable tour guide" at the Whitney Biennial. For three months he stalked the museum's gal-leries in Japanese carpenter trousers, using a battery-powered bull-horn to proclaim that "under no circumstances are the artworks in this room preliminary sketches by Saul Steinberg for a new design, commissioned by the Vatican, for the Christian cross" or that "all of Daniel Johnston's drawings are in fact produced by a Hong Kong teenager who's paid just five dollars for each sheet." There was un-settling advice ("Please ensure that your hairstyle does not infringe copyright, or represent anyone's prophet"), critique of Altria—the tobacco company sponsoring the exhibition—and perverse political commentary: "Without reductive stereotypes of racial essential-ism there can be no reductive politics of racial liberation. There-fore *viva* reductive stereotypes of racial essentialism!" It was what, in other contexts, would have been called "trolling" or "stand-up comedy," but since it happened in designated art spaces—and at a time when my conception of art was wholly triumphant—art is what we must call it. N's final New York exhibition happened in 2009 and was called *Love Is the End of Art*. Again he enlisted the help of a Japanese performer, this time the artist Aki Sasamoto.

Dressed as a *kuroko*—a black-clad Kabuki stagehand holding a follow spot—N interrupted Aki's set pieces (for instance, chopping up fruit with ice skates while standing on a school desk) speaking as an art critic unrequitedly in love with her. The stagehand-critic promised to write the review that would make Aki's career while nagging her to consult a therapist called Dr. Helen. Let's see, what else? There was a series of "emotional lectures" in which N played an academic celebrating a poet (or designer, or architect) who—it transpired in scenes of mounting rage—had fucked the critic's wife. There were text pieces in which gallerists were sent jokes to whisper into the ears of their visitors, or public tours in which London was presented as Pyongyang. There were proverbs gleaned from Facebook and beamed across LED displays, miniature operettas about flirtation, impersonations of Ivor Cutler, performative publishing in which bulletins were issued continuously from "false kiosks" and reports from entirely fictional architecture biennials. None of this made money, but the art world—as it had been in my day—was both affluent and affable, and it amused N to be given licence to play in its protected, privileged spaces. For me, everything could become visual art, but I suspect that his art decade was, for N, more about how to inject writing into new sorts of niche. And above all how to do something very private in public: invent, improvise in real time, lie, make stuff up, show zero becoming one, turn nothing into something and junk into culture. There is a neon sign by Martin Creed I like very much: THE WHOLE WORLD + THE WORK = THE WHOLE WORLD. That says it all. And more.

Graham Greene: It's a strange world wherever you are. You can trust no one but yourself, and not even yourself sometimes. N had been living a double life since the late 1990s—a life like a two-way mirror: private on one side, public on the other. The Cold War was over, so N's double life was no longer about the split between the two Berlins—us and them, capitalism and communism—although some of it did actually take place in Berlin. But it was still, in a larger sense, East versus West; a matter of visas, passports, credentials, identities, and above all, credibility. Without ever quite choosing the role, N became a double man, a confidential agent like the ones in my "entertainments" or the novels of Len Deighton and John le Carré. A metaphorical spy, outwardly confident but inwardly nervous, fretting constantly about being unmasked, defrocked. It happened like this. N began to cohabit with Japanese women, and this led to spending at least part of the year in the Orient. From the turn of the century onwards the span of his life was measured out in ninety-day tourist visas—if not his own, those of his partners, visiting from Japan. They were all, of course, lying to the immigration authorities—the "tourist" status was just a convenience, a bureaucratic catch-all. No real tourist spends eight months of the year for eight years in a single country. One got away with it by changing one's passport frequently. The British authorities asked no questions; previous visas were washed away, absolved like sins after confession. Sometimes it didn't work: Hisae spent a night in the cells at a Berlin airport and was temporarily banned after a couple of her attempts to enter Germany failed. N was interrogated for over an hour at Kansai International Airport, and had to vow to change his status at the first opportunity. He just changed his passport again and was waved through like a new man in clean paper skin. Alongside this administrative doubleness lurked a sexual duplicity: in bed, too, N began to live a double life. In Japan he could have a comfortable domestic life with Hisae, whereas on his travels he would usually be joined by *une voyageuse clandestine*. The bonds with these travelling companions were not always sexual. But photographs of the co-travellers were never shown, and no mention was made of them. Hisae had a more successful strategy than Shizu in dealing with this: whereas Shizu had tried to organise N's extracurricular life so that it happened under her nose, Hisae worked hard to ignore it. She treated the privacy of his laptop as sacrosanct and shunned social media. Shizu's libertinism had led to some sticky situations, for the rules were never quite clear: Could skirmishes with Miss X occur while Shizu was in the bath? Freedom soon came up against its own limits. Geographical distance may not make a moral difference, but it *feels* as if it does. With Hisae, in what was nearly a marriage, N resolved never to have a lover in the same city. That would feel too much like treachery. But, behind the scenes, Ayesha might pop up in Venice or Paris, Yuka in Tel Aviv or Oslo, and Hanni in Munich or Milan. Isn't it interesting that the other term for "a two-way mirror" is "a one-way mirror"? It all depends on who you ask, what they know, and which side they're on.

Kate Millett: Something like my book *Flying*. Nineteen seventy-four. The mess of my life, my Japanese husband Fumio, my woman lovers. *Sexpol* was dogma, this was experience. Messy but true. Not *should* but *is*. Not preaching but being. Me puking and crazy in airports. Personal/political. Any solution, any revolution, it's got to happen in the everyday. How we deal with things as they come up. And yet we're nutso. There is no normal. We're freaks, a ragged mess. Take N in 2005. He's always on the verge of moving to Japan. Like I did in 1961. His partner is Japanese, like mine. Hisae tolerates a lot, as Fumio did. N is living in Berlin. But Hong Kong, Osaka, Tokyo, San Francisco, New York, they're all in the neighborhood. In April he sings in London. At a library. Colliers Wood. A brick oblong filled with books and chairs. Praveen from Project Adorno has set it up. N is dressed in black. Rough felt sailor pants with a panel that buttons up the front. Birkenstock clogs, a woolen cape. Odd clothes grant permission to think oddly. N stands in front of the books. Singing here feels transgressive. He links the songs with a Laurie Anderson voice. Graphic design collective Åbäke are in the front row. Patrick, Benjamin, Kajsa, Maki. Talking to them is like inhaling from an oxygen tank of pure enlightenment. There's someone else here. N spots her outside but is too shy to engage. She's puffing on a skinny roll-up in a doorway. Hunched shoulders, woolly hat, tiny, very pretty. A darting smile in her eyes. Subcontinental Asian? With a ginger boy who looks like Bowie. Art students. N disappears off to a restaurant with Åbäke. A week later an email arrives. All lowercase. It's from the tiny pretty girl, N knows that immediately. She had Christmas cheeks all week, she says. N's birthday is the day before hers, she says. Always nice to discover other Aquarians, she says. She starts talking about thirteenth-century peasant funeral songs done in a Brechtian burlesque style. Signs off saying Hisae is very pretty. N tells her he noticed her. "I think you're one of the most attractive people I've ever set eye(s) on! The ginger-haired boy is lucky. I'd be happy if you wrote to me often." She writes every day. They exchange photographs, increasingly undressed. They chat on ICQ. N copies her lowercase style. In June he has to fly to New York for his art show with Mai Ueda. He buys a ticket via London and stays with Ayesha in her flat at New Cross. Ground floor. Damp and dingy in that British way. Messy but full of fascinating stuff. Ayesha studied art. Sculptures and installations. Animal rights, museums, postcolonialism, world music, bisexuality, mice, Sparks. Ginger Matt was there once, but he's moved out. She's shy in person. Her voice is whispery, her legs unshaved. N sits with her on the sofa. His knees push into her thighs as he gazes into her beautiful face. Big eyes, lank acrid hair, nasal-labial lines. Mother Malay Chinese, father Pakistani. N wants her enormously. To gobble up her body and her soul. To integrate and become her. Ayesha shows him his room. Her bedroom is nearer the garden. Please don't come in there. N gets gloomy, phones Aya in North London, asks if he can stay with her instead. Aya says she lives with a boy called Jeremy now. But Ayesha keeps coming into his room and talking to him during the night. What does she want? She's smoking grass. Nothing sexual happens. In the morning N can't stand it anymore and barges into the forbidden room, heart going fast as a bird's. Ayesha wakes, groans. He lifts her top, sucks her breasts. They fuck, and keep fucking. For the next fifteen months they text every day and meet to fuck whenever they can. *when am I going to see you again, mr currie?* N whisks her to New York, Paris, Venice. It's casual yet intense. She's also doing the tech guy at the art school. She's the unreliable tour guide's unreliable sidekick. Only after they split up in Paris—after that hellish night—does N realize his loss. So vertiginous! The sensation is physical. For two years his stomach feels ruptured, ulcerating, bloodied. All his songs are about her. He is still haunted. She's married now. It makes perfect sense. The husband is totally right for her. She moved to Los Angeles, Yangon, Malacca, back to London. She became an academic. An activist. Morally beautiful. If you've really loved someone you love them until you die. You integrate and become them. You never get over love, never. You shouldn't even try.

part
six

2010–2020

Survival. Never a wholly admirable story.

—George Oppen

Charles Bukowski: A new decade is like a page of fresh paper all ready to be smeared with the same old shit. At this stage—fifty to sixty—you're probably not going to change. Personality is destiny. They can't teach an old dog. You sniff your own hole and like it. The tail is wagging you. I'm sorry it's me here, by the way, to talk about this next thing. Because I'm a lousy old bum who talks filth. Being dead has just made me worse. Let me apologize in advance to the lady—the Japanese American princess this is going to be about. The JAP deserves Tao Lin or Miranda July, but they're alive and will be for some time. Good health is a terrible thing. N meets the JAP on Facebook, which is some bullshit I know nothing about. I'm guessing it's not really about faces and not really about books. Jesus Christ, you people. The JAP is a fan of Tao Lin and so is N, and N likes her face. So maybe it is about faces and books after all. The JAP lives in Los Angeles. She's an only child from a rich family in Tokyo. She has a Filipino boyfriend who does jerkoff shit like drive down the highway on the wrong side. The JAP writes poetry and N tells her it's good. Bull about dinosaurs and flowers and seeds and quaffing the nectar of life. There's sex so close to the surface that N can smell the pussy juice. Miranda July would have put this differently. Hisae is in Osaka and things are uncertain. N is supposed to join her out there by the end of the year. She's found a little corner house in an industrial area, next to a trash reprocessing plant. Coolies push handcarts stacked with flattened boxes past the door. Mumbling old broads collect aluminum cans. Just south is Nishinari, the poorest slum in Japan. There's the zoo, which stinks of giraffe dung, then Tobita Shinchi, where the whores sit in doorways. Prefab flophouse dorms burst with middle-aged sad sacks who line up at 5:00 a.m. to be picked by mafia crews to work construction sites for ten thousand yen a day. This is the Japan that awaits N when the JAP comes to Berlin for a pussy honeymoon, and possibly to save him from a life in the slums. She has long straight black hair that just shows a strip of face. She lets him come in her mouth, which is connected to her nose by pronounced lines. She's beautiful like dinosaurs, seeds, juice, stars, nectar. They're walking past an ice cream parlor one day when she suggests some Hal Hartley bullshit game: "I'll shut my eyes and you guide me." So N does that, describing everything. Well, somehow this gets flipped, because when they're in Tokyo it's the JAP who guides N through Shinagawa Station as if he's a blind old man. Her folks have a fancy apartment near there. Fountains, chandeliers. N breaks a chair by sitting down too hard on it. It all comes to a head the night N has to be presented to the father, a rich politician with a little devil beard who's more or less married to his daughter. The mother on the other hand is fun; she likes to sing N's songs back at him:

> *Women are attracted to the evil genius*
> *Probing for his inner being they find his penis*

N is wearing a pinstripe suit he bought in a secondhand shop in Nishinari for ten dollars. They all go to this Chinese restaurant and after small talk about Adam Smith's theory of moral sentiments the father opens his briefcase and produces a stapled document several pages long. Questions for N to answer. How much money has he saved for his retirement? Who'll get custody of the kids in a divorce? Is N prepared to take a role in the family's educational charity? Dad's hands are trembling. The stapled paper is really telling N that he's nothing but a grifter. No bum in a ten-dollar suit is going to grab my daughter. The next day there are storms of tears and N fucks the JAP girl for the last time before catching the bullet train back to Osaka. "It's my dad, he's ruined everything!" "No, no, don't blame your dad!" Marrying a woman is fine but nobody should have to marry parents. Because N hasn't told Hisae anything his Osaka life is still there to step back into. He returns to the corner house with its roller shutter doors and green industrial floor. For the first six months he lives there alone. Hisae is staying up at her family house in Tennoji. She says it's to look after Pok the black rabbit, but it's strange. Hisae is working for a phone company. Her art school pretensions have ebbed away. Her new interest is Takarazuka. It's a glitzy, kitschy type of musical theater where women play the men. Hisae and N have grown apart, but she and Osaka give him the freedom he needs to work. So for the next seven years that's what he does. With no distractions. Correction, a few.

Robert Lowell:
In a corner house in Den-Den Town N hangs like a macaque,
watching girls through fan-cracks in the ventilation shaft.
The friends he's made are two oceans away—let Dante and
    Homer squabble
over why—all N can do is cycle and recycle, pick the termites
    from his back.
And then it comes: a midnight shrill of grief from Debito, from
Bowie-Sama, hero of the silent sons. Where once he screamed the
    lines
of Rimbaud's "Royalty," posed like Heckel's *Roquairol*,

the old man now creaks out a croak: *Where Are They Now?* or
    Hell, What Hope?
or something of the sort. Just for a joke, at lunchtime N begins to
    ape the song;
by one he's added Roddy McDowall, strings from Glass,
and tinkling bells from Stomu Yamash'ta's soundtrack for
The Man Who Fell to Earth. Then—stupefaction!—
Bowie's seen the video, tells a friend in mail: "Yes, that's so cool!"
—which makes the monkey's day, the next day, and his life as well.

Bertolt Brecht: You think you're special? You're not special. I speak to you now in the voice of the city itself. You will have noted that life here is hard? You may have arrived from somewhere else, but now you live among the poor. Feel free to adopt their ways. Buy their clothes secondhand and wear them in shabby arcades. Men's clothes, women's clothes. You will never blend in. You can do what you like. Scribble obscenities in a psalter! Dress like a clown or a housewife in a cheap wig! Barge into the cram school! Post spy microfilms to Tumblr! You have gleaned next to nothing about me. I am made of opaque windows and corrugated iron shutters. I am made of concrete freeways slithering on stilts. I am made of mountains, pylons, forests, bays, and chiming temples. My ugly houses squeeze together for company. My people steep naked in the public bathhouses, men with men and women with women. One Cup sake costs two hundred yen in vending machines where moths and derelicts gather. You can gauge the desperation of a district by the price of its drinks. My love hotels are boxes without, filthy Neuschwansteins within. Bang a mama in Namba and wave bye-bye as she pedals off on her *mamachari*. Block your ears at Kabuki fleapits where ridiculous dandies hammer out the hits, waving swords. The homeless who live in plyboard and tarpaulin fail to reply when you question them. Why should they bring shame on their families? "Interview my cat!" jokes one. You hear the voices of carpenters drifting out of my karaoke bars at dusk as they sing—sadly and badly, but not without beauty. You like to cycle through my Korean districts at night. In the dark your Caucasian features fade. Now you are just another silhouette. If men piss on the street, so can you. If old women dance exuberantly in August, so can you. If dragonflies flit and fireworks explode, you can too. When my weather is hot you pause to hear the bleat of the sexual act. My walls are thin. You are invisible and intangible and might as well walk through my buildings. But you are also a citizen with an equal right to utter indifference. Commit crimes and my police will ignore you! Raid the old lady's porn bookstore for ancient paperbacks and read Shakespeare at the top of your voice near the ballet school overlooking the docks! We have a lot of crazy people here. Our moon is a big orange beast and our bridges span profundities of industrial darkness. Hoard your purple and orange Suhrkamps like a goblin! You are as dead as Ernst Bloch. You are as foreign as Bertolt Brecht. At first it stings to be blanked, but later you'll appreciate being a ghost. I couldn't give a shit about you. Take a dump under the freeway! Walk nude up the mountain, barefoot on sharp rocks! Scream beneath the holy waterfall! Only mosquitos and spiders care. When you croak another foreigner will replace you. The airport is that way, and the ocean also. Enjoy my gift of blankness. Fill it up with something.

Lafcadio Hearn: In the year 2011 I wafted like smoke across the Japanese archipelago from my old haunts in Matsue to resume my search for ghost stories in the Kansai prefecture. Since I was by this time a ghost myself, I figured my powers of apprehension might have grown more keen. This turned out, alas, not to be the case: I was, it seemed, only able to glean tales invented by one-eyed Japanophile anglophones like myself. Fortunately, there was one such creature living in a corner house near Shinsekai in Osaka, and his tales were decidedly unsettling, declaimed in mournful incantations which mingled all too readily with the soporific voice of the wind. Listening through the metal shutters of an industrial door, I jotted down all I was able to discern; a strain, I must admit, for the fellow—a genteel Scotsman, by the sound of it—did insist on whispering. I can report, then, that this restless spirit calls himself "Thunderclown" and dwells in a realm he calls "the Blankey-Bo." There he passes the time by reciting the tale of the Chinese willow pattern as seen by one of its deceased characters. He will be happy never to encounter love again, for love raises devils, he claims. He teases a precocious lady poet called Miss Calloway who makes a stir with "clever conversation studied from a magazine." Soon, however, a skeleton "that dances in a coat of human skin" is heard confessing to murderous urges in Paris. Now comes a turgid ballad commemorating "the drugs we took in 1992," and another in which we witness an awful revenge exacted upon a teacher by her lecherous student. I hear a dramatic monologue in the manner of Browning in favour of some kind of anti-natalist philosophy, a series of unverifiable propositions about the future, and a vision of the lost kingdom of Shangri-La formed in the mind of a man dying of cancer. In the final tale the Thunderclown returns as Heraclitus, "weeping over the obscure." Now comes a terrible earthquake, and a great tsunami licks the island of Honshu upon its eastern shores, unleashing a plume of radiation across earth and sea. When the clamour subsides it is the year 2012, and I find the doleful Scot no less morbid. He is hymning erasure, the death of Lycidas, necrophilia in the sand dunes, jackdaws in the rhubarb patch, holidays in hell, and the arson of Herostratus. He is shunned, he tells us (though it comes as little surprise), and feels like a set of "reflections on damaged life," an unread book shelved deep in some forgotten library stack. At this point I shudder and leave the Scot to his keening—which is perhaps no more than an eddying ululation, a figment of my imagination stirred by the brisk zephyrs that herald the approach of Pacific typhoons. I return not to Matsue but to Zōshigaya, where I rest under a simple stone next to my dear wife Setsu.

Emily Dickinson: The seasons pass, and thus must the continents exchange their places, as required by visas—those paper leases on life—and hastened by the glistening hives the moderns call airports, droning with the ceaseless clamor of their mechanical bees. My dears, how one longs for alternation! And yet how one fears it as an end to all comfort. At such times one wishes—oh how heartily!—for a sensitive soul with whom to correspond. Someone who might shine a lantern through the storm of life as if to call: "Though you be far, belong to me!" One afternoon in the Far Orient N is seated in a flying machine, about to launch once more into God's great blue heaven and hurtle toward Europe, when he receives a letter from me. My dear, I shall not lie and say it was *exactly* me; it was from a girl called Alice, a citizen of Summerville, South Carolina. She did much resemble me, though, in both face and temperament. With this fairy surprise began a sweet exchange that lasted nigh on four years and played midwife to N's record *Bambi* and his novel *UnAmerica*. "Bambi" was the familiar name N chose for his dear doe. His return, in these lyrical pieces, to the style of his own adolescence was intended as an act of fellowship with the lass, who was then just nineteen. I cannot speak to the merits of his verse; his lines resemble mine as little as a wolf does a feather:

> *I had a whale of a time up Clam Mountain being obscene*
> *Under the swarms of flies in the violent skies of the Holocene*

Has vulgarity really so flourished—and decorum so perished—in God's earthly paradise since my departure to his heavenly one? As for the account of our land in *UnAmerica*, I recognize nothing but whimsy and lampoon. Did the South really win the Civil War? Would God be working as a janitor in a Summerville soda parlor, and would He charge His servant Brad with the reenactment of the westward voyage of Saint Brendan, causing our United States to fall, at the last, into a renewed condition of obscurity? These are the scrawlings of a lunatic, a Lear, a Carroll. Four years after beginning their correspondence N and Alice will at last meet by the Asakusa temple gates and promenade through Tokyo for a few hours, arm in arm. There will be no question of romance, my dear, for theirs has been a friendship rooted in that affinity we must simply call affection. Let me offer my praise indeed: were they deer I should pat their speckled flanks—if cats, pull their tails.

Satyajit Ray: Something is restless in N's Osaka life. Japan is his spiritual homeland, and yet carnal demons—as well as the need to leave every three months to meet the requirements of his endless succession of tourist visas—prevent N from settling into a comfortable domestic life with Hisae. He would dearly have wished it were otherwise. Apu in my film *The World of Apu* brings his young bride Aparna back to his shabby room in Calcutta. Freed from the distractions of loneliness he writes his poems and plays his flute. With Hisae N can do the same. It turns out to be the longest continuous relationship of his life: almost fourteen years. The seven years in Berlin are happy—the pair enjoy an almost-continuous togetherness—but the seven in Osaka see a growing detachment or minimalism. Hisae takes a job with a phone company. She leaves their home early in the morning and comes back late at night. Her space becomes cluttered and messy while N's grows ever more tidy and austere. When Hisae does have a day off she devotes it to Takarazuka, the musical theatre whose romantic plots provide some of the passion and excitement she must feel she is lacking at home. From 2014 on the couple sleep in separate bedrooms, ostensibly so that "Hime" will not disturb her "Pasha" when she leaves for work, but actually because sex has ebbed away, leaving only affection and habit. They still tickle and giggle and play. N appreciates the lack of jealous possessiveness: there's no question of Hisae standing over him demanding that he erase videos of old girlfriends or destroy love letters. Averting her eyes from what she doesn't wish to see, Hisae gives N space to work, and—implicitly, on condition that he acts with tact and discretion—to develop relationships of various kinds with other women. These fall into two main categories: in the first are married Japanese women in their late thirties and early forties, often with children, who remember N's nineties fame and wish to rekindle a teenage crush. These women often claim to be separated or divorced, but turn out rather to be married. The affairs are highly erotic, and tend to take place in colourful love hotels—the shabby and quirky Yoshi's House in Namba, for instance. They fizzle after a year or so. The second category is the travelling companions: mostly art students, they're Western women in their twenties. These peripatetic friendships tend to be platonic, although beds are shared and the travellers usually crush together beneath the sheets naked. Hillary the Edinburgh hippie dances onstage with N dressed as a beekeeper and accompanies him to Mallorca. Colleen the Belfast vegan accompanies him to Madrid and Barcelona. Hanni from Munich comes to Edinburgh, the Hebrides, Pisa, Florence, and Venice. In a category of her own is Yuka, the theatre student with whom N spends a clandestine decade. N meets her first in Berlin, where he's conducting a performance art piece called *The Rice Experiment* with his nephew Robbie. The idea is to insult one pot of rice and praise another to see which rots quicker: in fact, the praised pot outlasts the slandered one. Yuka points out the Shinto aspects of the performance. She's an intellectual—a devotee of Meyerhold's constructivist experiments and exponent of a Japanese underground phenomenon called the Theatre Theory of the Apes. She reads N's *Book of Japans* as he's writing it, provides suggestions and guidance, and even drafts her own versions of some scenes. The pair travel together to London, Tokyo, Oslo, Paris, Madrid, Tel Aviv, Jerusalem, and Hanoi. Their relationship is unstable: sometimes platonic, sometimes sexual, it chafes constantly against the pressure Yuka is under from her elderly parents to get married. Her desire to be a wife conflicts with N's wish to live entirely in the moment, without promises or vows. "I am not happy to be your secret mistress" is met with a glib existentialism: "All we have is today and its pleasures. *Carpe diem.*"

David Bowie: It's just gone four and the Sea of Japan has never looked more leaden. N has passed Tsushima, a Japanese island that is actually closer to Korea. He'll be arriving at Fukuoka within the hour. Then—assuming there are no visa problems—he'll take the train to Osaka. On the Beetle jetfoil from Busan the Wi-Fi is bloody awful. But wait, what's this Facebook message? All lowercase. "bowie is dead." N gets a burst of adrenaline, an upswell of horror. Can this be a joke? If it is, it's in very bad taste. He tries to load the BBC News site. No joy. After much groaning and gurning the headlines finally appear on the MacBook. Nothing about me. It's got to be a hoax. N remembers something Iman once said in an interview: "David doesn't believe anything until he hears it on the BBC." Quite true, ha ha! But now Twitter sputters into life. N manages to get half a page of feed. One of the tweets is from my son. It's true, he says. There's a photo of me hoisting him onto my back. Duncan is going offline for a while. N does the same. He wants to be alone with this cataclysmic news. I've been his lodestar, the single most decisive influence on his life. N thinks of his father, who died last summer. To lose us within months of each other is really hard. N expected me to grow elegantly cadaverous like Balthus, the wily old artist I once interviewed for *Modern Painters*. Now that I remember everything—a big improvement on my living memory, which was like Swiss fucking cheese—I recall N asking me a question on Bowienet. What did I think of the art magazine *Frieze*? "*Frieze* tends to preach to the converted," I told him. Our sole exchange. All this is rushing through his head, little details to set against a huge fact. N imagines vicious people saying: "Oh, Momus just copies David Bowie a day later, let's wait and see if he dies tomorrow." Nobody on the jetfoil knows yet. N contemplates tapping the Western couple sitting in front of him on the shoulder and telling them, but what would be the point? Would the middle-aged Japanese man sitting next to him care? He envisions catching glimpses, from his *shinkansen*, of gigantic *Blade Runner*–esque billboards displaying images of people weeping. In fact the streets of Fukuoka are filled with radiant faces. Girls in kimonos and brilliant white stoles. It's Coming of Age Day, when students celebrate turning twenty. Schoolgirls in uniform float by, coyly aware of their youthful radiance and its transience. Neon signs float in the dusk. It's quite unlike all those romantically dark scenarios of mine in which the world is dying and the newsman weeps and corpses rot on the slimy thoroughfare. Life goes on in its innocent, incorrigible way. Joy, traffic, the light in the sky. Cakes and ale. It all keeps swinging. N remembers something I told Russell Harty when I was young: "What do I worship? Life. I love life very much." In one of my last interviews the theme returned: "I'm not going to enjoy being dead much." And N's mind goes back to the crossing. As the jetfoil hung above the mercury-grey sea something caught the bleary corner of his eye. A silvery flash, there and then gone, a big living thing breaking the surface of the water, leaping with what looked like joy, the pure joy of being alive. A swordfish? Too slow to see for sure, N decided it was a dolphin.

Keith Vaughan: My journals, kept from 1939 right up to my suicide in 1977, the blurring moment of my death visible on the page as I succumbed to the mixture of whisky and Nembutal. One million words, latterly detailing my slow artistic decline, my drunken solitude, my experiments with electrically operated masturbation machines. Perhaps some kind of comfort to others in my condition? Or mere self-soothing, horse whispering? When his artistic hero died N turned to his old diaries for solace, spending hours each day sitting in his *zaisu* chair—the fluffy one he'd picked up outside a whorehouse in Tobita Shinchi—transcribing the journals he'd kept in the late seventies and early eighties. It was a way of answering the basic existential question: Who am I? Painstakingly, he disentangled himself from the oedipal struggle with his father—a mild enough character—and the identification with Bowie, the idealised self. He made PDFs of the journals and posted them in three parts on his website: *Black Letts Diary* (1979), *Somewhere There Are People Like Me* (1980), and *The Bertie Wooster of Alienation* (1981). The 1980 volume was mocked up to look like a Folio paperback, as if it were Gide's journal. The 1981 one had the 1960s Chatto & Windus look, its cover grimy and stickered like an old library book. Two thousand sixteen was a bloody awful year: Leonard Cohen died, Trump won the American election, and Britain voted to leave the European Union. N was of course completely opposed to Brexit, except insofar as it made Scottish independence—and immediate rejoining of the EU—more likely. A darkening turn in the Western soul, a determination to turn the clock back, weighed heavily on him, even in Japan and even though his own life was actually going very well. Middle age felt like a warm glow. Women still liked him, apparently. Success was simply being able to keep at it. His musical work—now melding Japanese folk music with echoes of Harry Partch and Moondog—pleased him and his tiny coterie of listeners. Journalism kept N connected to the more pleasant parts of life: art biennials and the cheap restaurants of Osaka, which for a while he was chronicling for *The Japan Times*. Even money wasn't a problem: long practice in living cheaply seemed to be paying off, and—unlike me—N wasn't a smoker, a drinker, dying from cancer, or particularly troubled either by self-doubt or self-pity.

Frederick Rolfe: During his later years in Keihanshin N came to fulgurate in a sumptuous aseity. He and his silent acolyth moved in early 2015 to a warehouse apartment in the Osaka docks. There, a mere bridge-span from Osaka's only branch of Ikea, N's matutinal rituals would begin with Hisae's departure for her telephone company and, on his own part, a votive offering to Onan. After a dip in the caldarian labrum and a cursory inspection of the Akashi isthmus N would carefully prepare a cup of PG Tips with his excandescent Muji kettle, unsnarp a *mikan*, and draw a macilent streak of Japanese butter, galbanate as lactifuge, across two slices of that pallid spongiform the Lawson one-hundred-yen store dares to call "French sesame pan." Only now could N begin his tolutiloquent labour on pavonine productions as various and innumerable as they were, in all worldly senses, inconsequential: Momus records entitled *Turpsycore*, *Glyptothek*, *Scobberlotchers*, and *Pillycock*, experimental radiophonic productions or "hearspools," hauntological videos of academic imposture, collaborations with fellow Scots David McClymont and Joe Howe, a Faustian novel called *Herr F*, another entitled *Popppappp* . . . The work was unremitting because when idle our ghost found himself besieged by devils keen to coax him out on urban expeditions both voluptuous and velocipidean. After episodes of minor turpitude he might seal his effrenate, increasingly talpine days with the purchase of a winking beaker of iced latte at Antico Caffe Al Avis in Namba Parks or a mildewed Elizabethan paperback at Ehara Books. His methystine apex might be the discovery of a diaphotick chlamys featuring Benetton Art

Deco motifs in proximate tyrinathine hues—a bargain at just five hundred yen in a pop-up store called Emerald Famille on Amagasaki's purrothrixine Chuo Arcade. And so life could have continued indefinitely had Hisae not, in late 2017—shortly after the unexpected death of her father, an event for which N provided scant maritorious comfort—decided to suggest a "happy ending" to their partnership. Thus did it come to pass that, after extensive travels in Korea, Laos, Myanmar, Vietnam, and Malaysia, N returned to Europe, where an unlikely quirk of the Vatican's electoral process led to his surprise investiture, in the summer of 2018, as Bishop of Berlin, Vicar of Jesus Christ, Successor of the Prince of the Apostles, Supreme Pontiff of the Universal Church, and Servant of the servants of God: Pope Hadrian VIII.

Oscar Wilde: It is a fine early summer day in 2019, and the sun spills Ionian gold upon Père Lachaise. Two lovers have picked their way through undistinguished tombs to my own, a streamlined stone angel locked in a box of glass. Epstein's monument is the perfect symbol for my earthly fate—for, upon observing how dearly I had always longed to take wing, it must have amused a spiteful world thus to plumb and imprison me. These visitors are frail and yet healthy in their matching Repetto shoes, heads draped in the festive Japanese fabrics known as *tenugui*. They seem to be very much in love. Although he speaks softly, I hear the man—who has a genteel Scottish accent—tell the woman: "Of course you know that Wilde exploded when he died?" She—a Frenchwoman with features somewhat Siamese—asks whether this is not a legend. The Scot then produces a sliver of glass, a sort of pocket mirror, and consults an aerial encyclopaedia. He reads from his tiny oracle: apparently I died of encephalitic meningitis brought on by syphilis. A man called Ellmann is summoned to testify that no sooner had I rattled out my last breath than "the body exploded with fluids from the ear, nose, mouth and other orifices. The debris was appalling." The Scot adds, with horrid practicality: "They must have been scraping him off the wallpaper for hours. I'm sure the hotel manager was furious." I am not best pleased by this exchange, as you might imagine, but must confess with an Aeolian sigh that I have heard worse from the visitors who gather around my tomb. Idiocy runs rampant through your world more shamelessly than it did even in ours. Noémie and Nicholas will drift to the columbarium to see the niche of Léopold Fucker, reduced to ashes in 1980, and then to the memorial for Air France 447, which plummeted like Icarus to the deep. Further down that avenue of apocalypse they will encounter monuments to the victims of a syphilis far worse than my own: that of Friedrich Nietzsche. Some cause happiness wherever they go, others whenever they go. Farewell, then, living lovers, thou lovers of life! Farewell, Nicholas and Noémie! Live happily ever after, or at least until your time comes to explode! Write in our voices if you must, but let us, your great dead, get on with the important business of unbeing. Do you recall how beautifully my Canterville ghost described the Garden of Death?

> Far away beyond the pine-woods . . . there is a little garden.
> There the grass grows long and deep, there are the great
> white stars of the hemlock flower, there the nightingale sings
> all night long. All night long he sings, and the cold, crystal
> moon looks down, and the yew-tree spreads out its giant
> arms over the sleepers . . . Love is always with you, and Love
> is stronger than Death is.

A NOTE ABOUT THE AUTHOR

Momus, born Nick Currie, is a Scot who makes songs, books, and art. He is the author of six books of speculative fiction and has released more than thirty albums, the most recent being *Akkordion*. Momus divides his time between Berlin and Paris.